A BRIEF HISTORY
OF BOLIVIA

D0921056

A BRIEF HISTORY
OF BOLIVIA

WALTRAUD Q. MORALES

University of Central Florida

Checkmark Books®

An imprint of Facts On File, Inc.

A Brief History of Bolivia

Checkmark Books
An imprint of Facts On File, Inc.
132 West 31st Street
New York NY 10001

Library of Congress Cataloging-in-Publication Data

Morales, Waltraud Q.
  A brief history of Bolivia / by Waltraud Q. Morales.
    p. cm.
Includes bibliographical references and index.
  ISBN 0-8160-4692-1 (hardcover)
  ISBN 0-8160-5720-6 (pbk)
  1. Bolivia—History. I. Title.
  F3321.M76 2003
  984—dc21

Cover design by Semadar Megged
Maps by Dale Williams

Printed in the United States of America

MP Hermitage 10 9 8 7 6 5 4 3 2 1

This book is printed on acid-free paper.

To Carl,
my one and only,
and to Mom and Dad with love

CONTENTS

LIST OF ILLUSTRATIONS

LIST OF MAPS

LIST OF TABLES

LIST OF ABBREVIATIONS

ADN	Nationalist Democratic Action (Acción Democrática Nacionalista)
APDHB	Bolivian Permanent Assembly of Human Rights (Asamblea Permanente de Derechos Humanos de Bolivia); also Permanent Assembly of Human Rights of Bolivia
BAMIN	Mining Bank of Bolivia (Banco Minero de Bolivia)
CEPB	Bolivian Confederation of Private Entrepreneurs (Confederación de Empresarios Privados de Bolivia)
CIA	(U.S.) Central Intelligence Agency
CNTCB	National Confederation of Peasant Workers of Bolivia (Confederación Nacional de Trabajadores Campesinos de Bolivia)
COB	Bolivian Labor Central (Central Obrera Boliviana)
COMIBOL	Bolivian Mining Corporation (Corporación Minera de Bolivia)
CONADE	National Committee for the Defense of Democracy (Comité Nacional de Defensa de la Democracia)
CONDEPA	Conscience of the Fatherland (Conciencia de Patria)
CSTB	Confederation of Bolivian Workers (Confederacíon Sindical de Trabajadores de Bolivia)
CSUTCB	Sole Unionist Confederation of Peasant Workers of Bolivia, or General Trade Union Confederation of Peasant Workers of Bolivia (Confederación Sindical Unica de Trabajadores Campesinos de Bolivia); also Confederation of Peasant Unions of Bolivia
DEA	(U.S.) Drug Enforcement Administration
FPN	Popular Nationalist Front (Frente Popular Nacionalista)
FRB	Bolivian Revolutionary Front (Frente de la Revolución Boliviana)
FSB	Bolivian Socialist Falange (Falange Socialista Boliviana)
FSTMB	Bolivian Mine Workers' Federation, or Trade Union Federation of Bolivian Mineworkers (Federacíon Sindical de Trabajadores Mineros de Bolivia)

IMF	International Monetary Fund
IU	United Left (Izquierda Unida)
LEC	Legion of Veterans (Legión de Ex-Combatientes)
MAS	Movement Toward Socialism (Movimiento al Socialismo)
MIP	Pachakuti Indigenist Movement (Movimiento Indígena Pachakuti)
MIR	Leftist Revolutionary Movement, or Movement of the Revolutionary Left (Movimiento de Izquierda Revolucionaria)
MIR-NM	MIR–New Majority (MIR–Nueva Mayoría)
MNR	Nationalist Revolutionary Movement (Movimiento Nacionalista Revolucionario)
MNRA	Authentic MNR (MNR Auténtico)
MNRH	Historic MNR (MNR Histórico)
MNRI	MNR-Left (MNR Izquierda)
MPC	Popular Christian Movement (Movimiento Popular Cristiano)
MRTKL	Tupac Katari Revolutionary Liberation Movement (Movimiento Revolucionario Tupac Katari de Liberación)
NPE	New Economic Policy (Nueva Política Económica)
NFR	New Republican Force (Nueva Fuerza Republicana)
OAS	Organization of American States
PCB	Bolivian Communist Party (Partido Comunista de Bolivia)
PDC	Christian Democratic Party (Partido Demócrata Cristiano)
PIR	Party of the Revolutionary Left (Partido de la Izquierda Revolucionaria)
POR	Revolutionary Workers' Party (Partido Obrero Revolucionario)
PRA	Authentic Revolutionary Party (Partido Revolucionario Auténtico)
PRI	Institutional Revolutionary Party (Partido Revolucionario Institucional)
PRIN	Revolutionary Party of the Nationalist Left (Partido Revolucionario de la Izquierda Nacionalista)
PS	Socialist Party (Partido Socialista)
PS-1	Socialist Party–One (Partido Socialista Uno)
PSD	Social Democratic Party (Partido Social Demócrata)

PSOB	Socialist Workers' Party of Bolivia (Partido Socialista Obrero de Bolivia)
PURS	Party of the Republican Socialist Union (Partido de la Unión Republicana Socialista)
RADEPA	Reason of the Fatherland (Razón de Patria)
UCS	Civic Solidarity Union (Unión Cívica de la Solidaridad)
UDP	Democratic Popular Unity (Unidad Democrática y Popular)
UMOPAR	Mobile Rural Patrol Units, or "Leopardos" (Unidad Móvil de Patrullaje para el Area Rural)
USAID	U.S. Agency for International Development
YPFB	Bolivian State Petroleum Enterprise (Yacimientos Petrolíferos Fiscales Bolivianos)

ACKNOWLEDGMENTS

The generous assistance of friends and scholars of Bolivia and of private and governmental organizations has been invaluable. They have provided insight and the wonderful illustrations that enhance this book, gratefully acknowledged after the captions. In addition, I would like to personally thank the following individuals for their diverse contributions: Charles W. Arnade, Guillermo Delgado P., José B. Fernández, Martin Glassner, Robert H. Jackson, Kathy S. Leonard, Peter McFarren, Víctor Montoya, Marlene Nilsson, Nicholas A. Robins, Fred Savariau, Jim Shultz, Allyn MacLean Stearman, and Elayne Zorn. The Columbus Library of the Organization of American States, the Perry-Castañeda Library Map Collection of the General Libraries of the University of Texas at Austin—available online at http://www.lib.utexas.edu/maps/—and the United Nations Photo Library provided much appreciated materials and assistance.

I also owe a debt of thanks to the University of Central Florida and its Department of Political Science for the sabbatical leave that provided me the rare opportunity to undertake and complete this book and for the help of graduate students Teresa Lamar and Nicole Reale. Finally, I must extend my special thanks to the editor, Edward Purcell, without whom this challenging project would never have been started much less brought to fruition, and to Facts On File for its interest and support.

INTRODUCTION: PEOPLE OF SOUTH AMERICA'S HEARTLAND

Our lot has been to experience the change of century; now it is our task to initiate the century of change.

■

*— President Jorge Quiroga Ramírez, 2001 ("Mensaje de ...
Quiroga Ramírez ... en el día de su asunción al mando de la nación")*

The dawn of the 21st century and a new millennium coincided with the passing of an era in Bolivian history, and this turning point confronted Bolivia's leaders and citizens with the legacy of their past and the promise of their future. Present-day young political leaders represent a postrevolutionary generation born in the second half of the 20th century. Although they played no role in the 1952 National Revolution that fundamentally altered Bolivian society, they have inherited its powerful historical significance.

Once known as the land of 200 coups, Bolivia has maintained governmental stability and democratic continuity for more than two decades now. New political, social, and economic actors have emerged and are prepared to lead the country into a more prosperous era. In order for them to succeed, they must resolve Bolivia's traditional problems of instability, poverty, and geography. Nevertheless, this historical juncture represents a unique opportunity to overcome these long-standing national constraints and better the lives of Bolivia's people.

Prisoner of Geography

Bolivia is a nation in the geographical center of South America, with no direct access to the ocean. The people of Bolivia proudly present their country as the vital heart of the continent while rejecting its landlocked status. In their eyes, Bolivia has been a prisoner of geography and a victim of historical adversity. For more than 100 years, Bolivians have waged a relentless campaign to reverse their encirclement and redress the defeats of their history. Recent governments, however, have maneuvered

to transform geographical constraints into strategic geopolitical advantages. In their view, Bolivia can escape geographical confinement by becoming the land bridge between the two great oceans, thereby integrating east and west and opening up the interior of the continent to economic development.

The Andean republic's estimated 8.3 million people are territorially constrained by five neighboring South American nations. On the Atlantic side is Brazil to the north and southeast and Paraguay and Argentina to the south. Chile and Peru lie westward from Bolivia and block direct access to the Pacific Ocean. With the exception of Paraguay, Bolivia's continental neighbors are larger, richer, and more powerful. All of these neighbors, including the relatively weaker and poorer Paraguay, have gained territory at Bolivia's expense and impeded Bolivian attempts to break from its landlocked condition.

Almost three times the size of the U.S. state of Montana and larger than Texas and California combined, contemporary Bolivia extends 682,000 square miles and is the sixth-largest country in South America. Despite its size, Bolivia remains sparsely and unevenly populated with only one-fifth the population of comparably sized Colombia. This chronic low population density contributed to the nation's territorial dismemberment in the 19th and 20th centuries.

The country's founding fathers named Bolivia in honor of Simón Bolívar, the renowned and ambitious South American independence fighter, in an astute attempt to ensure the new nation's precarious political survival during the dangerous and chaotic postindependence wars of conquest and consolidation. From the beginning, there was great anxiety that Bolivia's more aggressive and powerful neighbors would swallow up the fledgling republic. Indeed, since independence in 1825, territorial aggression by close neighbors has reduced Bolivia to half its original size.

Bolivia became landlocked with the loss of its coastal Atacama province in the 1879 War of the Pacific against Peru and Chile. Far from Bolivia's highland cities and population centers, this desert province was sparsely settled and very difficult to defend. Historically, the Pacific ports connected directly with railway lines that traversed the high Andean passes and served the major mining centers of colonial and republican Bolivia. Although expensive and cumbersome, this maritime access was vital to the country's economy, which relied on the export of silver, tin, and other precious ores. Today, as one of only two Latin American countries without direct access to the sea (Paraguay is the other), Bolivia can reach world markets only through the Pacific and Atlantic seaports of neighboring countries.

Bolivia's landlocked status has impeded economic development and negatively influenced the country's history and the national psyche. Dependent on the goodwill of its neighbors for maritime rights, the Bolivian economy has failed to achieve its full potential and to support the nation's extremely poor indigenous population. Recent theories of economic growth emphasize the critical importance of a country's geography. From this perspective, not all of Bolivia's developmental failures can be laid at the door of political instability and bad government. Rather, Bolivians have suffered also the tyranny of geography.

GEOGRAPHY AND POVERTY

It seems clear that there is a connection—in Latin America at least—between geography and poverty, and Bolivia has epitomized the global gap between rich and poor nations. In 1995, Bolivia's gross domestic product (GDP) per capita ranked among the lowest quarter of all countries; however, there have been improvements in the standard of living of Bolivia's people in the last decade. The United Nation's Development Program reported the average GDP per capita of $1,380 in 1989 rose to $2,617 by 1995.

Economic instability and endemic poverty mean that income can fluctuate widely; thus, GDP per capita for 1998 fell again to $1,036 and was estimated to be up at $3,000 for 1999. Income also remains very unequally distributed, with the poorest 20 percent of the population earning an average of $703 GDP per capita, and the richest 20 percent bringing in $6,049 GDP per capita. The use of averages itself disguises an even greater income disparity, and an estimated 66 to 70 percent of Bolivians live below the poverty line, according to recent data.

Many Bolivians are forced to migrate in order to find work and survive. There have been significant population movements to more tropical regions within Bolivia since 1985, and about 20 percent of Bolivians live in neighboring countries. Bolivia's human development index (HDI), which measures quality of life through such indicators as education, life expectancy, housing, sanitation, and health care, remains low compared to the Latin American–Caribbean averages and the averages for industrialized nations. More than 40 percent of Bolivia's population lacks access to proper sanitation, and 37 percent lacks drinkable water.

Bolivia's distant inland location magnifies the transportation costs of exports and imports. Shipping goods over land is many times more costly than maritime shipping. Yet bulky, low-value-added goods, such as tin and other mineral exports, depend on maritime shipping. Recent development studies have concluded that the average landlocked country pays 50 percent more in transportation costs than a coastal nation. Without cheap access to maritime routes and a well-developed physical infrastructure (roads, railways, and ports), many Bolivian goods never reach potential regional and global markets

The landlocked geography of Bolivia has also had cultural and intellectual consequences. As a result, the country's population has developed an inward-looking orientation. Until well into the 20th century, the

An aerial view of the Andes Mountains of Bolivia (UN/DPI Photo by Milton Grant)

country remained largely isolated from global intellectual currents, technological innovations, and major population migrations. There were consequences for the national psyche as well. The defeat in the War of the Pacific and the seemingly irreversible loss of the seacoast nurtured a collective national guilt and obsession with territorial and historical vindication. At times, recovery of the seacoast consumed the national energy and embittered Bolivia's relations with its neighbors. The revenge-oriented policies drew four Bolivian generations into wars and misguided attempts to salvage the national patrimony and historical reputation.

On the positive side, the struggle for *la salida al mar* (an outlet to the sea) has served to inspire patriotism and national unity in difficult times. One way or the other, a reversal of Bolivia's continental containment will be a fundamental Bolivian goal in the century ahead. And perhaps one day Bolivians will be able to include a seacoast among their most valued resources.

Major Resources

For most of its colonial, independent, and modern history, Bolivia has been identified with its mines. Beginning in colonial times, abundant mineral wealth has been extracted from deep mines situated along the westward spine of the Andes and high intermountain plateau, the altiplano. Much depleted today, these mines supplied vast quantities of silver and gold to the Spanish royal treasury for nearly three centuries. Historians have estimated that the rich Potosí mines alone offered up to $1 billion in silver to the European colonizers.

Mining became the country's lifeblood, its salvation, and its curse. Virtually every aspect of Bolivia's cultural, social, economic, and political development responded to the mining monocultures of silver and then tin. This skewed economic dependence on mineral extraction gave rise to the oft-quoted description of Bolivia as "a beggar on a throne of gold." Indeed, extensive mineral extraction created a boom economy that enriched only a few, shamelessly exploited Indian labor, and ignored long-term development needs.

After the silver mines played out, Bolivia became one of the world's major producers of tin. During the high point of the tin boom in the first half of the 20th century, Bolivian mines provided 30 percent of the annual world production. However, tonnage declined steadily after the Great Depression, despite a brief resurgence during World War II when Bolivia mined the all-time high of almost half of the world's supply. By the 1980s, production had shrunk below 10 percent. Tin, which had once bankrolled Bolivia's wars and entire government budgets, was only 6 percent of exports in 2000.

Bolivia is, nonetheless, still a mining country. In 2002, it exported an alphabet soup of other important strategic and industrial metals, including antimony, bismuth, copper, gold, iron, lead, manganese, silver, tungsten, wolfram, and zinc. The number-one mineral export was zinc, followed by gold. Hydrocarbons, primarily natural gas, have largely replaced the mining monoculture, and energy constitutes the new economic boom.

Despite the historical importance of mining, Bolivia's population has primarily been agricultural, yet agricultural land has always been a valuable and scarce commodity. With its rugged Andean topography, arid altiplano, alternately wet and dry savannas, dense forests, and tropical jungles, only about 10 percent of Bolivia's land area of 270 million acres is considered arable. In 2000, only a tiny fraction—2 percent—was actually cultivated.

Most agricultural land belonged historically to a handful of powerful landowners, who controlled huge estates. Throughout the 18th and 19th centuries, independent Indian communities known as *ayllus*, competed fiercely to preserve their communally owned lands. As late as 1950, 72 percent of the economically active population—mostly Indian

Rural Population in Select Latin American Countries			
Latin American Country	Percent of Population in 1980	Percent of Population in 1998	People per Square Kilometer of Arable Land in 1997
Argentina	17	11	16
Bolivia	55	39	163
Brazil	34	20	63
Chile	19	15	111
Colombia	36	27	568
Ecuador	53	37	286
El Salvador	58	54	570
Guatemala	63	61	471
Mexico	34	26	98
Paraguay	58	45	107
Peru	35	28	187
Source: Latin America Press (2001).			

peasants, or campesinos—engaged in agriculture; at the same time, only 6 percent of landowners held 92 percent of the cultivable land. The 1952 revolution brought sweeping agrarian reform. Twenty-four million acres were distributed to 237,000 families in land reform carried out by 1955, and by 1970, 289,000 families had received 29 million acres of land; however, in the last three decades, a significant concentration of land inequality has recurred. Because of land scarcity and harsh rural conditions, thousands of campesinos migrated to the cities where they exchanged land-distribution problems with over-crowding, unemployment, exploitation, and poverty.

The Land
Bolivia's land mass covers three distinct and diverse topographical regions: the Andean, the transitional sub-Andean, and the lowland. The Andean region consists of the arid mountain plateau called the altiplano and lies at 13,000 feet above sea level. Historically, the majority of the population settled on the altiplano, only 80 miles wide and running 500 miles from north to south between two main branches of the

Andean range. The sub-Andean region consists of the rich temperate valleys (*valles*) nestled in the foothills of the Andes and the semitropical valleys (*yungas*) of the northeastern escarpment of the Andes. The eastern lowlands (llanos, also referred to as the Oriente) of the country include subtropical forests and grasslands, as well as the dense tropical rain forests of the Amazon Basin.

The altiplano functions as the South American continent's highest and most extensive landlocked water drainage system. It is believed once to have been a great intermountain sea encircled by peaks 40,000 feet high. Today's peaks, although more modest, still tower above 21,000 feet, and the magnificent Titicaca is one of the world's highest major lakes. Its deep blue waters extend more than 3,400 square miles and are more than 750 feet deep. To the west, rising out of the Cordillera Occidental is Mount Sajama, an extinct volcano of 21,291 feet. In the Cordillera Real to the east, the peaks of Illampu (21,500 feet) and Illimani (21,300 feet) loom over the capital of La Paz, situated in an escarpment 1,000 feet below the altiplano.

To the southeast is Lake Poopó, the altiplano's "dead sea." At 965 square miles in area but only 35 feet deep, this vast, extremely salty lake empties into the salt pan of Uyuni (Salar de Uyuni) and small salt flats in the south. It may be the geological remains of the long-evaporated and -lost waters of the ancient lakes that were once part of the high inland sea. Over the years, the great salt deserts have yielded trillions of tons of salt, which is collected, crudely processed, and sold by Indians in Bolivia's urban markets.

The climate on the altiplano varies from frigid to temperate, depending on the altitude, sun, and winds. Sundown brings a rapid temperature drop. Water is scarce, and the soil supports mostly scrub grass. Conditions are poor almost everywhere for agriculture, but the sheltered shores of Lake Titicaca are an exception. Along the lake, sufficient water, fertile land, and a moderate climate sustain crops of corn, oca (a highland tuber), potatoes, wheat, and highland grains. Hundreds of potato varieties native to the Andes were cultivated by the ancient Aymara and Inca civilizations, and there are more than 200 varieties in present-day Bolivia.

In the higher elevations and more rocky and exposed regions of the plateau, Indian herdsmen tend sheep and the distinctive Andean animals related to the camel, the llama, the alpaca, and the rare vicuña. Harvesting the wool of these animals is an important source of income for indigenous communities. The wool of the alpaca and especially of the dwindling vicuña is highly prized. When it is available today, the cashmere spun from vicuña yarn is the finest and dearest anywhere.

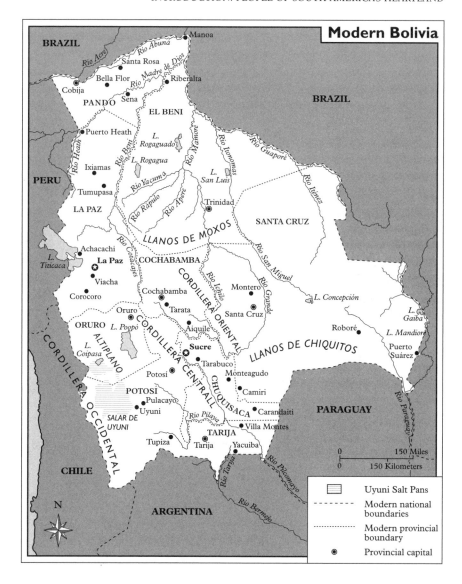

Mining has been the primary economic activity of the altiplano. The major mining complexes of Catavi (Llallagua) and Huanuni near the city of Oruro are situated close to the frigid and steep Andean passes. Isolated and completely dependent on outside resources for clothing, food, and housing, Bolivian miners have been a hardy, poor, and long-suffering class of workers.

The transitional upper valleys of the sub-Andean region lie between 10,000 and 14,500 feet and include the departments of Tarija,

The llama (shown here) and its cousins the alpaca and the vicuña are the distinctive domestic animals of the Andean region raised for wool and meat. (Kathy S. Leonard photo)

Chuquisaca, and Cochabamba. The city of Cochabamba, Bolivia's third largest, and its surrounding valleys are the granary and food basket of the nation. These broad upper valleys of the central Andes to the east and southeast of the altiplano enjoy a perpetual spring of Mediterranean-like climate. Water shortages, however, have been a problem, and rainfall is low and variable at the higher elevations. All the typical temperate and semitropical crops are grown in these valleys and transported to the cities on the altiplano.

At the lower altitude of 5,600 feet begin the warmer and more humid valleys of the *yungas* region. An Aymara word that means "warm," *yungas* are the semitropical to tropical valleys between the altiplano and the eastern llanos. The La Paz *yungas* sharply descend from the northeastern slopes of the Andes. These are the extremely lush mountain jungles of the narrow valleys and canyons that form part of the traditional growing area for Bolivia's coca leaf, which is the primary ingredient in the production of illegal cocaine. In the lower tropical valleys at 600 feet the ancient Aymara and Inca grew not only the sacred coca plant but also many semitropical and tropical fruits. Then, as now, crops such as coffee, tea, cacao, cassava (manioc), mangoes, citrus, and pineapples were transported more than 10,000 feet up the precipitous mountain roads to the highland population centers. And then, as now, no crop was more valuable or easier to grow and transport than coca.

If one considers the predominant physical geography, Bolivia is a low-land country: The third major geographical region, the Oriente, covers 70 percent of the territory and consists of the extensive and ecologically diverse eastern lowlands, or llanos. This plains region contains three distinct topographical and climatic zones: the gentle grasslands, the northern tropical rain forests, and the harsh scrubland of the Chaco to the south. Generally, the lowland climate is tropical and humid with well-defined seasonal variations—a dry season in the winter (May–September) and rainy summer months (December–February). From June through August, frigid southern winds can blow up from Antarctica and produce sharp cold fronts.

Bolivia's Pantanal region lies along the department of Santa Cruz's southeastern border with Brazil and is characterized by tropical rain forests and a vast inland system of marshes, river forests, and lagoons. Wetland ecosystems extend northward into the departments of El Beni and Pando and the wet forests of the Amazon. The northern plains include the Llanos de Moxos, whose wetlands once formed part of a great landlocked sea. Toward the east and the south are the dryer forests and grasslands (pampas), which offer natural pasture for intensive cattle ranching. Tropical rain forests cover most of the less-populated and inaccessible Pando department and also extend partly into the departments of El Beni, Santa Cruz, Cochabamba, and La Paz. The Chapare, once a major coca-growing region of Bolivia, is located in the tropical subregion of Cochabamba department.

The primitive slash-and-burn methods of early settlers continue to be used in these biologically rich subregions to raze thousands of acres of virgin rain forests. Consequently, the freed biomass of the very fragile tropical soils produces abundant crop yields for a short while, but soon the soil is depleted and more forest must be cleared. At the height of the coca-cocaine economy, extensive coca cultivation and hundreds of secret cocaine paste–processing labs that were hidden in the jungles contributed to their devastation. This destruction of the rain forest by human settlement, intervention, and depredation has drastically altered the delicate ecological balance of the region.

Agriculture, as well as animal husbandry, has been the economic mainstay of the lowlands. Sugarcane, rice, cotton, and soybean exports produced temporary economic booms in Santa Cruz department. Also in the 1970s and 1980s, the aggressive expansion of coca cultivation and the windfall capital infusion from the coca-cocaine economy put population growth and development in Santa Cruz on a fast track. After the first oil boom peaked in 1974, the city of Santa Cruz developed into

Bolivian campesinos harvest potatoes from a high-altitude Andean field. For centuries, Bolivians have relied on the indigenous potato as a major food source. (UN Photo/Helene Temblay)

the Oriente's financial center for agriculture and drug traffic. More recently, the new hydrocarbon bonanza in natural gas has driven the economy of the Santa Cruz region and stimulated the population increase of the departmental capital. The national census for 2001 indicated that the lowland metropolis surpassed central La Paz, the administrative capital, in overall population; however, if the population of all the outlying communities of the greater La Paz area is included, the highland capital maintains its traditional status as Bolivia's largest city. Even so, Santa Cruz is steadily gaining.

The Chaco comprises the third ecoregion of Bolivia's lowlands. An extension of the Gran Chaco of Paraguay and Argentina, the Chaco occupies the southern and southeastern portions of the department of Santa Cruz and the eastern territories of the departments of Chuquisaca and Tarija. This inhospitable, arid region of cacti, spiny scrubs, and dry quebracho forests is swamp for three months of the year and parched desert the rest of the time. The extremely poor land can sustain the grazing only of wild cattle and goats, although with irrigation and in the subtropical climate the Chaco produces cotton, soybeans, and corn. The Chaco's few cities supply petroleum and natural gas installations and pipelines to

Bolivia and railway lines into Argentina and Brazil. The Chaco was once the bloody battlefield of Bolivia's devastating war with Paraguay.

The People

Often described as a mosaic of race, ethnicity, and nationality, Bolivia is predominantly an Indian nation. Peoples native to the highland and valley regions of the country as well as the tropical rain forests and lowlands comprise 50 to 60 percent of the population today. The two largest and oldest indigenous groups in highland Bolivia are the Aymara, numbering 20 to 25 percent of the population, and the Quechua, who comprise 35 to 40 percent of Bolivia's population.

The Aymara believe themselves to be descended from the ancient Native Americans who founded the Andean kingdom of Tiwanaku hundreds of years before the conquest by the Quechua-speaking Inca. Modern-day Aymara populate the temperate shores of Lake Titicaca and the central altiplano, with the majority of Aymara speakers (90 percent) located in the department of La Paz and most of the rest found in the departments of Oruro and Potosí.

The Quechua, descendants of the Inca and the tribes they conquered, are Bolivia's largest indigenous group. Overall, Quechua speakers are also the largest ethnolinguistic group in South America. In Bolivia, Quechua speakers primarily live in the departments of Cochabamba and Sucre, but their communities also extend into the valleys of Potosí, Tarija, La Paz, and Oruro.

Fragments of other highland Indians and Aymara and Quechua subgroups can be distinguished by distinct customs, music, and dress. Traditionally, before the land reforms of the National Revolution in 1952, Bolivia's highland Indians lived as either serfs (known as *pongos, colonos,* or *peones*) on the rural haciendas or as communal

A Quechua woman in traditional clothing (Kathy S. Leonard photo)

A paceño, or resident of La Paz, of Aymara ancestry (Kathy S. Leonard photo)

freeholders *(communarios)* of indigenous *ayllus* (land cooperatives). Bolivia's lowland Indians are often overlooked when considering the country's rich Native American heritage. The indigenous tribes of the savannas and rain forests contributed significantly, however, to the multiethnic composition of Bolivian society. Very few pure descendants remain of these ethnically diverse lowland tribes. Fewer than 50,000 lowland Indians of four linguistic families presently live. The two major groups are the Guaraní and the Arawak. In the 18th century, the Guaraní were converted and organized into Jesuit religious settlements, the missions *(reducciones)*. When the Jesuits were expelled from South America in 1767, exploitation and slavery severely damaged and depleted the indigenous communities. Extermination, acculturation, deculturation, and intermarriage also reduced most lowland Indian populations and created a racial and ethnic mixture of the lowland mestizos. Anthropologists continue to study the diminishing tribes of the lowlands before they completely die out. At present, for example, there are only a few hundred Sirionó forest Indians remaining.

Mestizos form Bolivia's second-largest racial and ethnic group. Interracial unions between the Spaniards and the Indians were common from the time the conquistadores arrived in what was to become modern Bolivia. As a result, mestizos, or *cholos,* as they are called in Bolivia, of mixed Indian and white parentage now make up 30 to 40 percent of Bolivia's population, and their numbers are steadily increasing, gradually transforming Bolivia from an Indian to a mestizo nation. Members of a third group, who are primarily of white European descent, number perhaps from 5 to 15 percent.

The remaining elements of Bolivia's population are extremely diverse and include people of African heritage, who descended from the black slaves that were brought to Bolivia and forced to work the Potosí mines in colonial times. There are also a small number of Middle Eastern, Asian Indian, Chinese, Japanese, and eastern European settlers, as well as immigrant colonies of Dutch and German Mennonites and descendants of Jewish refugees from Nazi Europe. Bolivia was one of the few countries in the world to accept Europe's fleeing Jewish emigrants during the late 1930s, thus saving thousands of lives. The majority of these heterogeneous and multinational groups settled in urban areas, especially in the city of Santa Cruz and the department's lowlands.

In many cases, the race and ethnicity of Bolivian citizens have become so diluted as to be largely indistinguishable. Nevertheless, despite extensive population mixing and the leveling effect of the National Revolution, discrimination based on race and ethnicity persists. Indeed, race often refers to ethnicity and "social race," or a person's overt physical characteristics, cultural attributes, preferred language, socioeconomic status, and degree of social mobility and education.

Race has also been perceived differently in the many regions of the country. In the highlands, the whites, or *blancos,* who were identified with the descendants of the Spanish conquerors and the aristocratic upper class, are still considered a more cultured and elite class. In the southeastern valleys and lowlands, the *blancos* claim to be descended from pure European stock and therefore believe themselves to be superior to the white population of the highlands. The aristocracy of the lowlands has traditionally identified with the more Europeanized descendants of Argentina.

Regional Forces

From colonial times, Bolivia has served as a barrier to westward expansion by Brazil and northward expansion by Argentina. Bolivia not only separates these two ambitious continental rivals, it also divides the continent along its north-south axis into the northern tier and what is known as the Southern Cone. Because of their country's central location and buffering role, Bolivians have become involved in the political and economic developments of South America's three major regional subsystems: the River Plate region; the Andean region; and the Amazonian region.

Recent Bolivian governments have aggressively pursued an external policy of regional integration with neighboring countries. This outward-looking integration policy was expected to significantly expand intra- and interregional trade not only within Bolivia but also with the rest of South America. Therefore, the current regional initiative promised to accelerate Bolivia's future economic development overall, but especially in the less accessible and historically neglected lowland regions of the interior. In this way, the government hoped that a redefined and proactive strategy of continental regionalism would serve multiple purposes by also deflecting the internal divisiveness and traditional parochialism among the different regions of the country.

Powerful regional forces within Bolivia influenced the country's history and socioeconomic development. Bolivia inherited from Spain's decentralized colonial rule a tradition of localism and regionalism that hampered national integration and balanced economic growth. The colonial economy's reliance on mining further reinforced regional tensions and determined the seat of political power. Before the mining era, the colonial city of Chuquisaca (later renamed Sucre) served as the political capital of the country. The silver boom in the 16th century, however, shifted economic and political influence to the city of Potosí. For a time, Potosí was the most populated city in colonial Bolivia. Later, the tin boom in the 19th century once again shifted the power balance, this time northward along the altiplano to the mining centers of the department of Oruro and the city of La Paz. Today, Sucre remains Bolivia's constitutional capital, but its population is dwindling and its

Modern-day La Paz, the administrative capital of Bolivia, with volcanic Mount Illimani in the background (Copyright Daniel I. Komer, DDB Stock Photography)

significance is primarily historical. Political power is wielded from the highland and La Paz, which is the de facto administrative capital of contemporary Bolivia.

After independence and well into the 20th century, the negative aspects of regionalism continued to burden Bolivian governments. Harold Osborne characterized Bolivia as "a land divided," and James Malloy as "two" Bolivias separated by the outward-looking extractive economy and the semifeudal and inward-oriented agricultural economy. This economic bifurcation severely skewed the country's communications and transportation systems. As a result, goods flowed in and out of Bolivia primarily through La Paz, the country's real economic and political capital. In turn, La Paz was narrowly linked to the vital mining centers and few major cities, such as Oruro and Potosí, on the altiplano and Cochabamba in the inter-Andean valleys. It was easier and cheaper to import foodstuffs and distribute these in the highland from La Paz than to tap the abundant agricultural resources in the country's interior provinces.

Impressive topographical diversity also fostered Bolivia's intense regionalism. Politics, economics, and backward transportation and communication networks nurtured it further. Administratively, Bolivia is composed of the nine regional departments of La Paz, Oruro, Potosí, and Chuquisaca in the highlands; Cochabamba and Tarija in the valleys; and Santa Cruz, El Beni, and Pando in the tropical lowlands. The importance of a given department has generally depended on its exploitable economic and demographic resources and its accessibility. For most of its history Bolivia's deep interior (El Beni, Pando, and most of Santa Cruz) remained virgin or frontier territory. Even as late as the 1970s the bulk of Bolivia's vast lowland regions was little accessible by road or rail. Bolivia's lowland departments comprise 70 percent of the national territory. The altiplano and near valley settlements, however, have been home to 75 percent of the population. Traditionally described as an Andean country, two-thirds of Bolivia actually lies within the Amazon Basin.

Very early on in the country's formation, a strong highland versus lowland regional split developed that persists up to the present. The people of the highlands are known as *kollas* (after one of the ancient Aymara kingdoms) and distinguish themselves from the *cambas,* the people native to the semitropical and tropical lowlands of Bolivia's interior. The typical Bolivian highlander has more in common with a highlander from Peru or Chile than with a compatriot of the lowlands. And the Bolivian lowlander identifies more closely with his or her counterpart in Brazil and Argentina.

Historically, the central government confronted secessionist movements, especially in the country's southeastern departments, where lowlander citizens preferred Argentine to Bolivian rule. Although regional disparities have declined with development, more economic opportunities in neighboring countries encourage back-and-forth migration. After three decades of spectacular growth, the lowland city of Santa Cruz is no longer a rural backwater but on its way to becoming the country's most populous and powerful urban center. Bolivia's northeastern departments, on the other hand, have yet to be fully integrated with the rest of the country. Vast rivers, dense rain forests, and wetlands, although a source of great ecological wealth, isolate and enfeeble the economies of the region.

Today's Bolivia boasts great geographical diversity and a wealth of natural treasures. At times these assets have also been liabilities, attracting the aggression of neighbors, stirring regional separatism, and impeding the national integration of its people. Regionalism has influenced the unequal distribution and development of Bolivia's population, but it has also insulated Bolivians from outsiders and protected the country's multiethnic and cultural diversity. Nevertheless, uniting and ruling the disparate regions and peoples of this underpopulated country continues to challenge Bolivian governments.

1

THE ANCIENT INDIAN
PEOPLES

The history of ancient Bolivia encompasses primarily the Indian
empires of the Tiwanakan, the Aymara, and the Incan peoples.
These native Andean cultures never developed written records, but they
left behind extensive archaeological sites and a rich heritage of oral traditions and artifacts. Much of what is known about these civilizations
is drawn from the remains of their cities and villages, extensive centers
of worship, and public works projects. In addition, examples of their
material and artistic cultures are provided in the form of distinctive
woven textiles, gold and silver ornaments, and intricate pottery and
carvings. And, legends and stories that have been preserved by the
descendants of these peoples and in some cases were recorded by early
Spanish chroniclers also contribute to our knowledge of these indigenous civilizations. From the Pacific coast to the highlands and valleys
of what is now Bolivia, indigenous peoples settled and prospered from
prehistoric times until A.D. 1532, when Spanish conquerors arrived and
systematically destroyed the ancient Indian world and enslaved its
native peoples.

Pre-Tiwanakan Cultures

The earliest Indian civilizations of Bolivia inhabited the high plateau of
the Andean altiplano. A long-popular theory holds that these Andean
people, known to archaeologists today as pre-Tiwanakan, were originally descended from nomadic Asian tribespeople who had crossed
over on foot from Siberia into North America during a period in
Paleolithic times when there was a land bridge across the Bering Sea.
Over millennia, these tribes gradually moved down the continents into
South America, ultimately establishing permanent settlements along

I

the Andean coast and in the arid Andean altiplano. Although virtually no evidence of such migrations has ever been found in the far northern Arctic regions, there are several recently discovered ancient sites along or near the Pacific coast of South America that show humans were established there many thousands of years ago, although archaeologists disagree on how far back to push the date.

Modern researchers generally believe that the early tribal groupings, which ultimately became the pre-Tiwanakan peoples, settled below Lake Titicaca between around 1600 and 1400 B.C. Little is really known about these very early Andean cultures, and it is possible that some scattered Indian communities may have dated as far back as 7500 B.C. or even 10,000 B.C.

It is indisputable from the archaeological evidence, however, that very early Indian peoples lived on the coast and up into the Andean highlands to elevations of 15,000 feet. Coastal villagers fished in the mouths of rivers, and as they gradually developed agricultural skills, they began to grow cotton, corn, and potatoes and to domesticate guinea pigs for meat. In the highlands, the early Indian peoples hunted Andean deer and herded llamas for meat and alpacas for wool.

One of the first distinctively identifiable cultures is known as the Chavín, named after extensive ruins found on the eastern Andes of Peru. It is believed that the Chavín culture, which is preserved today primarily in the ruins of religious sites, exerted influence widely and spread across the Andean region from around 900 B.C. until it went into decline around 100 B.C. (There are remains of an extremely early Chavín religious center in a mountainous valley region about 150 miles northeast of Lima, Peru, that may date from 3000 B.C., but the best-known site is the much later Chavín de Huántar, also in modern-day Peru.) Remnants of Chavín temples and palaces reveal distinctive architecture and decorative carvings of snakes and jaguars and strange figures. The Chavín influence over the surrounding Andean region and into what is modern-day Bolivia was primarily religious and cultural. As converts to the Chavín religious cult spread among neighboring tribes throughout northern and central Peru, so did their gold artistry and intricately woven cloth and tapestries of alpaca wool.

By A.D. 300, there were other important Indian communities along the dry Pacific coast and highlands of modern-day Peru, Chile, and Bolivia. For example, south of the Chavín area, the Nazca and Paracas peoples, skilled in weaving and pottery, lived in small coastal towns. In the highlands 150 miles east of Lima, far to the north of modern-day Bolivia, the Huari people built an urban empire of cities with elaborate paved plazas and large palaces in the Chavín architectural and decorative style. For 500 years, from A.D. 300 to 800, the Huari held sway over an extensive area. These cultures were important in the prehistory of South America, and they doubtless had strong influences on the indigenous people who lived in the region that today is Bolivia, but the best-defined and most important political center was on Lake Titicaca.

Tiwanakan Civilization

Modern archaeologists speculate that Aymara-speaking people may have migrated from central Peru into the Bolivian altiplano (a region that is also often referred to as Alto Peru, or Upper Peru, when discussing this period) and taken up residence on the shores of Lake Titicaca as early as 700 B.C. The evidence is clear that a culture centered on the city of Tiwanaku (also spelled Tiahuanaco), less than 40 miles from Bolivia's modern capital city of La Paz, emerged between 100 B.C. and A.D. 100 and by 600, a powerful Tiwanakan empire had developed that came to dominate the Bolivian altiplano and to control the coastal settlements of the Nazca and Paracas peoples in what is modern-day Peru. The Tiwanakans may be thought of as the ancestors of the modern-day Aymara Indians of the Bolivian and Peruvian highlands who still live near Lake Titicaca and in the neighboring lowland valleys. Researchers believe that the Tiwanakan Empire preceded and even rivaled the more familiar empire of the Inca in many respects.

The Tiwanakan Empire's armies and engineers conquered and colonized huge areas and established an intricate paved road system linking agricultural colonies on the coast to those in the highlands and the tropical valleys and jungles beyond. This empire extended from the border of modern-day Ecuador in the north down the Peruvian and Chilean Pacific coastal lands southward, covering over half of Bolivia, and into the foothills of the Argentine Andes.

The imperial capital city of Tiwanaku probably had a population of 50,000 people and covered

A Tiwanakan pottery jar in the form of a mountain cat, made by the ancestors of the Aymara people (Peter McFarren photo)

3

an area of about four square miles. At the height of its development, the city was ruled by a divine emperor-priest who directed the religious rituals and cultural life of the people. With the help of the royal family, the emperor also controlled secular affairs of state. Similar to their subsequent Incan counterparts, the Tiwanakan rulers lived a luxurious life and maintained the power of their hereditary caste through close intermarriage. The Tiwanakans are also thought to have influenced the cosmological and religious beliefs of other pre-Incan and Incan peoples. The great creator god of the ancient Tiwanakans was Viracocha, or Pachacámac, whose shrine was located near modern-day Lima, in Peru. The Inca incorporated the Tiwanakan sacred shrine and the worship of Pachacámac into their own religion, and the site remains a sacred place for most native Andean religions to this day.

Tiwanakan technology was relatively sophisticated—artisans knew how to alloy copper and tin to create bronze, for example—and the civilization's complex social and economic organization made it possible for Tiwanakans to build an extensive system of roads and maintain communications over long distances. Their intricate farming system of raised agricultural fields permitted the Tiwanakans to reap great annual harvests, and they stored the surplus in public granaries against lean crop years. According to investigations by U.S. anthropologist Alan Kolata, the Tiwanakan agricultural system was so advanced at its height 1,500 years ago that the plains around the archaeological site of the Pampa Koani valley near Lake Titicaca may have produced enough food for 125,000 people. The same region barely supports its 7,000 desperately poor inhabitants today.

Archaeological ruins at the imperial city of Tiwanaku show extensive skill in architecture and knowledge of astronomy. Tiwanaku was laid out in several large plazas with the dominant central plaza paved with imposing stone slabs. The few architectural walls, semisubterranean temples, and gateways that survive today are adorned with Chavín-style figures and carved animals. Most impressive of these is the Puerta del Sol, or the Gate of the Sun, and the rebuilt Temple of Kalasasaya, which in Aymara means "stones standing upright" and refers to its basalt-sandstone monoliths that are astronomically aligned around a ritual platform.

As impressive as the achievements of the Tiwanakan culture were, the empire came to a sudden end around A.D. 1200. The reason for the demise of Tiwanakan power and the dispersal of its people remain mysteries, but Aymara oral traditions speak of cataclysmic disasters: a great flood, a massive earthquake, internal disintegration and feuding, and

4

The Gate of the Sun at the site of the imperial city of Tiwanaku, near modern-day La Paz. The elaborately carved doorway was cut from a single block of stone. (Peter McFarren photo)

external conquest. The most probable cause of the empire's collapse, according to several modern experts, may have been a widespread and prolonged drought.

The Kingdoms of the Aymara

Bolivian historians believe that the Tiwanakan Empire was succeeded on the Bolivian altiplano by numerous small, regional Indian kingdoms. The people of these kingdoms were the direct ancestors of Bolivia's Aymara. In modern times, Bolivians use the names Kolla and Kollasuyo to refer in a collective sense to the Aymara-based indigenous culture of the Bolivian altiplano and to all the Aymara kingdoms, respectively. (Kollasuyo means "empire of the Kolla.") There were specifically, however, 12 major kingdoms or nations, of which the Kolla, who were scattered around the shores of Lake Titicaca, were the largest and most powerful.

The political, economic, and social structures of the Aymara nations, including the Kolla and the Lupaca, were highly structured and rigidly stratified into a dual-layered system. Each Aymara nation or kingdom was stratified into two separate and unequal internal kingdoms—one high and one low—and each had its own king and its own ruling elite.

5

Two entirely complete political and socioeconomic structures existed stacked one upon the other.

The complex organization of Aymara society was believed to have been derived from the Tiwanakans and later adapted by the Inca. On the political side it included dual sets of powerful central military leaders, hereditary regional chieftains (curacas), local ayllu authorities who dealt with the land communes, state religious counselors, and councils of wise elders.

Although at first glance, this dual system seems cumbersome and unnecessarily complex, it served an important function. As has been true throughout Bolivian history, during the period of the Aymara kingdoms, the largest number of people lived on the high altiplano plateau, which had only a limited amount of agricultural land. The people of the altiplano had to rely on crops grown in the distant fertile valleys and in farm districts closer to the Pacific coast. When the Aymara kingdoms colonized or conquered regions that could supply food and other necessities to the population of the altiplano, they also transplanted their dual system of political and socioeconomic organization. This immediately created parallel functional structures in both the agricultural colony and the altiplano homeland. The system cut across differing ecological regions and climatic zones and allowed the Aymara to exploit the agricultural hinterland. In this way the dominant kingdoms, which were all located in the eastern highlands, benefited from the agricultural bounty of the subordinate kingdoms on both sides of the Andean mountain chain. According to the historian Herbert S. Klein, this integrated system exploited the agricultural potential of differing ecological zones to the fullest and made possible the production and exchange of different crops within the empire. These arrangements between the core society of the highlands and the agricultural colonies relied on an elaborate system of kinship, exchange, and labor obligations (the latter was called the mita system and was adopted by both the Inca and the Spanish).

The Aymara's dual organizational scheme was also applied on a micro level within the social class structure of the ayllu, the self-governing tribal community and collective landholding system based on kinship. These were divided into upper and lower parts with the nobility associated with the upper ayllus and the commoners with the lower. The Aymara social order, which also influenced Incan society, rested on the extended family and tribal agricultural cooperatives of the ayllu. Several ayllus formed a federation of ayllus. The primarily agricultural economy was organized around the communal cultivation of the native potato and highland grains.

Aymara cosmology and religion centered on nature and the sun, moon, and stars. Viracocha, or Pachacámac, was the powerful creator god; Khuno, the dark deity of evil; and Pachamama (Mother Earth), the feminine deity of fertility.

Around A.D. 1460, the aggressive and imperialistic Inca swept down from the north and rapidly conquered the decentralized kingdoms of the Aymara people. The defeated remnants of the dispersed Aymara communities on the Bolivian altiplano were subsumed into the southern region of the Inca Empire. Bolivian historians attribute the disintegration and speedy subjugation of the Aymara kingdoms to internecine feuding and bloody civil wars. In 1470, this fierce love of warfare and independence erupted into a major revolt against their new Inca rulers.

The Empire of the Inca

The empire of the Inca, founded near the sacred city of Cuzco in modern-day Peru at the beginning of the 13th century, ultimately dominated the entire Andean and coastal regions. At its head stood Sapa-Inca ("supreme Inca"), the hereditary emperor who claimed descent from the sun god Inti. Although the term the *Inca* or *Incas* is generically used to describe all the Quechua-speaking inhabitants of the vast, multinational Indian empire, the term specifically refers to the ruling caste or the royal princes of the Quechua people, as well as to the supreme emperor, Sapa-Inca.

The culturally unified pan-Andean empire that the Inca created by conquest and colonization was called the Tahuantinsuyo. Bolivian historians like to point out that the Inca Empire was the second pan-Andean empire of its kind—the empire of Tiwanaku came first by several centuries—but the Inca Empire certainly surpassed all others in scale and grandeur. By 1527 at the height of its territorial expansion, the Inca Empire's boundaries extended 4,000 miles in length, and covered more than 380,000 square miles from northern Ecuador to southern Chile, and probably contained 10 million subjects.

The origin of the Quechua-speaking Inca is the subject of competing legends and theories. Bolivian historians often theorize that the Inca were of Aymara origin. According to this interpretation, the Inca arose from the northern Aymara kingdom of Lupaca (the Lupaca were also known as the Chucuito after the name of their capital) and the specific *ayllu,* or kinship group, of the Ayares, a people who originally inhabited the region of Puno in Peru and near the Bolivian shores of Lake Titicaca. At some point, the Ayares migrated northward from Lake Titicaca to near Cuzco in Peru.

Both Bolivian oral traditions and a commentary compiled by the conquest-era Spanish historian Inca Garcilaso de la Vega recount that the movement was ordered by the chieftain of the Ayares, Manco Kapac, and his sister-wife, Mama Ocllo. According to the legendary story, the couple claimed to be children of the sun god, who instructed them to civilize the surrounding backward tribes. They set out from the Island of the Sun in Lake Titicaca with a golden staff, which guided them eventually to a mountain near Cuzco in modern-day Peru. There the divine pair established their kingdom.

The Ayares, who were Aymara speakers, intermarried with the more primitive regional Indian communities of the Quechua language family and adopted the Quechua language. Over time, the Cuzco Quechua, whose name means "people from the tropical lands," flourished and developed into the powerful Indian nation that became known as the Inca. Following this interpretation, the emerging imperial state of the Quechua-speaking Inca was derived from the preceding political and socioeconomic systems of the Aymara and Tiwanakan civilizations.

Inca Sinchi Roca, the successor of Manco Kapac, is believed to have divided the empire into four geographical sections that were ruled by viceroys and were internally further divided into provinces and subprovinces ruled by provincial officials. The subprovinces were made up of several *allyus,* headed by *curacas,* who were either elected or the hereditary chiefs of the conquered governments. At the next lower level of organization were the tribes and the villages, which consisted of 100 families, and at the very bottom were groups of 10 families served by a headman. In this manner, the Inca adopted and perfected the administrative system of the Aymara and transformed it into a complex but effective system of imperial control.

The oral traditions and chroniclers do not agree about which of the Incan leaders first began the imperial expansion of the Quechua people of Cuzco. Some accounts say it was Manco Kapac himself; others believe that the Inca Empire did not expand appreciably until several generations later under the leadership of the seventh Incan ruler, Viracocha (also spelled Wiracocha), who took the name of the all-powerful deity of the Tiwanakans. Viracocha was indisputably a great conqueror who subdued tribes and kingdoms as far away as modern-day northern Argentina and incorporated them into the empire. His successor, Pachacútec, conquered the Chimú Empire in what is today part of Peru and fostered the development of religious centers and public works, including the magnificent Inca roads and aqueducts. Later, the eleventh Inca, Huayna Capac, extended Incan rule over the kingdom of

Inca masons were superb engineers and craftsmen, who constructed massive buildings, walls, and waterways out of huge stones that they fit together without mortar or the help of metal tools. (Brown Brothers photo)

Quito, and the tribes of what is today modern Ecuador. The empire achieved its farthest extension during Huayna Capac's reign.

The Incan economic structure was a rigid pyramid based on the same pattern as the empire's political organization exploiting the agricultural potential of the empire to its fullest. Land was very precious; it was held in common and could not be sold. The rich natural resources of the gold and silver mines, the forests, and the vast flocks and herds of animals were tightly controlled by the Incan ruling class as state monopolies. The land's produce and resources were always divided into three parts and distributed among the Inca ruling caste, the priests, and the *ayllus.* Within the *ayllus,* land was collectively owned by the entire community as it had been in the Andean world for time out of mind but was distributed for cultivation according to the size and composition of each household in the *ayllu.* Generally, the land was divided into two-acre plots; one whole plot went to each male member of the family and a half plot to each female member. All members of the community were obligated to cooperatively farm the plots of land belonging to the Inca and royal family, the priests, and the community's widows and orphans,

THE GREAT INCA RULERS

Manco Kapac: founded the empire

Sinchi Roca: divided the empire into four regions

Mita Kapac: subdued the Kolla and other Aymara kingdoms

Kapac Yupanqui: conquered many tribes of the central Andean valleys and made teaching the Quechua language obligatory

Inca Roca: made Quechua the sole language of the empire and established schools for the children of the nobility in Cuzco

Yuhuar Huácac: weak ruler deposed by his son Ripac, who took the new name of Viracocha

Viracocha: extended the empire by far-reaching conquests and built grand palaces and canals

Pachacútec: conquered the Chimú Empire in Peru, founded schools and religious centers, constructed a system of aqueducts, and ordered the design of a calendar

Inca Yupanqui: extended the empire to the Maule River

Tupac Yupanqui: founded Copacabana, constructed the Temple of the Island of the Moon, and marched on Quito (Ecuador)

Huayna Capac: married the daughter of the ruler of Quito and ruled over the empire at its greatest extension; divided the empire between his two sons, Huáscar and Atahuallpa

Huáscar: Ruled over the southern part of the empire in Cuzco and began a war with his brother, Atahuallpa.

Atahuallpa: Ruler of Quito, defeated and killed his brother, Huáscar, and was himself captured and killed by the Spanish conqueror, Francisco Pizarro.

but otherwise, family plots were farmed only by that family. Additionally, there was an involuntary labor system called the *mita* that forced all able-bodied males to serve the Sapa-Inca. In this way the empire ensured that it had the necessary manpower to supply soldiers for the imperial army and laborers to build and maintain imperial roads and irrigation systems and to work the state mines.

The Incan social system was similarly hierarchical and rigid and served to reinforce the organization of the economy and political life. At the very top of the social pyramid was the supreme emperor (Sapa-Inca) and his royal relatives. Next came the imperial nobility, who served as the principal military, bureaucratic, and religious officers of the empire. They were followed by a provincial upper class composed of the hereditary chiefs of the conquered tribes and their sons and daughters, who were educated at the royal court in Cuzco. This regional aristocracy was permitted to hold private wealth in the form of jewelry and slaves. One level above the base of the pyramidal class structure was a free but propertyless peasant class, and at the bottom was a slave class mainly made up of captives from enemy tribes and criminals.

A large, powerful imperial army held the empire together militarily and politically and was the means of territorial expansion, a process of conquest and absorption of the conquered into the Inca imperial structure. The basic imperial colonization policy, intended to ensure loyalty to the empire, uprooted conquered peoples and whole communities and resettled them in safe territories that were friendly and loyal to the empire. Only the most trustworthy Quechua colonists were sent to colonize and control the strategically important agricultural zones such as the fertile valleys of Cochabamba and Chuquisaca in Bolivia.

The great Incan rulers unified this pan-Andean society of multiethnic tribes and kingdoms into a formidable imperial state. But Incan political hegemony was not achieved by power alone. These millions of people were joined and integrated culturally as well by one religion, a common body of laws, and the official Quechua language.

The Inca also developed an efficient system of communication that used royal runners (*chaski*) to carry oral messages and the knotted message ropes called *quipus* (adopted from the Aymara) from all corners of the empire to the central government in Cuzco. The messengers traveled along two parallel coastal and Andean highways radiating outward from Cuzco and traversing the length of the 4,000-mile empire from north to south. The great Inca Road was a marvel of ingenuity and engineering skill. The road, level and paved with stones, was designed for foot travel because the Inca had not discovered the wheel. The road traversed fearsome rivers by means of hanging bridges made of the twisted fibers of the maguey plant and plunged down into large underground tunnels and up steep staircases. Historian Victor Von Hagen writes that Sapa-Inca in his palace in Cuzco could dine on fresh fish from the coast carried along the Inca Road over the highest Andes, a distance of 200 miles, in only two days.

Shortly before the coming of the Spanish in the 16th century, the highly developed Inca Empire began to decline. Critical to its demise were the division of the empire and resulting civil war between the brothers and dual rulers Huáscar and Atahuallpa, as well as growing local

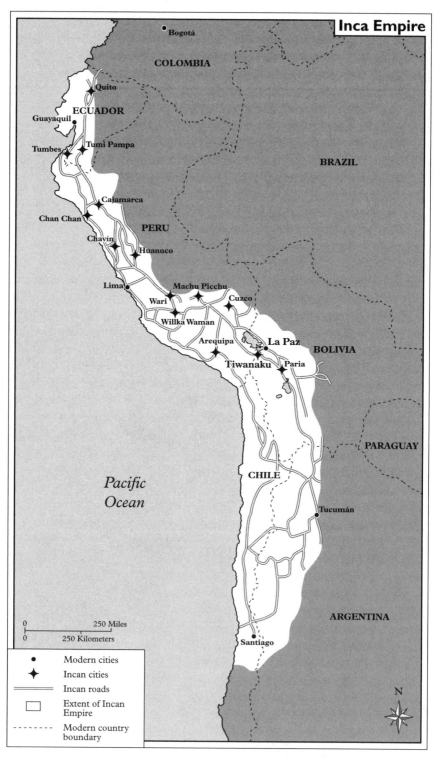

Inca Empire

Bogotá

COLOMBIA

Quito

ECUADOR

Guayaquil

Tumbes

Tumí Pampa

Cajamarca

Chan Chan

Chavín

PERU

Huanuco

Lima

Machu Picchu

Wari

Cuzco

Willka Waman

Arequipa

La Paz

BOLIVIA

Tiwanaku

Paria

BRAZIL

PARAGUAY

CHILE

Tucumán

Pacific
Ocean

ARGENTINA

Santiago

0   250 Miles
0   250 Kilometers

● Modern cities
✦ Incan cities
═ Incan roads
▢ Extent of Incan Empire
- - - Modern country boundary

N

12

uprisings among distant and partially subdued tribes such as the one in 1470 by the Bolivian Aymara-Kolla, who had retained their Aymara language and distinct cultural identity despite the repeated waves of Quechua conquest and colonization. When the European adventurers arrived in South America early in the 16th century, the vast Inca Empire of thousands of soldiers and millions of inhabitants was easily conquered by a combination of Spanish treachery and advanced military technology. Within a year, the great capital of Cuzco capitulated and the victorious Spanish marauders regrouped and marched against the recalcitrant Indians of Bolivia's altiplano.

The Inca Huáscar, who inherited half the empire from his father, Inca Huayna Capac. Huáscar was defeated, dethroned, and imprisoned by his younger half-brother and rival, Atahuallpa, during the "Brothers' War." Atahuallpa was later captured and killed by the Spanish. (Art Today)

2

COLONIAL BOLIVIA
(1532–1780)

We came here to serve God, but also to get rich.

■

Bernal Díaz del Castillo (Hamill 1992, 14)

Some of the prophecies of the Indian peoples of the Americas fore-
told the arrival of the Spanish, but nothing could have prepared the
native population of Bolivia for the stunning impact of the brutal, avaricious conquerors who came in search of gold, silver, gems, and—as an
afterthought—to Christianize native populations in the name of the
cross and the Crown. Francisco Pizarro, an illiterate military adventurer, overnight destroyed the glorious empire of the Inca, and in the
following years, Spanish explorers, priests, and royal administrators
consolidated a New World colonial empire.

Pizarro's Conquest of the Inca Empire

> ...these men were so bold they did not fear dangerous things;
> they were stuffed into their clothes, which covered them from
> head to foot; they were white and had beards and a ferocious
> appearance.

■

Father Bernabé Cobo, 17th century (1979, 160)

Francisco Pizarro, the illegitimate son of an obscure Spanish officer,
fought as a young man in the Indian wars in Central America and later
became prosperous. But in his comfortable middle age he became

obsessed by reports of a mighty kingdom and legendary riches to the south and launched a late career as an explorer and conqueror. In 1524, Pizarro, in league with Diego de Almagro, led a disastrous expedition down the South American coast. On a second voyage, however, Pizarro and his men luckily intercepted a small shipment of gold and silver and other treasure from the northern Incan outpost of Tumbes on the Peruvian coast, and the booty whetted his appetite.

Pizarro, convinced that there were more riches in the interior, sailed to Spain to find men and money for a new expedition. He won the favor and support of King Charles I of Spain, who named Pizarro governor of Peru and hereditary *adelantado* (military governor) for life. With reinforcements from Pizarro's hometown of Trujillo, including his three half-brothers, Hernando, Juan, and Gonzalo, Pizarro returned to South America and launched his expedition.

When Pizarro and his small army of experienced and well-equipped conquistadores marched inland from their landing on the Pacific coast, they discovered an Incan empire in the aftermath of a terrible schism. Fortuitously for the Spanish, the discord had decisively damaged the power of the Inca to resist an outside force. The trouble had begun with the death of Huayna Capac, who had been emperor for 34 years. He may have succumbed to the epidemic of European smallpox that swept down the Pacific coast during the 1520s ahead of Pizarro and his men.

On his deathbed, Inca Huayna Capac had divided the empire between two of his sons. Huáscar, the eldest, was to control the southern empire from the traditional capital in Cuzco. Atahuallpa, Huayna Capac's

THE ADVANCE MEN

Pizarro and other illustrious explorers and soldiers of fortune were granted the title of *adelantado* (from the Spanish verb *adelantar*, or "to advance"). These *adelantados* were private individuals who preceded or advanced Spanish conquest and rule. The Spanish king extended to private individuals royal grants to explore new territories at their own expense (or sometimes with royal favor) and to found a colony and govern it in the name of the Spanish Crown. Once the New World was settled, the honorific and administrative term was used to designate a colonial governor of a frontier district or province. Pizarro was named *adelantado* for life before he had even set foot in the heart of the Inca Empire.

favorite and the better soldier of the two, was to lead the professional army and rule the recently conquered northern lands of the empire (modern-day Ecuador and Colombia) from the court in Quito. For two years following their father's death, the half-brothers maintained a delicate political status quo, but eventually Atahuallpa challenged Huáscar's rule, and a long and exhausting civil war followed.

The strife and dislocations of the bloody Brothers' War threw the Inca Empire out of balance. The Inca system was strictly hierarchical and authoritarian; without a clearly designated Sapa-Inca and the officialdom he commanded, the empire, including the army, was paralyzed. Whom were the layers of officials to

Francisco Pizarro led an amazingly small number of Spanish soldiers in the stunning conquest of the mighty Inca Empire. (Brown Brothers photo)

look to for instruction? Whom were the people to obey? Huáscar or Atahuallpa? Moreover, the civil war drained off manpower into two opposing armies, and as a consequence, fields were left unplanted and unharvested.

Eventually, Atahuallpa's military superiority tipped the balance, and he defeated his half-brother in the Battle of Quipaypampa (Huanuco Pampa), which took place several miles outside Cuzco in 1532. Huáscar was captured and held as a prisoner, and thousands of his supporters were slaughtered.

In the climax of this desperate internecine struggle, Pizarro and his avaricious adventurers arrived. Pizarro's timing could not have been more favorable for quick conquest. Although the Inca Empire was defended by more than 40,000 soldiers, the bitter internal war allowed the meager contingent of 168 Spanish invaders to infiltrate and enslave one of the last great civilizations of the Americas.

Pizarro encountered Atahuallpa's victorious forces near the city of Cajamarca. The Spanish leader realized the potentially desperate situation he was in, facing a huge army of Indian warriors, so he put in place a plan of savage deceit whose success exceeded what must have been his wildest hopes. He enticed Atahuallpa to a meeting in the town plaza of Cajamarca, and the Sapa-Inca, who apparently felt invincible after his recent victory and unthreatened by these strange outsiders, came with only a small bodyguard, leaving the bulk of his army encamped nearby. Pizarro first sent out a priest to meet Atahuallpa and to offer the emperor conversion on the spot to Christianity. When the Sapa-Inca quite naturally refused, Pizarro had all the pretext he needed, and the Spaniards unleashed a vicious, unforgiving ambush. The attack by cannon, harquebus, crossbow, lance, and sword caught the Inca entirely unprepared, and a slaughter ensued. Several hundred, perhaps more than 1,000, Inca were killed there and then, and Atahuallpa was taken captive without the loss of a single Spanish life. In the space of a few hours, the balance of power shifted completely from what had seemed like a vast and all-powerful Indian civilization to a mere handful of scruffy Spanish soldiers.

For the Inca, this disaster, coming on the heels of the succession crisis and brutal purge of Huáscar's supporters by the victorious Atahuallpa, destroyed the foundations of the empire. With Atahuallpa in Spanish hands, there was no one to direct the response, no one to give orders to the generals or the legions of imperial officials. The huge Incan armies, which could have crushed the handful of Spaniards at any time, did nothing. Moreover, the remnants of Huáscar's loyalists (among them highland Bolivia's Aymara nations) eyed the Spanish invaders as potential allies in their struggle against Atahuallpa.

Atahuallpa, fearing a renewed threat from his brother more than from his Spanish captors, ordered Huáscar killed and offered to ransom himself with enough gold and silver to fill three sizable rooms. Pizarro promised to return the captive supreme Inca to his northern capital in Quito once the ransom was paid. Soon, an amazing horde began to flow into Cajamarca. While Atahuallpa dickered complaisantly with his captors, his subjects amassed a ransom that may have amounted to nearly 40,000 pounds of gold and silver.

Unfortunately, Atahuallpa had misjudged Pizarro's intentions, and in the end, Pizarro ordered Atahuallpa's execution. Since the young Inca had converted to Christianity in the last hours of his life, Atahuallpa was garroted to death rather than burned at the stake as a pagan and heretic. The Sapa-Inca had deeply feared the destruction of his body, a sacrilege in the Andean world that would preclude its mummification and an assured afterlife. Contemporary chroniclers reported that Atahuallpa accepted his fate with equanimity.

Pizarro moved quickly to begin to consolidate his victory and assert Spanish dominion over the Indian peoples of the Inca Empire. Since

ATAHUALLPA'S RANSOM

F rancisco Pizarro extorted from Atahuallpa the most fabulous ransom in history, which was delivered to the Spanish in the form of finely worked gold and silver. The Spaniards melted down these priceless treasures into 13,420 pounds of 22-carat gold and 26,000 pounds of pure silver (Burkholder and Johnson 1994, 46). Each foot soldier in the Spanish expedition received 45 pounds of gold and 90 pounds of silver; a cavalryman received 90 pounds of gold and 180 pounds of silver; an army captain's share was greater yet. As *adelantado,* Francisco Pizarro received 630 pounds of gold and 1,260 pounds of silver (Burkholder and Johnson 1994, 46). A fifth of the treasure went to the king. The men commanded by Pizarro's erstwhile colleague Diego de Almagro arrived too late to take part in the massacre at Cajamarca, so their shares were much less, feeding the factionalism that would lead to civil war in later years.

there was no clear succession, the Spanish decided to crown puppet Incan rulers as a means of control. The first was Tupac Huallpa, but he died only a few months later, apparently of poison. Pizarro then appointed Manco Capac II (Manco Inca Yupanqui), a half-brother (or relative) of the former Sapa-Incas, to the throne.

Pizarro and his army had captured Cuzco, brushing aside Atahuallpa's generals on the way, and stripped the Inca capital of its remaining wealth. To distract the feuding Spanish factions, Pizarro appointed Diego de Almagro to command an expedition into Chile and then himself headed for the coast. In January 1535, he founded the Ciudad de los Reyes ("city of the kings"), which later became known as Lima, the capital of his Peruvian province.

Both contemporary chroniclers and modern historians marvel at the rapid collapse of the Empire of the Sun, as the Inca called it. How could a few hundred Spaniards defeat an army of tens of thousands and control a population of 10 million natives? The traditional answer is that the Spaniards had superior military technology: steel swords, cannons, matchlock firearms, and horses—unknown and mysterious things that greatly terrified the Inca. The Spanish were also cunning, daring, and greedy; at times they were diplomatic and often extremely lucky. In addition, they expertly exploited the ethnic and tribal differences among the Indians; their military tactics were innovative, and they were able to manipulate circumstances in their favor.

On the other hand, the Inca lacked most of these qualities. Atahuallpa routinely underestimated the Spanish invaders. Indeed, often the strange white men were not even treated as invaders but welcomed with great curiosity and respect. Atahuallpa believed that his superior numbers provided him the luxury to determine when, where, and how he would confront the Spanish threat. He had been disastrously wrong.

Conquest of Upper Peru and Founding of Colonial Cities

Finders keepers was not only the Pizarros' maxim, but the rule of life everywhere in the Indies, repeatedly recognized by the crown itself.

■

(Lockhart 1972, 180)

In the years immediately following Pizarro's capture and execution of Atahuallpa, the Spanish conquest of South America—although never seriously in danger—ran over very rough ground, primarily because the main actors bickered over the spoils of the Inca Empire and came to hate and despise one another more than they feared the native population. Within a few years, all the Pizarro brothers excepting Hernando and their rival Almagro were dead, either captured by enemies and executed, as happened to Gonzalo Pizarro and Diego Almagro, or assassinated, like the elderly Francisco, who was killed by Almagro's revengeful mestizo son (who was himself executed for his crime).

The supposed puppet Inca, Manco Capac II, meanwhile, took advantage of the discord among the Spanish and escaped their control. He organized the first large-scale Indian resistance to the conquest and was briefly successful, laying siege to both Lima and Cuzco. The Spanish finally paused in their internal strife long enough to defeat Manco Capac II, however, and the Inca withdrew his rebellious forces to the distant, hidden city of Vilcabamba.

During the turmoil of the disputes between the Spanish factions and the revolt of Manco Capac II, the Aymara kingdoms of Bolivia had found themselves divided and forced to choose between Spanish or Incan overlords. While the Lupaca nation aggressively favored Manco Capac II's uprising, the Kolla failed to support the Inca's revolt and sided with the Spanish forces. After Francisco Pizarro defeated the Inca rebels, the victorious Spaniards took their retribution against all

Indians who had supported the Inca revolt. For Kolla loyalty, the Spanish rescued the Kolla from an attack by the remaining Inca-Lupaca rebel armies in the region of Chuquito and Desaguadero. There, the Pizarro forces defeated the very last of the Inca rebel holdouts and were able to promote serious colonization. Upper Peru, which became modern-day Bolivia, had originally been part of Diego de Almagro's territorial claim but was colonized by Hernando and Gonzalo Pizarro. By 1544, the region, which became known as Charcas, had been completely pacified.

In the years 1538 to 1606, the Spanish founded the major cities of colonial Bolivia. The first Spaniards to enter the region had been a contingent of Almagro's forces—570 Spanish and more than 10,000 Indians captained by Juan de Saavedra—that had marched along the shores of Lake Titicaca near Desaguadero en route south to Chile in 1535. Three years later, Gonzalo Pizarro advanced into Upper Peru along Lake Titicaca and moved southward into Charcas, located in the ancient valley of Choquechaca, which belonged to the Charcas people. There, despite the very aggressive resistance by the local Indians, who were subdued only after Hernando Pizarro rushed in urgent reinforcements from Cuzco, Gonzalo established the great colonial city of Chuquisaca, renamed Sucre in 1840. Near Chuquisaca was the reason for the city's founding, the fabulously rich Porco silver mine, which funneled wealth into the coffers of the Pizarros and the Spanish Crown, and drew hordes of fortune hunters to the region.

Initially, Chuquisaca served as the administrative and agricultural supply center for the entire Potosí mining region. But the silver boom was so fantastic that in 1545 the city of Potosí, or the Villa Imperial de Carlos V (imperial city of Charles V), became the second major city to be founded in highland Bolivia near another amazing discovery: the Cerro Rico (rich mount) mine. The unbelievable silver riches of this mine transformed Potosí into the greatest and most important city of the Spanish New World.

The city of Nuestra Señora de La Paz (Bolivia's current de facto capital, named for Our Lady of Peace) was not founded until 1548 by Viceroy Pedro de la Gasca. At the time, the city served, according to historians, primarily as the way station on the route from the silver mines of Potosí to Lima. Bolivian historical sources emphasize that La Paz was also established to exploit the discovery of gold in the Choqueyapu River that runs through the valley.

The concentration of Aymara and Quechua Indian populations and the immense silver and mercury deposits in the province of Potosí

FOUNDING OF BOLIVIA'S MAJOR CITIES

1538 Chuquisaca (also called La Plata or Charcas, later renamed Sucre; the colonial capital and the constitutional capital of modern-day Bolivia)

1545 Potosí (center of the fabulous 16th- to 19th-century silver mining boom)

1548 La Paz (originally a way station, the present-day political and de facto capital)

1561 Santa Cruz de la Sierra (currently the second-largest city; center of the sugar, cotton, and oil booms of the 20th century)

1571 Cochabamba (center of colonial wheat and corn production; presently the third-largest city)

1574 Tarija (frontier city near prosperous haciendas in the 19th century)

1606 Oruro (center of 18th-century silver and 19th- and 20th-century tin mining booms)

made the central altiplano and southern valleys the natural site of Spanish colonial rule in Bolivia. Silver wealth, of vital and strategic importance to Spain, assured that distant Bolivia would not become an insignificant and isolated backwater of the empire. In 1558–59 the semiautonomous Audiencia of Charcas (Upper Peru) was established with the city of Chuquisaca serving as the region's judicial and administrative seat.

Because highland Bolivia was accessible from the coast only by traversing steep Andean passes and roads, the Spanish conquerors also approached Bolivia from the eastern and southeastern lowlands. These pampas and wetland regions were inhabited by tropical forest Indians of the Tupi-Guaraní linguistic family and other warlike tribes. On the northeastern savannas and tropical forests of Moxos, the city of Trinidad was founded in 1556 by Captains Tristán de Tejada and Juan de Salinas. Despite fierce Indian resistance, in 1561 the Spanish explorer Nuflo de Chávez proceeded westward from Asunción, Paraguay, and discovered and established the subtropical, lowland city of Santa Cruz de la Sierra. Territorial rivalries between the Paraguayan and Peruvian explorers loyal to Spain, as well as encroachments by aggressive Portuguese adventurers from Brazil, occurred over the rich

Bolivian spoils. These were partially resolved by the Spanish Crown and the new colonial governing structure. In 1776, the Audiencia of Charcas was joined to the newly established Viceroyalty of Río de la Plata, based in Buenos Aires, Argentina.

City of Silver and Silver Mining

> *The motor of this capitalism was mining, carried on first in the footsteps of the Indians, later in deep deposits discovered by Spanish prospectors.*
>
> ■
>
> *(Wolf 1959, 176)*

Mining dominated the colonial economy of Charcas (Upper Peru, or modern-day Bolivia) from the 16th to the 18th centuries, making Potosí, the fabled City of Silver, into the wealthiest and most populated in the New World. In 1650, at the zenith of silver production, Potosí boasted 160,000 inhabitants (five times its current population). Major silver production occurred during the 16th and first half of the 17th centuries, with the first veins producing unprecedented quantities of virtually pure silver.

During the first two decades of spectacular silver exploitation, from 1545 to 1565, rich silver ore could easily be mined from the surface of the famous Cerro Rico. But by 1560 production began to falter and mining was in full crisis. One problem was a severe shortage of laborers to work the mines; a second was the depletion of the almost pure surface deposits. With lower-content less-accessible ore, the process of extraction became more complex and costly in labor and capital. For a time production increased with the introduction of new mining and refinement technologies such as the mercury amalgam process suitable for high altitudes and hydraulic power used to sink deeper shafts and create large refining centers. But the silver revival would have been impossible without a large and steady labor supply. To this end, the Spanish colonial viceroy Francisco de Toledo reintroduced a draft Indian labor system adapted from the Incan *mita* system, thereby ensuring practically free unskilled labor to the mine and mill owners. Other changes included a new mining code, a rationalized taxation structure, royal control of silver production, and a royal mint in Potosí.

According to historians Herbert S. Klein and Jeffrey Cole, these developments dramatically reordered the mining economy and the social and economic life of the Indians. The mercury amalgam process was

23

A view of Cerro Rico, the enormously wealthy mountain of silver, as seen from Cobija's Arch in the city of Potosí (Copyright Christian Inchauste, DDO Stock Photography)

especially significant because it broke indigenous control over refining, which the Indians had dominated previously. Fifteen thousand small open-hearth smelters (known as *guayra*, or "wind ovens") used by the Indians were replaced by several hundred large Spanish refineries driven by hydropower. Viceroy Toledo also created a royal monopoly of mercury with the Huancavelica mine in Peru, which became the exclusive supplier. By controlling this necessary input the Crown could reduce tax evasion and contraband and monitor fairly accurately the actual production of silver ore by the mill and mine owners.

Further, all ore had to be smelted into bars and bullion in the royal mint, where taxes and the royal fifth of all production could be extracted directly and most efficiently. The mining code was also important to the preservation of order and rational operation of the industry. With more than 600 individually owned mines in Potosí, all representing different shafts, elaborate rules of ownership were essential. As a result of these innovations, silver production revived and continued to the end of the 17th century.

In the 18th century, even as silver extraction was declining, the magnificent colonial city of Potosí flourished. Its impressive churches, architecture, and works of art were produced in this golden century. Unfortunately, when the great silver era finally ended by the early 19th century, Potosí lapsed into penury and sleepy solitude. During the independence wars between 1810 and 1825, the royal treasury in Potosí remained depleted. Briefly, further improvements in extraction technologies and the discovery of new mines permitted the last resurgence of silver production at the end of the 19th century, which served to bankroll the construction of the first Bolivian railroad.

Colonial Agriculture

> These Spanish enterprises—mining, agriculture, stock-raising, manufacture—inevitably changed the face of the land and the relation of men to the land they inhabited.
>
> ■
>
> (Wolf 1959, 179)

The indigenous populations under Spanish rule struggled to cope with widespread deprivation and social inequality, although some colonial historians believe that life in Upper Peru did not change fundamentally for the Indians, who were now subject to Spanish, rather than Inca, overlords. Even though hardships were the common lot of the poorest classes under both systems, other historians have emphasized the exploitative nature of Spanish rule. In particular, two socioeconomic institutions have been singled out for censure: the Spanish colonial version of the *mita* and the *encomienda* system.

The *mita* originated under the ancient Aymara civilization and was later reinstituted by the Inca. Both cultures used the *mita* to provide compulsory labor by Indian vassals to the imperial elite. Reintroduced yet again under Spanish rule by Francisco de Toledo, viceroy of Lima, in the 1570s, the *mita* assured an abundant supply of free labor for state and private enterprises in such activities as agricultural production and especially silver mining. Historian Jeffrey Cole believes that Toledo expected the *mita* system to be only temporary and had intended to create sufficient monetary incentives to renew the voluntary labor pool in Potosí, which had become depleted because of declining profits and increasing hardships for the miners. But several decades after its implementation by the Spaniards, the *mita* had degenerated into a harsh and racist peonage system that was finally abolished by Simón Bolívar in 1825.

Back in 1503, the Spanish Crown had also adopted a legal device known as the *encomienda,* which assigned the legal rights over Indians in the Spanish colonies of the Americas to designated Spanish explorers and conquerors. A grant served as both a reward and an obligation to the recipient: The *encomendero,* as the "one who is entrusted," was charged with supervising the physical and spiritual well-being of the Indians; in return, he benefited from the free labor and the communal lands of the Indians in his trust. The *encomienda* system was initially conceived as a humane reform of the *repartimiento* (from the Spanish verb *repartir,* or "to divide up") under which the Spanish conquerors and colonists had brutally seized and enslaved the native peoples and appropriated their communal lands. (Often *encomienda* and *repartimiento* are used interchangeably, with the latter simply meaning "an allotment of land and labor.")

The *encomienda* system deteriorated, however, and instead of civilizing the indigenous peoples, the *encomenderos* became their feudal overlords, exploiting their labor and expropriating their lands and mines. Abuses of the *encomienda* paved the way for the hacienda landholding system that has impeded Latin American economic and social development in many countries to the present day. The Spanish Crown attempted to abolish the repressive *encomienda* system in the 16th and 17th centuries, and finally succeeded near the end of the 18th century, on the eve of the national independence revolutions.

Under colonial rule, both the *encomienda* and the *mita* served several functions. As an institution the *encomienda* served to consolidate the conquest by granting to Spanish military governors new territories to administer. The Spanish *encomendero* (later the hacendado, or hacienda owner) in what would become Bolivia was entrusted to oversee a specific Indian population within an *ayllu*. Aside from free Indian labor, the Spanish overlord enjoyed other benefit such as having the right to tax all male Indians, although the Spanish Crown attempted to withdraw these rights in the New Laws of 1542 and later reforms. Historian Rafael Varón Gabai scrupulously catalogued the extensive properties and resources that were transferred to the Pizarro family and their men who conquered and settled Lower and Upper Peru; this research confirmed that the great conquests were about capitalism and commercial gain. Human labor and land were as much commodities as silver and gold.

The Spanish Crown created two types of compulsory laborers: the *yanaconas* and the *mitayos*. The *yanaconas* were exempted from *mita* service and were basically serfs or slaves permanently bound to large private estates where they worked the fields or served in the household of the landowner. The *mitayos* were Indians organized under the *mita* to provide low-paid or unpaid labor for a percentage of the year, working in the mines. The *mita* combined the Incan system of tribute labor with the Iberian medieval feudal system of obligatory labor and adapted it to the capitalistic needs of the New World entrepreneurs, particularly the mining industrialists.

The Incan *mita* had been limited to the period between the harvesting and the planting of crops. Initially the Spanish *mita* was also limited to Indians between 18 and 60 years old to work without pay in the fields or the mines three months of every year. Over time the *mitayos* were abused and treated as slaves year-round. Indians, who were the unskilled ore carriers, perished by the hundreds of thousands in the silver mines. The Bolivian historian Fellmann Velarde states that in the mines at Potosí in any one year the death toll ranged from 2,500 to 12,000 men. The high cost of food in Potosi, which had to be brought in from the distant valleys of Cochabamba, meant that *mitayos* were often chronically underfed and so desperate for food that they were reduced to eating their own llamas. Many Indians fled Potosí to undeveloped areas or to the agricultural estates to evade the onerous *mita* service.

The *encomienda* reinforced this harsh system of colonial exploitation. Despite attempted reforms by the Spanish Crown, grants intended for one or perhaps two generations at most had been consolidated by the 18th century into the permanent hereditary property rights of the colonial aristocracy. Most Indians were either outright feudal serfs or marginal sharecroppers of tiny subsistence plots rented for a portion of their harvest and personal service obligations to the wealthy hacendado and his family. After independence, the hacienda landowning structure created and perpetuated the feudal or semifeudal society in which the hacendado was the autocratic lord of the manor who exercised ultimate political, social, and economic control over everything and everyone on his lands. In Bolivia, these conditions remained basically unchanged until the 1952 revolution.

Spain's Administrative Bureaucracy

In Spain, royal authority was absolute and this exclusive control was replicated as much as possible in the New World. In 1524, King Charles I established the Council of the Indies as Spain's chief agency to govern the New World. The members of the council were nobles from wealthy families and former colonial officials. Its staff was extensive and included accountants, solicitors, mapmakers, and historians. The council resided at court, met in secret, and promulgated the king's colonial policy. It submitted the list of nominees for important political positions for the king's approval and prepared the voluminous laws and decrees governing the colonies. Additionally, the council served as a final appeals court, supervised all colonial officials, and maintained detailed records and reports of their activities.

The Spanish Crown governed the distant New World colonies through an elaborate bureaucracy composed at its apex of viceroyalties and *audiencias* (royal courts). Although all power, favor, and legality emanated from the king, the sovereign granted sweeping powers to the early explorers and conquerors from Columbus to Pizarro. Most of these *adelantados* only held power as such for a few years, although Pizarro was named *adelantado* for life. Usually, the king, in the meantime, appointed a governor whose office could be terminated by the Crown. As these *adelantados* and governors became too powerful and threatened the prerogatives of the Crown and the court, their privileges were easily curtailed or revoked and central authority reasserted.

In the case of Upper and Lower Peru, with the outbreak of the conflict between the Pizarros and Almagro, the king sent the region's first viceroy, Blasco Núñez Vela, from Spain to pacify and govern the Viceroyalty of Peru from the seat in Lima. A viceroy was the highest

Viceroyalty of Peru, c. 1650

Santa Marta
Cartagena
Panamá
Cumaná
Caracas
Antioquia
Bogotá
Cali
Popayán
Pasto
Quito
Guayaquil
Tumbes
Piura
Moyobamba
Cajamarca
Trujillo
Lima
Cuzco
Arequipa
La Paz
Arica
Chuquisaca
(Sucre)
Potosí
Salta
Asunción
Tucumán
Corrientes
Córdoba
Valparaíso
Mendoza
Santiago
Buenos Aires
Concepción

*Pacific
Ocean*

Atlantic Ocean

N

| | 0 | | 300 Miles |
| | 0 | | 300 Kilometers |

	Unexplored areas
	Audiencia of Panama, 1538 and 1567
	Audiencia of Lima, 1542
	Audiencia of Santa Fe, 1549
	Audiencia of Charcas, 1559
	Audiencia of Quito, 1563
	Audiencia of Chile, 1565 and 1609
	Boundaries of the Viceroyalty of Peru
⊗	Audiencia capitals
•	Major provincial cities

personal representative of the king with extensive power and responsibility; a good viceroy, according to Antonio de Mendoza, the first
viceroy of New Spain in Mexico, was expected "to do little and to do

that slowly." With absolute power and so far from Spain, only the most trusted and loyal of individuals were chosen by the king as his viceroys. At first, the term of office was three years; later it was changed to five. The viceroy's salary was extremely generous, providing him a regal lifestyle in the colony. His duties encompassed administration, colonization, law enforcement, tax collection, and trade expansion; he was commander in chief. The Viceroyalty of Peru was more prestigious and extensive than that of Mexico and incorporated all of the territories colonized by Spain in South America. By 1600, the Viceroyalty of Peru included six *audiencias* in Lima, Panama, Bogotá (or Santa Fe), Charcas, Quito, and Santiago de Chile.

An *audiencia* was a vital administrative institution of Spanish colonial rule, second only to the viceroyalty. In addition to being the highest court of appeal, it served as the center for all executive, administrative, and judicial action in the colony. Often the *audiencia* rivaled the power and influence of the viceroy, and it acquired, according to historian Charles Arnade, political, economic, legislative, ecclesiastic, and military functions. Further, the Laws of the Indies stipulated that the *audiencia* review the viceroys; thus, the viceroyalty and *audiencia* acted as a reciprocal checks-and-balance system. In 1551, the Council of the Indies advised the Crown to create an *audiencia* in Charcas and in 1559 a royal decree establishing the Audiencia of Charcas was issued. At the same time the new administrative center of Upper Peru was placed on an equal status with the Viceroyalty of Lima.

The Audiencia of Charcas began to exercise its jurisdiction in 1561 over a radius of 320 miles outward from its seat in the city of Chuquisaca. Although limited at first, the audiencia for Charcas expanded to include present-day Bolivia and, at its height, territories in Peru, Chile, Paraguay, Argentina, Uruguay, and Brazil. The extensive boundaries of the *audiencia* were constantly changing, sowing confusion and fractious postindependence and contemporary territorial disputes between Bolivia and neighboring South American countries. Nonetheless, Arnade describes the judge of the Charcas *audiencia* as virtual sovereign of the Spanish colony who arrogantly scoffed at the orders of his often distant rival, the viceroy in Lima.

After extensive administrative reorganization in the 18th century, the Audiencia of Charcas was placed under the newly established Viceroyalty of Buenos Aires in 1776. The reorganization was intended to dilute the political autonomy of the very independent highland *audiencia*. In the end, the viceroy in Buenos Aires was as distant from

Chuquisaca as Lima had been, and so the power of the Audiencia of Charcas was not effectively diminished. When two more *audiencias* were created, in Buenos Aires and Cuzco, however, the territory and power of the Audiencia of Charcas was effectively reduced. Moreover, the system of eight intendancies established in 1782 to centralize and reinforce weakening Spanish control in the vast territory of the *audiencia* successfully limited the *audiencia's* sway. Each intendancy was headed by an intendant, who reported directly to the viceroy in Buenos Aires. As a result, most political and administrative functions were performed by the intendancies, limiting the influence of the *audiencia* as it served primarily as a court of appeal.

Despite the elaborate bureaucracy established by the Spanish monarchs to govern the New World under a regime of law, the rigid centralization and uniformity often defied the spirit and intentions of the laws. Indeed with over 6,000 laws on the books by 1681, confusion as well as widespread disregard and corruption were critical problems for Spanish rule.

Decline and Revolt of the Indian Population

The Spanish brought with them many European diseases—smallpox, measles, influenza, and tuberculosis—unknown in the New World. These killed more than 15 percent of the indigenous highland population in the first 50 years of the colony. More epidemics followed roughly 20-year cycles well into the 17th century. The harsh and hated Potosí *mita* also killed thousands of Indians. The system brought about the decline of the indigenous population by destroying their communities and way of life, forcing many to choose among evils: migration, servitude on the haciendas, or the *mita*.

The colonial reorganization of their traditional *ayllus* and many scattered, small villages into *reducciones* ("reductions," or the regrouping and resettlement of dispersed Indian populations into larger, centralized villages) often forced ethnically distinct Indian communities to function as one. This administrative system was created by the Spanish to facilitate their exploitation of Indian labor. The *reducciones* destroyed the cohesiveness of original communities and led to conflict among Indians and widespread Indian flight and migration.

Similarly, the *encomienda* system operated to extract surplus from the indigenous population in the form of taxes, silver, forced sale of imported Spanish goods, or their labor. And the *encomendero* grants became efficient ways to appropriate more and more indigenous lands. Routinely, Indians were taxed far and above what the royal laws allowed. This heavy taxation coincided with major subsistence crises, especially in the fertile valleys of Cochabamba in the 1700s. One of these crises occurred between 1782 and 1785 during the great Indian rebellions of Upper Peru.

All these administrative and socioeconomic changes contributed to the social breakdown and demographic collapse of the native population, and the vicious circle of exploitation continued. As the population declined, Indians and their labor came into shorter supply, and it became necessary to tax and work even more the dwindling number of Indians. According to Herbert S. Klein, reforms of the tax tribute structure in the 1700s and a gradual increase in the rural population alleviated indigenous hardships somewhat for a time.

The extensive interbreeding among Spaniards, Indians, and black African slaves also represented an assault against the indigenous population, creating the new racial class of the mestizo. In Bolivia, mestizos came to be known as *cholos*.

The Catholic Church played its role in the decline of the Indian population as well. The Crown and its Spanish administrators forcefully promoted Catholicism in Upper Peru. The conquest had brought a flood of secular clergy and missionary priests from the major religious orders— the Dominicans, the Franciscans, the Augustinians, and the Jesuits. In 1552, the bishopric of Chuquisaca was created, giving colonial Bolivia its first independent ecclesiastical authority, and in 1605, a second bishopric of La Paz was established. In 1561, the church in Upper Peru initiated aggressive evangelization, translating the catechism into Quechua and later into Aymara. The church authorities worked with the village chiefs to establish churches in villages and Christian religious shrines and festivals across the altiplano. The first was the shrine of the Virgin of Copacabana, still revered today. Rapidly the blending of Christianity and preconquest religions formed a unique syncretic religion that infiltrated into indigenous culture and native spirituality.

Another consequence of Spanish colonial misgovernment was Indian unrest and numerous local revolts. More threatening was the series of Indian uprisings that erupted in the late 18th century as part of the Tupac Amarú rebellion. This bloody indigenous uprising attempted to reestablish the glory and independence of the Inca Empire and to drive the hated Spaniards and their allies definitively from the highlands.

Remembered in the history books as the "Great Rebellion," these massive and well-orchestrated revolts by the native people of the altiplano initiated a terrible race war that rocked the foundations of the colonial world. While this awesome multiclass and multicaste movement extending from southern Ecuador into northern Argentina appeared to leave no lasting impact, it actually served as harbinger of the South American independence revolts. By the end of the 18th century the rigid Spanish social and juridical system that favored the peninsular-born and the revolutionary ideas of the French Enlightenment had heightened the desire of Bolivia's homegrown aristocracy for autonomous rule.

3

INDEPENDENCE WARS AND THE NEW NATION (1780–1839)

Success will crown our efforts, because the destiny of America has been irrevocably decided.

■

Simón Bolívar, "The Jamaica Letter," September 6, 1815 (Lynch 1994, 308)

The Spanish colonial territory that became the Republic of Bolivia was a land of revolution from the beginning. Both the indigenous peoples and the Spanish colonists burned with a zeal for autonomy. When Napoléon Bonaparte's invading armies in faraway Europe crushed Spanish continental and imperial ambitions, bringing to a conclusive end Spain's great power status in 1807, the resulting confusion over who ruled Spain, coupled with corruption and misguided reforms in the colonies, spawned independence rebellions throughout the Spanish New World. Upper Peru transformed itself into the Republic of Bolivia, even though it was one of the last colonies to consolidate independence. The birth of Bolivia in 1825 brought more turmoil as the fledgling nation struggled to preserve its political existence from the expansionist schemes of its neighbors and the grand designs of its liberators.

The Native Seeds of Revolution

Popular rebellion anticipated the revolutions for independence in many parts of Spanish America, and continued throughout the revolutionary period and beyond.

■

(Lynch 1994, 21)

Decades before the first independence movements in South America, an escalating wave of Indian uprisings engulfed the central and southern

Andes. These indigenous rebellions were unequaled elsewhere in the New World and precipitated a major crisis of colonial rule. Incited by Spain's increasingly restrictive bureaucratic and economic policies, the Indian populations embraced a truly revolutionary path.

The first outbreak of rebellion in Upper Peru was in the city of Cochabamba in 1730, followed by a revolt in Oruro in 1739. In varying degrees these early revolts involved shared grievances and tentative multiclass and multiethnic alliances of Indians, mestizos, and Creoles (whites born in South America) against increased Spanish taxation and trade restrictions. The especially important radical millenarian manifesto of the Oruro insurgents anticipated and perhaps inspired the widespread Indian revolts in Peru-Bolivia more than 40 years afterward.

The first of the later revolts broke out in Cuzco, Peru, in 1780. It was led by José Gabriel Condorcanqui, better remembered as Tupac Amaru II, who claimed lineal descent from the Inca Tupac Amaru. Condorcanqui had been granted the title of marquis by the royal *audiencia* and was a leading *curaca* (local chief) in Cuzco. Moreover, he was an educated member of the Indian nobility, who read Latin and Spanish but not Quechua. He had served as a royal Indian agent and had taken his grievances against the colonial *mita* system to the royal court in Spain for adjudication. When his legal attempts to abolish the *mita* failed, he organized an Indian army and pronounced himself emperor of Peru.

Tupac Amaru and his supporters seized most of the province of Cuzco and laid siege to its capital from November 1780 to March 1781. The Spanish colonial officials of the Audiencia of Charcas immediately organized a large army and sent it against the Indian rebels. The colonial army defeated and captured Tupac Amaru, and the government brought his rebellion to an end by having him drawn and quartered in a public execution.

Meanwhile, the second phase of the Great Rebellion had already begun with a revolt near Potosí in January 1781, by Tomás Catari, a *curaca* of Upper Peru who had been denied his office. In March, Andrés Tupac Amaru, a nephew of Tupac Amaru II, led an uprising that engulfed the entire area along the eastern shores of Lake Titicaca. In August, Andrés Tupac Amaru captured the provincial capital of Sorata and killed all the Spanish defenders. He then marched on the regional capital of La Paz, where he joined the local leader Julián Apaza, who had taken the name of Tupac Catari. Together, they laid siege to La Paz and fought pitched battles across the altiplano that pitted tens of thousands of Indian rebels against Spanish colonial troops. The rebels were ultimately defeated, however, when colonial officials in Buenos Aires sent an army of 15,000 troops northward to aid the government of Upper Peru. Tupac Catari and Andrés Tupac Amaru, as well as Tomás Catari and other rebel leaders, were ultimately captured and executed.

These Andean revolts had important elements in common that distinguished them from typical Indian rebellions elsewhere in Spanish America. First, the Bolivian-Peruvian revolts were essentially utopian and nativist. Like the earlier Oruro insurgents, the Indian rebels of the 1780s fought to restore the Inca monarchy and a pre-Spanish social order. Second, they also fought to abolish the *mita* labor system and the abuses of the district officials. Third, unlike earlier, more general rebel movements, which represented the interests of mestizos and whites as well as Indians, the Amarist and Catarist agendas centered on the full restoration of rights and power for the indigenous peoples of Bolivia and Peru and were inspired by pan-Andean nationalism.

Millenarianism also helps explain the powerful appeal of Tupac Catari's insurgency. Historian Nicholas Robins writes that Catari's charismatic leadership was infused with a millenarianistic outlook that predicted the triumphal return of the Inca and the establishment of a divinely ordained new order. In this golden age, indigenous peoples

A modern-day Indian woman weaver near Lake Titicaca, working on an ancient style of hand loom (UN Photo by John Isaac)

WHO WAS TUPAC CATARI?

Tupac Catari was an Aymara Indian of humble origins. He was born Julián Apaza in the town of Ayoayo in the Bolivian province of Sicasica around 1750. Orphaned at a young age, he was raised by a Catholic official in his hometown. Tupac Catari spoke only Aymara and remained illiterate all of his life. He labored as a sugar mill worker, a miner, a baker, and an itinerant trader of coca leaf and textiles, traveling extensively between highland La Paz and the tropical valleys. Very little else is known about his life before 1781, when he assumed the name of Tupac Catari in honor of Tupac Amaru and Tomás Catari and emerged as a charismatic revolutionary leader.

In January and February 1781, he raised an indigenous army in the provinces of Sicasica and Pacajes, and in March he began the protracted siege of the city of La Paz. Despite many fierce assaults, the Indian armies never took the city. Nevertheless more than 10,000 inhabitants, or a third of the city's population, died, largely of disease and starvation. After consuming all the horses, donkeys, dogs, and cats in the encircled city, the hunger-crazed residents were reduced to eating leather goods and trunks to survive. At the height of his insurgency, Tupac Catari commanded an army of 40,000 Indians from more than a half-dozen provinces of Upper Peru. In November 1781, he was captured and subsequently drawn and quartered (Robins 1998, 128–39).

would be liberated once and for all from white culture and oppression. Although Catari at first distinguished between "good" Creoles and "bad," in the end, he declared that there would be no coexistence with the whites or their culture. With the reestablishment of native rule, white culture and all non-Indians in the region would be exterminated.

Catari was, nevertheless, inconsistent, even bizarre, in his approach to Spanish culture. On the one hand, he ordered his followers to speak only Aymara and avoid Spanish dress. Violators of these strictures were executed. On the other hand, Catari himself often wore Spanish-style clothes, alternating between a black velvet shirt and Inca noble dress. He also remained ambivalent about Catholicism. He mistreated and persecuted priests, yet he celebrated mass daily and claimed divine revelations and special powers from the Christian god. These supernatural powers included the alleged ability to control the elements and bring to life Indian ancestors previously killed in battle. María Eugenia del Valle de Siles, a noted Bolivian colonial historian, referred to this assimilation of Spanish elements as the "cultural mestization" of the Catari rebels.

The Catarist and other indigenous revolts, even the more conservative and reformist ones, were clearly dangerous to the white Creole class of Upper Peru. The Creoles themselves had also begun to differentiate their interests from those of the Spanish motherland, but although they also protested against the exacting fiscal and administrative policies of the Spanish

A Bolivian woman in traditional dress, including an elaborate hat. (Kathy S. Leonard photo)

Bourbon monarchy, in the end the Creoles could not make common cause with the indigenous rebels. The radical socioeconomic and nativist goals of the Indian revolutionaries promised the destruction of the Creole class and race. *Gente decente* (literally, "decent folk") of the white, educated, and propertied classes of Upper Peru were also racists. For these reasons, a united anti-Spanish revolutionary front for independence never emerged in Upper Peru. This lack of social cohesion— and an absence of political cohesion as well—largely doomed the earliest independence uprisings in the Audiencia of Charcas.

The 1809 Revolts

Patriots, I may die, but the torch of liberty that I have left burning, can never be extinguished.

■

Pedro Domingo Murillo (Ayala 1980, 71)

In 1809, Charcas exploded again when an insurrection broke out in Chuquisaca, followed by a revolt in La Paz. In standard textbooks, the Creole rebel Pedro Domingo Murillo is celebrated as the leader of the La Paz uprising. Charles Arnade's careful research, however, indicates that the priest José Antonio Medina was the real mastermind behind the La Paz revolt. Another indispensable figure was Mariano Michel, a freethinking graduate of the University of San Francisco Xavier in Chuquisaca and the most radical member of the revolutionary cell there. Michel was appointed the secret delegate to La Paz, where he was to incite revolution. Arnade describes Michel as rebellious but "not an advocate of complicated political theories," and endowed with "the gift of stirring the masses" (1970, 26).

The La Paz uprising was the product of a complex situation. With the Napoleonic invasion of Spain and the forcible deposition of the Spanish king Charles IV in favor of his son, Ferdinand VII, going on across the Atlantic, a local power struggle broke out in Upper Peru. Key political and ideological forces divided into opposing factions: the radicals, the royalist-absolutists, and the loyalists. The radicals favored independence; the royalist-absolutists remained true to the imprisoned King Charles IV and absolutist government; and the loyalists supported the integrity of the empire and Spanish imperial rule by whoever was the rightful successor of the Bourbon monarchy

The radicals were made up of the law students, graduates, and legal scholars and law professors of the Universidad Pontífica y Real de San Francisco Xavier in Chuquisaca, the seat of the *audiencia*. Philosophical debates and satiric political pamphlets against Spanish rule proliferated, and Enlightenment-inspired liberal treatises circulated widely in this closed intellectual environment. Although these freethinkers of the generation of 1809 were influenced by the liberal and democratic thought in France and the United States, their radicalism was primarily rooted in Roman Catholicism and the politically explosive philosophy of Francisco Suárez and Saint Thomas Aquinas. By supporting papal supremacy over the ruler, both philosophers justified resistance to a bad ruler and provided moral grounds for revolutionary action against tyranny.

The radicals, however, were the minority in Upper Peru. The majority of the Creoles and common people loved the Spanish king and solidly supported Bourbon rule. Thus, when news arrived in 1808 of the formation of a popular junta in Seville against the French usurpation of the throne and occupation of Madrid, the bulk of the population in Upper Peru responded conservatively. The Seville junta claimed to rule in the name of Ferdinand VII and sent José Manuel de Goyeneche to the Viceroyalty of Rió de la Plata to secure the allegiance of the colonials to their authority.

In the Audiencia of Charcas the reaction of the authorities was confused and divided. The three offices that represented the highest echelon of Spanish authority—the judges and the president of the *audiencia* and the archbishop—responded quite differently. The esteemed judges

THE CHURCH FATHERS, MACHIAVELLI, AND REVOLUTION

One of the most studied philosophers at the university in Chuquisaca was the church father Thomas Aquinas. Students could recite whole tracts of the *Summa Theologica* from memory. Aquinas defended good government and full civic participation, and he believed if a ruler ceased to govern for the common good and his rule degenerated into tyranny, citizens had the right to depose the tyrant and establish a just government.

Similarly, the Jesuit theologian Francisco Suárez weighed in on the great controversies between church and state and "concluded that government was to serve the physical needs of men. Should a ruler forget this basic responsibility it was within the rights of the people to replace him with one who would not ignore his duty" (Arnade 1970, 7). Thus two celebrated Catholic writers and thinkers promoted the right to revolution.

The great Italian philosopher and strategist Niccolò Machiavelli rounded out the revolutionary education of the Upper Peruvian intellectuals. From Machiavelli they learned the importance of deception and patience in statecraft—that is, the ends justify the means. And from their legal studies they developed the syllogistic reasoning that refashioned these philosophies into the radical agenda for self-rule.

of the *audiencia*, who could only be Spanish-born nobility—a source of great resentment to the ambitious native elite—assumed a highly conservative posture. Representing the royalist-absolutist faction, they were suspicious of the unsubstantiated claims of Seville and ideologically opposed to a governing authority founded upon popular revolution. They insisted on a written order from the king or the Council of the Indies, an impossible demand since the king was imprisoned and the council was controlled by the Napoleonic usurpers.

Meanwhile, the president of the *audiencia*, Ramón García León de Pizarro, and the archbishop, Benito María de Moxó y Francolí, supported allegiance to the junta in Seville and enthusiastically welcomed its representative in the Viceroyalty of Río de la Plata, Goyeneche. As loyalists, they viewed their response as the only patriotic action that could protect the Spanish Empire from certain disintegration. The archbishop, moreover, used his position (even threatening excommunication) and great personal zeal for the beloved motherland to mobilize public opinion in Upper Peru behind allegiance to the junta of Seville. His actions brought him into head-on conflict with the autocratic judges.

Ironically, both the narrow-mindedness of the *audiencia* judges and the emotional patriotism of the president and archbishop played into the hands of the radicals. The radicals recognized that it was in their immediate interest to support the archconservative judges of the *audiencia:* Favoring the pro-Seville forces would ensure maintaining the unity of the empire; support for the *audiencia,* however, would achieve a temporary quasi-independence until Upper Peru could completely separate from Spain. According to Charles Arnade, the radical law professors of Upper Peru reasoned that "Chuquisaca, the intellectual center of the Viceroyalty of Río de la Plata, would lead the way to independence" (1970, 15).

On November 11, 1808, José Manuel de Goyeneche, representative of the junta of Seville in Río de la Plata, arrived in Chuquisaca from Buenos Aires. The shrewd Goyeneche quickly sized up the bitter factionalism within the Audiencia of Charcas. When the judges were finally willing to receive him, he presented royal letters from Carlota Joaquina of Bourbon, who was the daughter of the dethroned Spanish king, sister of the king's legal heir, and also the princess-regent of Portugal and ruler of Brazil. Carlota claimed the Spanish colonies in the name of the royal family of Spain. The letters threw the *audiencia* into heightened confusion. In effect, Carlota represented the claim of Portugal, a bitter colonial rival of Spain.

The president and archbishop naively endorsed Carlota's claim. This act allowed the radicals to accuse the loyalists of treason because they urged submission to a foreign power and rival of Spain. An elaborate campaign of subversion, engineered by the radical conspirators, soon undermined the dwindling support for the loyalists. On May 25, 1809, the radicals; the executives of the *audiencia;* the *cabildo,* or town council; and members of the university deposed the president and began an open insurrection. By the light of that evening's full moon, an uncontrolled mob joined them and marched toward the president's house, shouting, "Viva Fernando!" The revolution engulfed Chuquisaca. Carlota's letters had accelerated events and precipitated the War of Independence in Charcas.

In the name of King Ferdinand VII of Spain, the Audiencia of Charcas assumed all power at four o'clock in the morning on May 26, 1809. Furthermore, the *audiencia* declared independence from the Viceroyalty of Buenos Aires (which had supported the junta of Seville and Carlota) and the illegitimate authorities in the Iberian homeland. The briefly successful revolution in Charcas had been effected by no more than 50 people. The three most important figures were Jaime Zudañez, a lawyer for the *audiencia;* Manuel, his brother and an office holder in the town council and university; and Bernardo Monteagudo, another lawyer with the *audiencia* and an influential member of the university.

The *audiencia* quickly sent delegates to the larger cities of Charcas. Along with the official mission, the delegates carried secret directives from the revolutionaries to bring others into the rebellion. Mariano Michel, the delegate to La Paz, was instrumental in the celebrated revolt there. Officially, he was instructed to inform the intendant of La Paz to arrest anyone supporting Carlota's claims; secretly, he was to engineer the arrest of the intendant and the takeover by the *cabildo.* The intendant was deposed with the assistance of José Antonio Medina, the parish priest of Sicasica, near La Paz, and a graduate of San Francisco University and an extreme radical of the generation of 1809.

The revolutionaries, however, did not stop there. Patriots of La Paz formed a governing junta and elected Pedro Domingo Murillo as its president. This new governing body proclaimed its independence and self-rule in the name of Ferdinand VII. Unfortunately, Murillo and the La Paz patriots had gone too far too soon. The independence movement was premature and produced internal dissension. Charles Arnade holds that the public declaration of independence "was a great mistake," which "proved to be the downfall" of Bolivia's revolutionary generation (1970, 28).

Meanwhile, the Spanish viceroy in Lima, José de la Serna, dispatched 5,000 soldiers led by the new president of the *audiencia* in Cuzco, Goyeneche, to crush the revolution in Upper Peru. Outnumbered and betrayed by the moderates, the revolutionary government in La Paz collapsed. Mercilessly, Goyeneche hunted down the leaders of the uprising. Few escaped his retribution; most were either executed or sentenced to hard labor in the mines. As a priest, Medina, the real leader of the revolt, was given a life sentence. Murillo, the nominal head of the revolution, and other rebel leaders were hung in the central plaza on January 29, 1810. Today a statue of Murillo stands in the center of the plaza that bears his name to commemorate the first declaration of independence in Spanish America.

With the news of Goyeneche's defeat of the La Paz movement, the judges of the *audiencia* in Chuquisaca reconsidered their actions, ultimately repented, and compromised with the royalist authorities on the condition that Goyeneche's army would not be sent against the city. The new president of the *audiencia*, Vicente Nieto, conducted an investigation and the Zudañez brothers and Monteagudo were imprisoned. By early 1810, most of the revolutionary generation of 1809 had perished in Upper Peru. For the revolution, however, all was not lost, although Bolivian independence would take another 15 years.

The 15 Years' War

> Because successes have been partial and spasmodic, we must not lose faith. In some places the fighters for independence triumph, while in others the tyrants have the advantage.
>
> ■
>
> Simón Bolívar, "The Jamaica Letter," September 6, 1815 (Lynch 1994, 309)

The radicals in Buenos Aires, the seat of the Viceroyalty of Río de la Plata that had gained jurisdiction over Upper Peru, declared independence on May 25, 1810. In the Andean highlands, local allies against the Spanish forces eagerly supported the rebellion in Buenos Aires, and Upper Peru spontaneously rallied to the cry of independence by the revolutionary Argentine junta. Sympathetic uprisings swept across the Audiencia of Charcas: Cochabamba in September, Potosí in November, and Tarija and Santa Cruz in the following months.

In time, however, the men and women of Upper Peru desired not only independence from Spanish bureaucracy, but also autonomy from all external encroachments, including those of Argentina. With territorial interests in mind, the newly independent Argentines hoped to wrest the prosperous northern provinces of the former Viceroyalty of Río de la Plata from the weakened grasp of colonial authorities in Lima. The liberating auxiliary armies from the south proved to be ruthless marauders, who left an angry citizenry in their wake.

Between 1810 and 1817, several Argentine expeditionary armies confronted the royalist forces of General José Manuel de Goyeneche. The royalists defeated each of the three auxiliary armies dispatched by Argentina. The brutal Juan José Castelli marched the first auxiliary army into Upper Peru in 1810. By the time he retreated, most of the region's citizens hated him and had turned against the Argentine liberators. The capable general Manuel Belgrano headed the second army in 1813 and almost succeeded in liberating the north. In 1815, the ineffective general José Rondeau commanded the third unsuccessful Argentine army. Finally, the brief incursion of a small force in 1817

MOTHERS OF REVOLUTION

In the second half of the 20th century, mothers in authoritarian Chile and Argentina became international celebrities because of their determination and courage. Mothers in Chile demonstrated against the military dictatorship of Augusto Pinochet and cleverly crafted political messages into their artistic *arpilleras,* or embroidered tapestries, depicting everyday Chilean life. In Argentina, the desperate Mothers of the Plaza de Mayo began to march every Thursday, demanding an accounting of their missing loved ones, who had been "disappeared" by repressive military juntas.

In the 19th century, Bolivia's mothers were no less courageous. On May 27, 1812, the heroic women of Cochabamba defiantly fought in the second independence revolt of the city. When the men had been killed in the revolutionary fighting and there was no one left to hold back the royalist armies, the *cochabambinas,* or women of Cochabamba, fiercely battled against professional Spanish soldiers. A statue and small park in Cochabamba commemorate their great personal sacrifice of life and limb. Fittingly for a country with a proud revolutionary heritage, the women's day of struggle and heroism, May 27, is traditionally celebrated as Mothers' Day throughout Bolivia.

under the command of Lieutenant Colonel Gregorio Araoz de la Madrid also failed. Despite their tenacity and assistance from sporadic urban revolts and roving rural bands and guerrilla forces of Upper Peru, a tense stalemate between the Lima royalists and the Bolivian-Argentine independence forces ensued.

Upper Peru once again presented the classic dilemma that had accorded the Audiencia of Charcas relative autonomy under colonial rule. Its main population centers were too distant from Buenos Aires but still too close to Lima, Spain's traditional stronghold in South America. Royalist forces from Lima could easily suppress unrest in Upper Peru, but at the same time external revolutionary forces sent from Buenos Aires were unable to sustain a unified and indigenous proindependence revolution there.

A period that Bolivians term the Heroic Era of the 15 Years' War followed these initial revolutionary uprisings. From 1810 to 1816, a diffuse and protracted guerrilla insurgency bubbled in the highland. Rural *republiquetas,* or independent "little republics" of local resistance, sprang up in the countryside, harassing Spanish forces and royalists.

There were six areas of concentrated guerrilla activity and control that seriously challenged Spanish hegemony in Upper Peru. Identified by their powerful guerrilla leaders, these republics were Arenales, Ayopaya, Camargo, Muñecas, Padilla, and Warnes. Geography and political economy largely determined the boundaries of these guerrilla zones. Two towns of strategic importance were Potosí, with its rich silver mines, and Chuquisaca, the political capital of the *audiencia*. The other major cities of Upper Peru—La Paz, Oruro, Cochabamba, and Santa Cruz—were important because of mining and agricultural activity. The six *republiquetas* were distributed along the royal highway and these critical urban centers.

In his extensive analysis of the armies of the independence movement and partisans of Upper Peru, Charles Arnade emphasizes the unstable and fluid nature of these guerrilla republics. In addition to the six major republics, there were numerous minor republics, smaller republics within larger republics, and factions within these that were led by virtually independent partisan leaders. Often these guerrilla leaders failed to communicate or coordinate operations. Despite this crazy-quilt resistance, by 1816 the republics posed a major threat to Spanish forces in the region. A fierce royalist offensive that year, however, destroyed all but the Ayopaya *republiqueta,* which remained active until Bolivian liberation in 1825.

The leader of the Ayopaya Republic was Miguel Lanza, who controlled the roads between La Paz, Oruro, and Cochabamba. He survived the independence war and became a trusted lieutenant of Bolivia's president Antonio José de Sucre. Lanza was the only guerrilla leader to participate in the birth of the Bolivian republic. For Bolivian historians, the story of this isolated republic has become one of legendary heroism. Most that is known about Ayopaya is drawn from the diary of a soldier and drummer simply known as Vargas. Although patriotism is generally assumed to have been the major incentive of the Upper Peruvian guerrillas, Charles Arnade's reading of the drummer's diary indicates that a free life of adventure outside of established society and the law was a greater factor.

The role of the highland Indian in the War of Independence of Upper Peru was even more complex. Although on both sides the "great Indian masses offered a large reservoir of able fighting men," the native peoples were often very ignorant of the reasons and factional dynamics of the war (Arnade 1970, 50). The Indian was a dangerous element, Arnade writes, because he would often shift allegiances and fight for whichever side was more convenient; after all, Bolivia's indigenous people had been mistreated by the *criollos,* and to some, the Spaniards were the lesser evil. Both sides wooed the Indians with sweet offers of privileges and equality that they had no intention of fulfilling. Indians were simply so much cannon fodder, which neither side ever considered emancipating. Most Indians may have preferred the elimination of both elements; nevertheless, there were staunchly loyal Indian forces on both sides of the War of Independence in Upper Peru.

By 1820, the independence struggle in Upper Peru had ground to a halt. The guerrilla wars by the *republiquetas* and the repeated incursions by the auxiliary armies of the United Provinces of Buenos Aires had proven inconclusive. More great heroes were needed to rekindle the revolution that Bolivia's Creole patriots had precipitously ignited in Upper Peru more than a decade earlier. The successful culmination of Bolivia's 15-year war for independence rested with the great liberators of South America.

The Great Liberators and Bolivian Independence

On July 28, 1821, José de San Martín, an Argentine general who had led a liberating army across the Andes and defeated the royalists, proclaimed the independence of Peru. However, San Martín then withdrew from the scene, leaving the celebrated Venezuelan Simón Bolívar at the helm of liberation forces in Upper Peru. The unified armies of Bolívar and San Martín confronted the remnants of loyalist resistance, the armies of Viceroy de la Serna in Peru and General Pedro Antonio Olañeta in Upper Peru. On August 6, 1824, the independence and royalist armies fought the decisive Battle of Junín. Although outnumbered, Bolívar's troops defeated the royalists. More revolutionary victories steadily followed.

In the Andes near Lake Titicaca, the independence commanders General Andrés de Santa Cruz and General Agustín Gamarra crushed the royalists in the Battle of Zepita. In the Battle of Ayacucho on December 9, 1824, Antonio José de Sucre defeated royalist forces and captured the commander, Viceroy de la Serna. Only one royalist general remained. On April 2, 1825, Colonel Carlos Medinaceli, who later became a founder and general of the Bolivian army, betrayed General Olañeta. On the morning of April 9, 1825, Sucre proclaimed the decisive end of the independence war.

Both Santa Cruz and Sucre became celebrated figures in the history of Bolivian independence. The mestizo general Andrés de Santa Cruz was a local revolutionary leader from the region near La Paz. Although he had been a former royalist commander, Santa Cruz had defected to the revolution and become one of its ablest generals. Sucre was a

Simón Bolívar, the Liberator, was a Venezuelan who led the independence movement in northern South America. He was the founder and namesake of the modern Bolivian nation. (Reproduced with permission of the General Secretariat of the Organization of American States)

Venezuelan and Bolívar's chief lieutenant.

The destiny of Upper Peru as an independent republic was unresolved, however. Its future turned upon the designs of Sucre and Bolívar. Marshal Sucre indicated in his letters to Bolívar and other revolutionary generals that the people of Upper Peru desired autonomy and should decide their own fate. Bolívar, on the other hand, opposed the autonomy of the Andean region. Bolívar's dream was a continental federation of states that could withstand European and North American influences. He had already unified the northern South American states under the Federation of Gran Colombia. At the very least, Bolívar intended Upper Peru to remain an integral part of Lower Peru and subject to the administrative control of Lima.

The Argentines, moreover, had proclaimed the United Provinces of South America in 1816. This act incorporated the administrative region of the former Audiencia of Charcas within the territories of the former Viceroyalty of Río de la Plata. After 1825 and the end of the independence wars, the competing claims of sovereignty and the conflicting territorial ambitions of Argentina, Peru, and Gran Colombia presented serious problems. The creation of an independent buffer state in Upper Peru might provide a logical and feasible solution.

Sucre decided to act. While Bolívar was being honored in distant Lima, Sucre promulgated an important decree in La Paz on February 9, 1825. The decree called for an assembly of notables to meet in Oruro on April 29 to decide the fate of Upper Peru. The assembly, which had to be postponed several times, actually met on July 10 in Chuquisaca, the seat of the Audiencia of Charcas. The assembly hall was in the University of San Francisco Xavier, the intellectual home of the revolutionary generation of 1809.

THE MEANING OF PATRIOTISM

Why did the men and women of Upper Peru fight in the long independence struggle? The historical record indicates that except for vague expressions of discontent with Spanish rule and protest against the Crown, one word was mentioned time and time again: *la patria*.

La patria means "the fatherland." The guerrilla units were referred to as the "armies of the *patria*," as opposed to the armies of the *realistas* or the Royalists. But what exactly was meant by the word *patria*? There was as yet no country to which the term referred.

Upper Peru in 1809 was the Audiencia of Charcas and an administrative province in the Viceroyalty of Río de la Plata. In 1810, when Buenos Aires declared independence, the Viceroyalty of Lima annexed Upper Peru.

Historian Charles Arnade provides an answer from the diary of the guerrilla soldier Vargas: "*Patria* is the soil on which we step and on which we must defend at all costs; for the *Patria* we must sacrifice our interests and our lives" (1970, 52).

Patria meant the love of freedom and the love of place. From the very start—even before there was officially the country of Bolivia—*bolivianos* have held a special attachment to the soil, which, as the Bolivian historian Humberto Guzmán states, "inspired the origin and meaning of *Patria*" (Arnade 1970, 53). A beloved Bolivian *queca* (traditional Andean scarf dance) begins with the words *"Viva mi patria Bolivia!"*

There, the constituent assembly debated three propositions: The first supported an independent Andean state; the second, unification with Peru; and the third, unification with Argentina. The dominant voices in the historic assembly were for independence. After lengthy debates and delays, the actual vote was taken on August 6. The final vote was not unanimous. Two of the 47 delegates voted in favor of union with Lower Peru. The 48th delegate was the heroic guerrilla leader General Miguel Lanza, who served as honorary president for the historic occasion and counted the votes. When all was said and done, however, all 48 delegates of Chuquisaca unanimously signed the Declaration of Independence that created the new Bolivian state.

The Chuquisaca delegates anticipated that Bolívar would disapprove of their actions. They, therefore, christened the new nation the Republic of Bolívar, hoping to appeal to the general's pride. In addition, the

Antonio José de Sucre, chief lieutenant to Simón Bolívar, was a pivotal figure in the Bolivian movement for independence and the founding of the nation in 1825. (Reproduced with permission of the General Secretariat of the Organization of American States)

Upper Peruvians honored the Liberator by appointing him the country's protector and first president. They designated August 6, 1825—the date of the critical vote and Bolívar's triumph in the Battle of Junín a year earlier—as Bolivia's day of national independence.

By this stratagem, the elected delegates of Chuquisaca secured Bolívar's tacit acquiescence in the founding of the República Bolívar. Nevertheless, Bolívar recognized Bolivian autonomy only reluctantly. In office, he continued to refer to Bolivia as Upper Peru and signed his presidential decrees as the dictator of Peru. Only in 1826, after he had stepped down as the country's president, did he approve the independence of Bolivia.

The Presidencies of Bolívar and Sucre

With what may have seemed the more difficult task achieved, the Bolivians turned from the revolutionary struggle to the challenge of self-rule. The 14 years following Bolivian independence were mixed, but generally positive, ones for the new nation. The country's first three presidents—Bolívar, Sucre, and Santa Cruz—provided a degree of integrity and stability that would be greatly missed as the century progressed.

Two days after the declaration of independence, Bolívar was enthusiastically welcomed in La Paz. His residence in, and administration of, the Andean republic was brief, lasting a mere five months. In that short time, Bolívar issued a stream of experimental and liberal decrees. He reduced tax levies by half, promulgated a land reform that benefited the indigenous population, declared the equality of all citizens, and secularized government and politics.

Unlike his triumphs in the wars of independence, however, Bolívar's civil administration of Bolivia was less successful. In part, Bolívar was of two minds when it came to government. Although he favored democratic rule in principle, in practice, he discovered that only a strong hand could restrain the willful and fractional South Americans. His reforms, too ambitious for the times and under difficult conditions within Bolivia, remained unimplemented. Nevertheless, Bolívar's idealistic governing principles are enshrined in Bolivia's first constitution of 1826, which was written by the Liberator himself.

The first constitutionally elected president of the young republic was Antonio José de Sucre. In January 1826, before departing Bolivia for Lima, never to return, Bolívar handed the government over to Sucre, his handpicked successor. Sucre ruled by decree until May of that year when a Bolivian Constituent Assembly formally elected him president. Despite controversy among Bolivian and non-Bolivian historians, Sucre is sometimes recognized as the "father of Bolivia." The claim to this honor rests on Sucre's promulgation of the decree of February 9, 1825, which initiated the chain of events that led both to the country's creation and his election as Bolivia's president.

WHO IS THE REAL FATHER OF BOLIVIA?

Casimiro Olañeta, the nephew of loyalist general Pedro Antonio de Olañeta, holds a hallowed but debated place in the history of Bolivian independence. Respected historians differ over his role and contributions: Some glorify him as the ultimate patriot and true "father of Bolivia"; others describe him as "perverse," "crafty," and "self-serving."

Olañeta's glory derives from his claim to have inspired Marshal Antonio José de Sucre with the idea of the independence of Upper Peru, and, as Olañeta wrote, with "the foundation of a new republic, which came to be called *Boliviana* by the assembly of deliberation to which I belonged" (Arnade 1970, 166). Bolivian historian Humberto Vázquez Machicado calls this the "myth of Olañeta" and believes that it should be revised.

He and other historians, including Charles Arnade, argue that Sucre supported Bolivian independence and promulgated the famous decree of February 9, 1825, solely out of his own personal conviction and without Olañeta's influence. Sucre, therefore, is the rightful "father of Bolivia." Arnade suggests that perhaps both are "fathers" of the new nation, Olañeta deserving this acclaim because of his "shrewd intrigues and scheming," and Sucre, because of "his honest, forceful, and clear policy" (1970, 168–69).

In the two and a half years of his able, yet unpopular administration Sucre struggled to rebuild the country. Sixteen years of war and severe economic conditions had depopulated the highlands, ruined the mines, and bankrupted the treasury. Sucre instituted ambitious political, economic, and social reforms. Despite implementation of fiscal reforms and a system of direct taxation to fuel the economic recovery, within a year Sucre believed it necessary to renew tribute payments, a type of regressive head tax that Bolívar had abolished. The Creole government, more so than the colonial one, relied on these tribute payments by the country's 800,000 indigenous citizens for 60 percent of its tax receipts. Sucre also authorized the seizure of the extensive properties of the Roman Catholic Church, reducing the church's economic and political influence in Bolivia.

Sucre's reforms had little time or support to succeed, however. His progressive policies alienated the established political and economic interests in the country. As his government became increasingly unpopular, Sucre's Bolivian opponents used their newly found nationalism against him. A Venezuelan by birth, Sucre was branded by his enemies as a foreign interloper. In turn, the honest, sober, and dedicated Sucre was appalled by the rampant greed and incivility of the officers and citizens around him. Political intrigues, fueled by renewed Peruvian and Argentine designs on Bolivia, worked to unseat him.

The year 1827 proved to be a critical turning point. In Lima, a military coup ousted Bolívar from the lifetime presidency of Peru, and its perpetrators declared war on Bolívar's Colombian regime. In Bolivia, an attempt on Sucre's life failed, but a mutiny swept the ranks of his unpaid army in December, and the Peruvian general Agustín Gamarra amassed an army along the Peru-Bolivia border. In April 1828, Sucre was seriously wounded during another revolt in the army. At this juncture, with the pretext of protecting Sucre from his own troops, Gamarra invaded Bolivia. Betrayed by the Bolivian generals, Sucre was forced to capitulate to Gamarra in the Treaty of Piquiza on July 6. Finally, in August 1828, Sucre resigned in despair and returned to his native Venezuela.

General Gamarra was now the powerful arbiter of Bolivia's fate. He installed Pedro Blanco, a Bolivian general, to succeed Sucre as president. Within five days, this obvious Peruvian puppet was assassinated, and another Bolivian general, José Miguel de Velasco, became interim president. From Colombia, Bolívar sent Sucre to deal with Gamarra. Commanding a Colombian army, Sucre defeated General Gamarra's more formidable force of 8,000 soldiers in the Battle of Tarqui on

February 27, 1829. Gamarra returned to Lima and on May 4, 1829, became the president of Peru. The Bolivian assembly of notables invited Marshal Andrés de Santa Cruz, then in Arequipa, Peru, to assume the presidency of Bolivia.

Santa Cruz: Bolivia's First Caudillo

From 1829 to 1839, the presidency of Andrés de Santa Cruz achieved remarkable political and economic stability in an era generally known for postcolonial anarchy. The administrative reforms that Santa Cruz implemented greatly influenced the institutions of modern Bolivia. He compiled Bolivian law into one of the first legal codes in the new republics, expanded higher education and public works, balanced the budget, and reduced the public debt. Santa Cruz reorganized the Bolivian army and created a new coastal department with its capital at the free port of La Mar, better known as Cobija. He established a ministry of interior and foreign relations and a major university in La Paz in 1831. Still, many of his innovations could not be implemented because of Bolivia's limited economic resources.

Politically, Santa Cruz is remembered as Bolivia's first native-born military strongman, or caudillo. President Santa Cruz favored authoritarian government and superseded Bolivia's second constitution of 1831, a slightly more democratic document that replaced the first constitution of Bolívar. By the time the inconstant Bolivians exiled him in 1839, he was reviled as a dictator. But unlike his successors, who treated Bolivia as their private fiefdom over the next 40 years, Santa Cruz tempered one-man rule with scrupulous honesty, efficient public administration, and true patriotism. He brought peace and stability to the country.

Santa Cruz had greater ambitions than the presidency of Bolivia. A *cholo* (to use the Bolivian term for mestizo), Santa Cruz was born near La Paz to a Spanish father and an Indian mother. He was strongly influenced by the Quechua heritage of his aristocratic mother, Juana Basilia Calahumana. She claimed royal ancestry with Tupac Amaru, the last Inca. Her son dreamed of resurrecting the glorious Inca political order and reuniting Upper and Lower Peru.

On his father's side, Santa Cruz was well connected to the ruling elite of Cuzco. Critics would rightly say that he was always more Peruvian than Bolivian. Santa Cruz, moreover, had served as provisional president of Peru from 1826 to 1827 until ousted by the Peruvian caudillo General Gamarra. These two leaders, despite having been boyhood friends and comrades in arms, became formidable rivals and hated enemies.

53

Santa Cruz continued to be enmeshed in Peruvian politics and obsessed with his goal of creating a greater Peru-Bolivia. Civil war in Peru provided him with his first important opportunity to effect his plan. An 1834 treaty with beleaguered Peruvian president Luis José de Orbegoso invited Bolivian intervention in a three-way dispute between warring Peruvian generals. In June 1835, the army of Santa Cruz invaded Peru. By early 1836, he had defeated the forces of the government's two rival Peruvian caudillos, Generals Gamarra and Felipe Santiago Salaverry.

Finally, in October 1836, Santa Cruz realized his burning ambition to unify the two countries and create the Peruvian-Bolivian Confederation. In May 1837, he convened a congress to formalize the pact of unification. Peru was reorganized into two autonomous states: South Peru governed by Orbegoso, and North Peru by President Pío Tristán. General José Miguel Velasco administered Bolivia. Santa Cruz became their "protector," or dictator of the confederation.

The historian Herbert S. Klein has noted that the confederation "brought both peace to Peru and respect for its power along the entire Pacific region" (1992, 117), and the territorial union also made Bolivia "a major power of contention" in South America (1992, 119). Some Bolivian historians, nevertheless, have considered the confederation "completely disadvantageous to Bolivia," by subordinating it to Peru (Vázquez Machicado 1988, 356).

At first, anarchy within Peru prevented effective internal resistance to the grand designs of Santa Cruz. Bolivian opposition to the unity pact was repressed for a time as well. External reaction to the confederation, however, was fierce and devastating from the outset. The confederation reminded Peru's neighbors of the hated Spanish viceroyalty of Lima that had once lorded over them. By consolidating the dominance of Peru, moreover, the confederation destroyed the precarious geopolitical equilibrium of the Southern Cone and Andean regions. This power imbalance directly threatened the national interests of Argentina and Chile. In 1837, both countries declared war on the confederation and invaded Peru.

Santa Cruz was able to repulse the Argentine expedition of General Juan Manuel de Rosas. He then confronted the Chilean armies of Minister Diego Portales and General Manuel Bulnes. In 1839, the tenacious Chileans defeated the confederation forces in the decisive Battle of Yungay. Chile's victory terminated the Peruvian-Bolivian Confederation and the ambitions of Santa Cruz, and ensured future Chilean commercial and territorial expansion at the expense of Peru and Bolivia.

Santa Cruz, one of the great Bolivian independence figures, was forced into exile in Ecuador. He attempted to return to Peru but was intercepted and imprisoned by the Chileans on the island of Chillán. In 1845, he was accorded a liberal pension and the following year sent into permanent exile in Europe. Once there, Bolivians relented and allowed him to serve in various diplomatic posts.

Far from South America and his Andean home, Santa Cruz died in France in 1865. Although in defeat Santa Cruz was reviled as a dictator and traitor unworthy of being called a Bolivian, his contemporaries came to judge him less harshly before his death. History has been even kinder. After the presidency of Santa Cruz, more Bolivian leaders of grandiose visions and great egos emerged. Their historical legacy was not as benign.

4

THE AGE OF CAUDILLO RULE
(1839–1879)

*States are slaves either through the nature of their constitution
or through its abuse. A people is therefore enslaved when the
government, by its nature or its vices, encroaches on and usurps
the rights of the citizen or subject.*

■

Simón Bolívar, "The Jamaica Letter," September 6, 1815 (Lynch 1994, 308)

After 1839, violence and venality characterized the governments of
the young Bolivian republic. In retrospect, the capable administrations of Bolivia's first presidents, Antonio José de Sucre and Andrés de Santa Cruz, proved to be notable exceptions to postindependence history. For the next 40 years, a succession of corrupt military strongmen, known as caudillos, controlled the country's political and economic destiny.

Who Were the Caudillos?

A question often posed in Latin American history is whether the caudillos who emerged in most of the newly independent nations during and after the 1820s were heroes or villains, or both. Some observers argue that the Latin American caudillos brought order and stability out of chaos, thereby providing a service to the new nations of the hemisphere. Also, caudillos supplanted the extreme regionalism of local warlords and established a necessary centralized authority. The majority of the critics, however, have condemned Latin America's caudillos for their cupidity, brutality, and despotism.

Bolivia's caudillos, in most respects, were no different than the other colorful military strongmen throughout Latin America. Some historians, nevertheless, have claimed that they were more flamboyant and notorious. Certainly a comparison with other, famous Latin American caudillos of the period suggests that Bolivia's military rulers damaged the country's immediate and long-term national interests more extensively than most. *Caudillismo* became so endemic and destructive in the country's history that the Bolivian philosopher and acerbic social critic Alcides Arguedas distinguished between *los caudillos bárbaros* (the barbarous caudillos) and *los caudillos letrados* (the cultured caudillos).

The exile of Santa Cruz initiated this age of chronic misrule and instability, the age of *caudillismo*. The officers and generals of the new Bolivian army, unaccustomed to peaceful civil society, used their forces to carve out private fiefdoms. When they managed to gain enough military and political power, these warlord generals made themselves dictators of the hapless country. Militarism and authoritarianism became a chronic pattern in the life of Bolivia. Once reinforced, this pattern has also plagued modern-day Bolivia.

Rebellion and Misrule

The age of the caudillos in Bolivia began with the internal power struggle between Generals José Ballivián and José Miguel de Velasco. These generals had cooperated in the overthrow of Santa Cruz in early 1839, but by July they were bitter rivals. Ballivián revolted when the constituent assembly that met in Chuquisaca turned against him and declared Velasco president, frustrating Ballivián's own ambitions. This same partisan assembly, reflecting the country's turmoil, excoriated Santa Cruz and drafted Bolivia's fourth constitution in 14 years. (The delegates also renamed the city of Chuquisaca in honor of Sucre and reconfirmed its status as the constitutional capital of the republic.)

Ballivián's first of several revolts against the Velasco government failed, and he fled to Peru. There, he secured the support of Peru's president and caudillo, General Agustín Gamarra. As in 1835, a faction in the Bolivian civil war irresponsibly invited the Peruvians to intervene in Bolivian affairs. The Velasco regime opposed the potential return of exiled Santa Cruz and confiscated the former president's property. In June 1841, a pro–Santa Cruz uprising by Bolivian general Sebastián Agreda ended the shaky Velasco government. Intending to capitalize on Bolivian instability and annex the province of La Paz, General Gamarra invaded Bolivia for the second time in July, and the powerful Peruvian army swiftly seized the city of La Paz.

Bolivia's factions ceased feuding over the return of Santa Cruz and united behind General Ballivián and defense of the country. Ballivián overthrew General Agreda, who had supported the restoration of Santa Cruz and been president less than four months. A key instigator of the political intrigues and revolts, General Ballivián finally became president. He rallied the disorganized Bolivian forces and defeated Gamarra in the Battle of Ingavi on November 14, 1841. This historic and decisive victory consolidated Bolivian independence and lifted at last the palpable threat of a Peruvian reconquest of Bolivia.

During the next six years of Ballivián's rule, the country could focus on territorial exploration and economic development. As president, Ballivián encouraged constitutional reform and a greater civilian role in national life. Historians consider his presidency as the last stable government in an era of increasing unrest.

Revolts by the youthful colonel Manuel Isidoro Belzú and Generals Agreda and Velasco forced Ballivián's resignation in late 1847. After a 10-day interim government, General Velasco became president for the fourth time in January 1848, but his presidency did not last out the year. In December, Belzú, now a general, removed Velasco from national office for the last time. Belzú's presidency ushered in the period of misrule by Bolivia's "barbarous caudillos."

Belzú, the Plebeian Caudillo

Comrades, private property is the principal source of transgressions and crimes in Bolivia. It is the cause of the permanent struggle between Bolivians.

■

Manuel Belzú (Bethell 1985, III:571).

Manuel Isidoro Belzú became interim, then constitutional president of Bolivia, governing for seven years, from 1848 to 1855. Unlike Ballivián, who was an educated, white aristocrat representing the powerful oligarchy of the new republic, Belzú was a plebeian in birth and tastes who had fought his way to power. He represented a new force in Bolivian politics—the urbanized, up-and-coming *cholos*—a threatening and "dangerous" development for the Creoles. Despised by the oligarchy because of his inferior pedigree, Belzú appealed to the impoverished classes of the country. He was one of them, and they granted him their complete adulation and loyalty. For the first time in Bolivian history, these men and women of humble station discovered in Belzú a voice and a decisive role in national politics.

Since colonial times, burros have been used extensively as beasts of burden in rural Bolivia. (Kathy S. Leonard photo)

The country's economic and political elite proved unable to oust Belzú from the presidency despite an assassination attempt in 1850 and more than 42 subversive plots against him. He was affectionately called Tata (Father) Belzú by the *cholo* masses who loved him. The commoners rescued their idol repeatedly, defying the guns of the organized army.

Belzú is often recognized as Bolivia's first populist caudillo because his policies flagrantly curried the favor of the Indians and oppressed classes. He implemented numerous beneficial reforms and protectionist economic legislation. His government produced a nationalistic Mining Code, Bolivia's fifth constitution in 1851, and an important population census in 1854. In particular, the mercantilist trade policies that Belzú pursued generated great internal and external opposition.

The nationalist Belzú was convinced that the flood of foreign goods inhibited the development of Bolivia's own domestic market. As a result, he constrained the activity of foreign merchants and investors. This protectionist policy led to a confrontation with the British representative in Bolivia, who was ultimately expelled. The expulsion generated numerous unsubstantiated, but colorful and uncomplimentary legends about Belzú and Bolivia. Historians discount the anecdotes that

THE 1854 CENSUS

The national census of 1854 indicated that the country's population, long in a downturn, had increased to 2.3 million inhabitants—over two-thirds of Bolivia's population in the 1950s, and a quarter of its population in 2001. Many important demographic patterns that have influenced Bolivia's historical development were already evident in this early census.

In the mid-19th century, great portions of the country remained relatively barren of Bolivian residents, especially in Bolivia's coastal province (El Litoral) and the port of La Mar, or Cobija. This territorial vacuum proved to be critical. The great Uruguayan philosopher José Enrique Rodó correctly observed in his book of essays *Ariel* (1900), "To govern is to populate." Bolivian governments, by failing to populate the whole of the national territory, did not fully govern Bolivia. As one can see, the 1854 census should have rung early alarm bells.

Population of Departments and Departmental Capitals, 1854 Census

Departments	Population	Departmental Capital	Population
Chuquisaca	349,119	Sucre	18,002
La Paz	593,779	La Paz	68,118
Cochabamba	382,919	Cochabamba	35,837
Potosí	254,728	Potosí	25,588
Oruro	91,751	Oruro	5,654
Santa Cruz	255,599	Santa Cruz	5,625
Tarija	277,724	Tarija	3,473
El Beni	114,922	Trinidad	not available
El Litoral	18,000	Puerto La Mar, or Cobija	1,703

Source: Vázquez Machicado (1988, 371)

Belzú humiliated the British consul, clipping his earlobes and parading him around on the back of a donkey, or that Queen Victoria imperiously eliminated Bolivia from her world map when told of Belzú's effrontery. Nevertheless, one can see from these tales that Belzú was a man of extremes, both passionately loved and hated.

Whatever Belzú's populist sentiments, he was a typical military autocrat, addicted to excesses and terrified of assassination and rebellion by rival caudillos. He knew that impatiently waiting in the wings were formidable foes—Mariano Melgarejo, Agustín Morales, and José María Linares. Nevertheless, Belzú survived as president for seven years, long enough to hold elections and leave office voluntarily—a notable record for Bolivian dictators of the day.

Tata Belzú's successor was General Jorge Córdova, his politically inexperienced son-in-law. In March 1855, a national congress elected Córdova president. Historian Herbert S. Klein described the event as a "controlled election" in which some 13,500 electors voted. The election, however, brought only brief tranquility for the pro-Belzú forces. Having scant confidence in his soft son-in-law, Belzú is said to have voted for the opposition candidate, José María Linares, who represented

THE FATE OF BELZÚ

O ne might say that Manuel Isidoro Belzú not only benefited from a great deal of luck, but also his sense of timing for when to leave office was excellent. Neither of these assets, however, would last. After he stepped down as president, Belzú wisely left Bolivia to travel abroad. He later served as Bolivia's representative on various diplomatic missions in Europe. In 1861, Belzú returned to his native Bolivia.

Once in La Paz, his old power base, Belzú soon became drawn into political plotting and regional feuding. Surrounded by his mob of supporters, Belzú renewed his dormant presidential ambitions. Ironically, the fear of assassination that had haunted him during his dangerous days in office also returned and was finally realized. In a wild confrontation in the presidential palace, his rival General Mariano Melgarejo shot and killed Belzú in an argument over the presidential succession.

According to a popular account of the affair, Melgarejo rushed to the presidential balcony after the cold-blooded murder and defiantly proclaimed to the mob below, "Belzú is dead! Who lives now?" The crowd roared back, "Long live Melgarejo!"

the free trade lobby. Moreover, when Córdova ascended the presidential dais, Belzú reportedly quipped he would not last. Indeed, within two years General Agreda and Linares cut short the undistinguished and unstable Córdova government.

The Civilian Interlude

The presidency of José María Linares, Bolivia's first civilian president, from 1857 to 1861, interrupted the pattern of caudillo rule. A member of an aristocratic Spanish family from the city of Sucre, Linares had advanced in politics not because of the advantages of a military career but because of his legal and administrative skills. He had first tried constitutional means of gaining power, running against Córdova in the rigged elections of 1855. In spite of the impossible electoral odds, Linares still received 4,000 votes. He and his supporters then succeeded with extraconstitutional methods: an armed coup.

As president, Linares instituted needed fiscal, administrative, and judicial reforms. Unlike Córdova and Belzú, President Linares catered to the mining bourgeoisie, the free traders, and the foreign capitalists eager to invest in Bolivia and grow rich on the profits. Although he ended the extensive government's monopoly of the mining industry, Linares retained control over the refining and minting of silver. His government, nevertheless, encouraged the formation of an official interest group to represent the powerful mining sector. Herbert S. Klein indicates that the mine owners of three large companies alone represented investments of 1.5 to 2 million pesos annually, which was almost "the total income generated by the national treasury in any one year" (1992, 131–32).

Although he broke with General Ballivián, Linares remained tied to the Red Party, or Partido Rojo, that Ballivián had founded. An important predecessor to the civilian political parties of the 1880s, the *rojos* opposed militarism and advanced the interests of a new political ruling class made up of silver magnates, lawyers, and the educated class. To stay in office Linares imposed unpopular authoritarian measures. In September 1858, he created a formal dictatorship, and in 1860, his harsh rule resulted in a large-scale revolt and an infamous Indian massacre at the holy shrine of the Virgin of Copacabana on the shores of Lake Titicaca.

Chronic coup plotting against Linares and the *rojos* intensified. Finally, before he could organize national elections, his opponents and traitors in his own cabinet launched a military revolt against him. In January 1861, the minister of war, General José María de Achá, seized power. The Bolivian Congress, recently elected and controlled

63

by opponents of Linares, sanctioned the takeover by formally select-ing Achá as the next president. After only a brief interlude of civilian rule, the military men were back in power.

The government of Achá may not have been more brutal than its antecedents or that of Melgarejo soon to come; nevertheless, in terms of its repression of political opponents, Achá's rule has received a reputation as the most violent government in the 19th century. In 1861, the local mil-itary commander in La Paz, Colonel Plácido Yañez, summarily executed 70 high-profile opposition politicians, including former president Jorge Córdova, who were known supporters of ex-president Belzú. The La Paz commander claimed that a revolt by Belzú had necessitated his ruthless reprisal. The atrocity became known as the Massacre of Loreto, after the old convent where the majority of the political prisoners had been held.

During Achá's presidency, there were few political and economic changes in overall government policy from the Linares period. Bolivia, however, moved closer to open conflict with Chile. In 1857, rich guano and nitrate deposits had been discovered in Mejillones, an isolated and underpopulated region in El Litoral province along Bolivia's Pacific sea-coast. A dispute between rival claims of Chilean and Brazilian investors over the exploitation of these lucrative resources erupted in 1863. With a puny Bolivian army that had dwindled to fewer than 2,000 men, Achá was unable to mount an effective resistance to the Chilean incursions. And, before he could organize either a defense or the upcoming presi-dential elections, Mariano Melgarejo, a close relative and the most infa-mous of Bolivian tyrants, deposed him on December 28, 1864.

Melgarejo, the Consummate *Caudillo Bárbaro*

> For the caudillo time is pressing. If he is not rich, he must become rich as soon as possible.
>
> ■
>
> (Chevalier 1992, 34)

A *cholo* of illegitimate birth from Cochabamba, Mariano Melgarejo lived up to the stereotype of a 19th-century caudillo. He was a brutal and dis-solute despot who squandered scarce state resources on mistresses and drunken orgies, and he suffered fits of outright madness.

Insisting on the title of "the most illustrious man of the century," Melgarejo compelled his officers to frolic and roll around on the floors of the national palace imitating overexcited pet poodles. He personally conducted horrifying rampages of pillage and rape down the streets of La Paz. When pesos dwindled in the national treasury, Melgarejo debased the currency and issued his own money—worthless *melgarejos*.

In one of his most infamous acts, Melgarejo practically gave away 40,000 square miles of Bolivia's tropical Matto Grosso territory to Brazil. Some historians emphasize that Melgarejo "meant well" by signing the 1867 treaty with Brazil that was intended to gain Bolivia an outlet on the Atlantic Ocean, but it was also under Melgarejo that Bolivia relinquished its legal claim to the extraordinarily valuable guano and nitrate deposits in the Atacama Desert.

The 1866 Mejillones Treaty, which the Melgarejo government signed, permitted Chile greater control over Bolivia's coastal territories on the Pacific Ocean. By its terms, all the land below the 24th parallel was ceded to Chile and exempted from Bolivian taxes levied on mining and other exports from Pacific ports. As a result of his secret machinations with the Chilean nitrate interests, Melgarejo filled his personal coffers at the expense of the nation, and his greed and irresponsibility hastened the War of the Pacific between Bolivia and Chile.

Melgarejo was hated by the country's traditional upper classes, consisting of the aristocratic families of Sucre and the Creole landed elite of southern and central Bolivia. Not only was Melgarejo's crude behavior repugnant to them, but he represented the rise of the nouveau riche mining elite on the national scene. During the independence wars, the colonial mining industry—the major engine of Bolivia's economy—had been virtually destroyed. After 1839, the increasingly liberal trade policies of Bolivian governments, the infusion of local and international capital, and modernized machinery and mining methods led to a resurgence of the silver mining industry and the national economy.

For 40 years since independence, Bolivian governments had depended on a severely limited tax base. Income from the extraction of quinine from cinchona, or Peruvian, bark dominated Bolivian commerce and treasury receipts from 1847 to 1855. But the brief monopoly was lost to Colombia, and as a result, by 1860, quinine exports were down to a trickle. By 1864, exports of guano and nitrates produced vital revenue and investment capital for the cash-starved economy.

President Melgarejo's social and economic policies benefited the free trade capitalists and the resurgent silver mining oligarchy, and investors scrambled to carve up the resources of Bolivia's Pacific Litoral province, which harbored the Caracoles silver mines and guano and nitrate deposits. The majority of these new owners and merchants were foreign or connected to Chilean interests. Melgarejo exempted them from silver export taxes and dismantled the state control of silver production and pricing.

Bolivian historians have excoriated the Melgarejo regime for selling the lucrative resources of the nation to the highest bidder. On the other hand, historian Herbert S. Klein has wondered whether other Bolivian governments, if also faced with flat revenues and deficit budgets, would have acted differently from Melgarejo. Klein has further questioned whether the new mining elite was truly concerned with the lucrative concessions the Bolivian governments extended to foreign interests in this period given that venality appeared to be widespread among the Bolivian ruling class of the day.

Indeed, in 1865, bountiful natural and capital resources were available to the country and those who controlled it for the first time since independence. The hungry generals, and Melgarejo was obviously one of the hungriest, could not pass up this unique opportunity for unheard-of personal gain. The loans and long-term contracts that Melgarejo signed enriched all the greedy special interests. Unfortunately, these deals, mostly corrupt and irresponsible, did not benefit the country as a whole or the majority of the people.

Many of Melgarejo's policies hurt Bolivia's indigenous people. Under the unpopular 1866 land decree, Indians were required to purchase individual land titles to replace communal claims. These individual titles were not permanent, however, and had to be renewed every five years to maintain effective ownership. If Indian farmers failed to comply, their lands reverted to the state and were auctioned off to the highest bidder or exchanged for the debts the state owed private individuals. Lands that were not purchased remained state property, and landless Indian farmers had no choice but to rent them from the government.

The majority of the indigenous population could not afford the new titles or the rents. Typically suspicious of the government, many simply ignored the law. Despite the guise of reform, the actual intent of the insidious law was to transfer communal lands to the white and *cholo* owners of the country's rural haciendas. It also provided a golden opportunity for Melgarejo's favorite mistress, Juana Sánchez, her family, and his favorite cronies to buy up indigenous properties for a pittance.

Melgarejo's comprehensive attack on the properties of the independent Indian communities provoked desperate and violent resistance. To enforce the land law, the national army ruthlessly killed thousands of Indians. Public outcry was so great, however, according to Herbert S. Klein, that the confiscation scheme was aborted and temporarily reversed when Melgarejo was ousted from power.

The disastrous six-year rule of Melgarejo became known simply as *"el sexenio"* (the six years). Bolivians tired of his despotism and misrule, but as revolts followed revolts—each one bloodier than the last—none succeeded in ridding the country of the tyrant. Finally, in December 1870, *paceños*, the people of La Paz, rose up, assisted by Colonel Hilarión Daza, who was the commander of the city's crack Colorado Battalion and who was well paid for this betrayal of Melgarejo. On January 15, 1871, in a terrible struggle in which more than 1,000 Bolivians died, Melgarejo was defeated and deposed by Colonel Agustín Morales.

THE LAST DAYS OF MELGAREJO

After his defeat, Mariano Melgarejo fled across the altiplano, hounded along the journey by vengeful Indian pursuers, who had not forgotten his seizure of their lands and the massacres of entire villages. According to the Bolivian historian José Fellman Velarde, of the 300 soldiers who escaped from La Paz with Melgarejo, only five reached Peru. The deposed tyrant arrived safely in Arequipa, where he was well received at first.

In La Paz, Melgarejo's distraught mistress, Juana Sánchez, remained a hostage. She found herself imprisoned and unable to pay her debts, which she claimed in a flowery and ingratiating letter to Colonel Agustín Morales not to have contracted. Sánchez implored the victorious Morales to allow her to sell her property in order to buy her freedom. Portraying herself as the victim of cold ingratitude, bad faith, and betrayal, she pleaded with him to release her and permit her exile.

Disturbed over the desperate plight of his beloved "Juanacha," Melgarejo hurried to Lima and begged and borrowed money from friends to send to Bolivia to rescue Juana. Unfortunately, Melgarejo's devotion to his mistress proved to be his undoing. Once freed and comfortably established in Lima, Sánchez heartlessly rejected the former president. Melgarejo tried to recover some of the wealth he claimed the Sánchez family owed him, and a lengthy, public litigation ensued that aired many intimate details of their relationship.

Finally on the night of November 23, 1872, Melgarejo, nearly destitute, half crazed, and reportedly inebriated, attempted to gain entry into Sánchez's house. There Sánchez's brother, and Melgarejo's own son-in-law, José Aurelio Sánchez, shot Melgarejo dead in the street. The remains of the reviled tyrant were buried in Lima and have never been repatriated to Bolivia.

The Madness of General Morales

In 1871, Agustín Morales, a native of La Paz and newly appointed a general, became the provisional president of Bolivia. He had been exiled during Belzú's rule but later returned to serve in the governments of Achá and Melgarejo. Under the guise of honoring this dangerous rival, Melgarejo appointed Morales to various consular posts abroad. Even from outside the country, however, Morales managed to engineer Melgarejo's violent overthrow.

The regime of General Morales promised to be as authoritarian and erratic as its predecessor. After serving only as provisional chief executive, Morales was elected constitutional president in May 1872. Unlike his predecessor, however, Morales conducted the state's financial affairs with integrity, and despite the chaos and corruption he inherited, he seriously attempted to extract the country from its indebtedness.

In order to restore a degree of calm in indigenous relations, the new government immediately annulled Melgarejo's disastrous agrarian reform decree; however, the return of communal lands, or *ayllus,* that had already been sold created a legal tangle and thorny political dilemma that was eventually resolved in favor of the landowning class. Also, now that the Bolivian government had steady revenues available to it, Morales could pursue general fiscal reforms and some greatly needed public works, for example, the minting of new currency to replace the debased coinage of previous governments, the additional freeing of trade and silver exports from governmental control, and the establishment of the semiprivate National Bank of Bolivia to reorganize the nation's money.

The Morales government also renegotiated the more onerous foreign contracts and trade concessions of the Melgarejo years. Unfortunately, for one reason or the other, some corrupt loans were continued. The companies that were affected negatively demanded and received monetary damages. The contract with U.S. financier George Church to establish a steamship company to ply Bolivian rivers in the east and open up a Bolivian port on the Atlantic Ocean proved to be a major scandal. Of the 2 million pounds raised for the company, according to Herbert S. Klein, the Bolivian government received practically nothing. Several railroad concessions granted foreign investors the construction of rail lines, which when completed would link commercial activities in Antofagasta, Mejillones, and the Caracoles silver mines in Bolivia's Pacific coast province with the new seat of government in La Paz.

By 1872, the world market price of silver had declined, and the descent continued at a rate of approximately 5 percent annually. The historian José Fellmann Velarde writes that this decrease advanced the concentration of wealth in the hands of a very small number of silver mining entrepreneurs. This process had been building steadily and had created a new economic elite, the silver mining oligarchy. Bolivian historians refer to these three or four major silver entrepreneurs as "Big Silver." Generally more focused on profits than politics, during the government of Morales these interests converged. Big Silver began to flex its political muscle in proportion to its increasing economic power.

In 1872, the Bolivian Congress approved a tax that favored the large producers at the expense of the small silver miners. Because of this tax, the concentration of mining wealth in a few hands received an enormous new impetus. After 1871, the intensive exploitation of the rich silver lodes found in the coastal mines of Caracoles revived silver production, which once again became the mainstay of the indebted Bolivian economy. Indeed, the decade of the 1870s culminated with the beginning of an important new politico-economic period, the Great Age of Silver. By 1880, according to Herbert S. Klein, silver output was phenomenal, with one enterprise alone generating more income than the central government.

According to historian Humberto Vázquez Machicado, the inconstancy and violence of Morales's character obviated his good intentions as president. Despite his displays of public modesty and reticence, Morales hungered for national power; for example, in a dramatic incident at the constitutional assembly of June 1871, Morales renounced his position as provisional president, then reversed himself and compelled the delegates to accept his retraction. In May 1872, the return to Bolivia of Adolfo Ballivián, the son of the popular ex-president, threatened Morales's election chances.

President Morales left office as violently as he had entered it. Congress, which was about to act against the designs of the president, was forced to suspend its activity because of a disruption by Colonel Hilarión Daza instigated by Morales. The next day, before an empty chamber, the choleric Morales dismissed Congress and his entire cabinet and declared himself dictator. Morales, who was directly challenging the silver mining and landowning interests, withdrew to the presidential palace, where he met a dramatic end. His behavior became more and more demented (Bolivian historians have described it as that of a frenzied caged beast) and on November 27, Morales's nephew, Lieutenant Colonel Federico La Faye, tried to intervene as Morales attacked one of his own aides. Morales, a giant of a man, turned against the frightened La Faye. Morales advanced toward his nephew, and La Faye emptied the entire contents of his service pistol, killing Morales.

After Morales's assassination, Tomás Frías, a distinguished civilian politician and doctor of law who had been Antonio José de Sucre's private secretary, served as interim president. On May 6, 1873, Adolfo Ballivián became president. Although also a military man, Ballivián was well educated and the son of a former national hero and president, José Ballivián. His brief rule consolidated the return to power of the civilian constitutionalists, or the *rojos*.

To his credit, the capable Ballivián negotiated important loans and seriously attempted to rescue the country from imminent bankruptcy. The external national debt at the time exceeded the fantastic sum of 1.5 million pounds sterling. Unfortunately, Ballivián was incurably ill and soon died of stomach cancer. With President Ballivián's untimely death, Frías, the leader of Congress and the Constitutionalist Party, became president once again in 1874.

These civilian governments struggled unsuccessfully to resolve the escalating territorial conflict with Chile. And, despite the bravado of the military as the international crisis heightened, the nation remained largely unprepared for the outbreak of war. The civilian *rojos* were impotent against the unruly and hawkish army and popular mood, which became ever angrier with the disastrous international contracts and negotiations. Moreover, the populist politicians of the day exhibited few reservations in personally capitalizing on the harsh economic conditions and volatile internal and international climate.

As the constitutionally mandated elections of 1876 approached, the dominant political groups remained severely divided, all vying for the coveted presidency. It seemed probable that no single candidate or strong leader would emerge to unite the country. In order to run as a candidate, General Hilarión Daza, who was minister of defense and commander of the Colorado Battalion, would have to resign his military offices. He feared that in the process the military would lose power and that he would lose control of the military. He decided not to rely on the doubtful institutional outcome and to thwart the scheduled elections instead. General Daza and his troops voted with their bayonets. On May 4, 1876, Daza deposed President Frías and became the last of Bolivia's military caudillos before the outbreak of the great Pacific war.

The Last 19th-Century Caudillo

The presidency of Hilarión Daza was landmark in Bolivian history. During his administration, the legislature approved the historic Liberal Constitution of 1879 (the county's ninth since independence), which remained, with slight modifications in 1880, Bolivia's fundamental governing charter until the 1930s. It protected private property rights and the economic concerns of Bolivia's Big Silver industrialists and their Chilean interests.

General Daza's rule, however, figures most tragically in the nation's collective memory because it marked the loss of Bolivia's access to the Pacific Ocean. His government and Congress of 1878 passed the infamous 10¢ tax on the nitrates exported by the British-Chilean Nitrates and Railroad Company of Antofagasta. This tax, which the bankrupt Bolivian treasury desperately needed, provided Chile with the perfect pretext to occupy Bolivia's seacoast and launch a war with its neighbors.

President Daza cannot be blamed entirely for the war and the loss of the seacoast. Years before his government, Chilean, British, and U.S. capital had extended financial tentacles into virtually every profit-generating enterprise available to Bolivia: guano, nitrates, borax, even silver. The economic concessions of the Bolivian Litoral province produced an estimated 28 million pesos annually, according to historian José Fellman Velarde. By his calculations, this bonanza

THE UNCOUTH GENERAL DAZA

Bolivian historians have bestowed on Hilarión Daza the epithet *"el soldado mandón"* (the imperious soldier). According to historian Humberto Vázquez Machicado, Daza was born in the constitutional capital of Sucre around 1840 the illegitimate son of an itinerant Italian snake-oil salesman named Grossolín. As a child, Daza had difficulty pronouncing his father's surname, and from these attempts he received the ludicrous nickname of "Chocholín." Not pleased, he started to use the surname of his mother.

Daza received his limited education on the tough streets of Sucre as a small-time crook and con artist and in the rough barracks of the army. He showed a talent for being in the right place at the right time and rapidly rose in the military ranks with Mariano Melgarejo, whom in the end he betrayed for 10,000 pesos. Daza was overthrown in 1879, while at the battlefront in Tacna, and headed for Europe. There, he lived the good life until the enormous fortune that he had pilfered became depleted. He returned to Bolivia intent on heading another military coup but was killed in 1894.

exceeded 14 times the Bolivian budget and eight times that of Chile at the time. This appropriation and Bolivia's semicolonization by domestic and foreign capital caused the War of the Pacific as much as the incompetence and venality of Daza and earlier Bolivian regimes did. Already, on the eve of Daza's military coup of May 1876, Chile in effect controlled the bulk of Bolivia's coastal assets demographically and financially. By the time General Daza was overthrown in December 1879, the Chilean forces had also militarily occupied the entire Bolivian Litoral.

5

REPUBLICAN RULE AND THE NEW OLIGARCHY (1879-1932)

People who cannot read will not have the right to vote; and since almost all Bolivians speak Quechua or Aymara, know nothing of the Castilian language, and cannot read, only a handful of select males will have that right.

■

(Galeano 1987, 130)

Two major wars—the War of the Pacific and the Chaco War—frame the historical period of 1879 to 1932. Bolivia's devastating defeat in the War of the Pacific left a deep imprint on the national psyche, serving as both a catharsis and a catalyst. At the war's end, blame and guilt completely discredited Bolivia's military strongmen and brought the era of caudillo rule to an abrupt close. The war also marked a significant turning point in the nation's development: the establishment of civilian, republican rule.

In this critical period, Bolivia realized a measure of political stability and economic growth, albeit under the tutelage of a new oligarchy. The narrow new ruling class—the silver- and tin-mining elite and landed aristocracy—was represented by civilian political parties, so the system's success depended on the franchise remaining limited to the privileged few. More than a half century later, the Chaco War shattered the republican status quo that the War of the Pacific had created.

On the Eve of the Great Pacific War

No war breaks out over guano, of which little remains. It is salt-peter that throws the Chilean army into the conquest of the deserts, against the allied forces of Peru and Bolivia.

■

(Galeano 1987, 218)

The War of the Pacific was a war over resources, although territorial rivalry was its most immediate cause. The conflict also involved geopolitics, economic rivalry, greed, corruption, and personal ambitions. Indeed, the basic ingredient of the war—rivalry for power and economic dominance—first came into play with Bolivian independence. Because of this endemic regional rivalry, some historians have argued that the War of the Pacific was inevitable.

In the 1870s, the conflict of national interests and increasing disparities in economic and political power among the three neighboring South American countries of Bolivia, Chile, and Peru reached a critical climax. The new power distribution greatly favored Chile, and Chilean statesmen seized this opportunity to consolidate and further expand their nation's influence and control along the Pacific coast.

Since its founding as a sovereign nation, Bolivia's survival had been tentative. At first, Lima and Buenos Aires considered Bolivia's very existence suspect. Bolivia, after all, had been capriciously carved out of the colonial *audiencias* that they had jealously controlled. Once established, Bolivia was troublesome and unstable. The new country seemed unable to rule itself, much less populate and effectively administer its vast and dispersed territory. Bolivia's rich natural resources were the constant envy of its more powerful and aggressive neighbors in the Southern Cone. Debilitated by corruption and instability, Bolivia dismally failed to preserve its territory and resources when challenged by Chile.

In great part Bolivia's geopolitics and unique national conditions facilitated this disastrous war and the loss of its Pacific seacoast. As late as the 1880s, the altiplano region remained the geopolitical center of the shaky new republic. The majority of the country's territory, however, was neglected and isolated from the highland by formidable natural barriers—impassable and hostile mountain ranges, rivers, deserts, and jungles. Bolivians in these frontier regions were forced to fend for themselves. Moreover, Bolivia's population was largely indigenous with only a thin upper crust of Spaniards and other Europeans. Neither social group had the necessary mobility or motivation to migrate to the less hospitable parts of the country.

These factors had a devastating impact on settlement of Bolivia's Atacama province. Even after the discovery of guano and nitrate deposits in the Atacama Desert, which stretched from Peru in the north to Chile in the south, the Bolivian government was unable to incorporate and fortify this distant, sparsely populated coastal province. The unexpected bonanza in natural fertilizers brought a sudden influx of new settlers, prospectors, and entrepreneurs to the region; however, this population increase only compounded Bolivia's problems since Bolivian citizens were now outnumbered 10 to one by Chileans and

THE LEAST HOSPITABLE PLACE ON EARTH

The Atacama Desert stretches along the Pacific coast of South America from approximately 21° to 27° south latitude. The War of the Pacific was fought over this most inhospitable terrain. Today the territory belongs to Chile, but the region remains exceedingly poor. As in Inca times, the economy depends on a few natural ports and fishing, but between 1840 and 1885, it was the scene of economic boom and huge wealth derived from extracting natural deposits of guano and sodium nitrates.

Off the coast, the cold waters of the Humboldt current meet the shore and the wall of coastal mountains rising 4,000 feet above the sea. A perpetual cloud cover forms over the peaks and the coastal plateau beyond. About 100 miles wide and stretching 1,000 miles north and south, this barren plateau is one of the driest places on earth. With an average annual rainfall of less than an inch per year, the Atacama may see no rain for decades at a time.

The region is also subject to terrible earthquakes that can be followed by devastating tidal waves. After an offshore earthquake in August 1868, a massive tidal wave ravaged the coast from Ecuador to Chile and swept out of existence the Atacama seaports wedged between the sea and the surrounding hills. Before modern transportation, the scarcity of water also encouraged plagues of yellow fever and cholera. The region was hell for prospective colonists (Farcau 2000, 5–6).

other immigrants, including thousands of Chinese coolies brought here by Peru and Chile as cheap, captive laborers.

With other nations and foreign firms competing for the profits from the bird droppings and saltpeter, Bolivia's share of the bonanza steadily shrank. The remainder was squandered by the corrupt caudillos on profligate living and ill-advised foreign concessions and loans. Bolivian entrepreneurs' resources were depleted or invested elsewhere, primarily in the highland silver mines. As a last resort, with the economy stagnant and the country heavily indebted, Bolivian governments permitted and encouraged British and Chilean capital to exploit the desert windfall on their behalf. In short, Bolivia's inherent political and economic weaknesses directly contributed to the outbreak of the war.

Chile, on the other hand, stood in a position of relative strength. Unlike Peru or Bolivia, Chile's exceptional political stability and economic growth since 1830 had helped make it the dominant power in the region. Chileans held regular elections for civilian governments and enticed foreign investors by the credibility of their sound political and financial systems. Chile's cities were modern, and its people were mostly European immigrants, rather than Indians. Its economy was more diversified, and its territory was more integrated and cohesive. Chile had what both Peru and Bolivia lacked. Indeed, one Chilean president boasted in 1858 that the country had "the honor to have proved to the world that the Spanish American people can govern themselves by their own unaided efforts and can continue to prosper" (Bader 1967, 25).

This is not to say that all was well in Chile at the time. The country had its share of shortcomings and crises, and it was precisely a national crisis—the depression of 1878—that pushed Chile closer to war. By the mid-1870s, Chilean progress had come to a halt. Chilean exports had declined and the foreign debt had skyrocketed at the same time that droughts and diseases ravaged the country. Upward of 50,000 Chileans—mostly *rotos,* or landless peasant farmers of European descent—were forced to emigrate. Many would slave in the grueling guano and nitrate operations in Bolivia's Atacama Desert.

Chile's economic decline was an incentive to resolve the territorial dispute with Bolivia aggressively. Chile saw in the great riches of the coastal desert an immediate solution to the 1878 financial crisis and reliable long-term financing for the national debt and future commercial and territorial expansion. Decades later, Chile's foreign minister, Abraham Köning, dissected Chilean motivations succinctly: "The area is rich and worth many millions" (Siles Guevara 1960, 68). Indeed, in the 20 years from 1880 to the end of the century, the gross value of the

MINERS OF THE ATACAMA

On a moonscape of parched sand and rock, virtually devoid of plant life, mountains of guano, or bird droppings, were "discovered" in 1840. (In the early 1800s, entrepreneurs had tried unsuccessfully to market the natural fertilizer in Europe, and it is thought that the Inca used the nitrate-rich guano as fertilizer for their fields.) The cold current rising up from Antarctica created ideal conditions for plankton, and the waters teemed with fish, attracting tens of thousands of sea birds to nest on the shore. And since it never rained, millions of tons of bird droppings had accumulated practically undisturbed for centuries.

The grayish-white guano needed no further processing; it was directly shoveled up into bags and loaded onto nearby ships. But the work was grueling and dehumanizing. The guano workers lived on these piles of excrement that formed the ground. Their digging raised an acrid and fetid dust that irritated their eyes, choked their mouths, contaminated their water, and blanketed their meager food. There was an "appalling stench that could be detected miles out to sea, an odor not just of hundreds of sweating bodies that would not be washed for weeks on end, but of rotting fish, salt, and excrement from which there was no escape" (Farcau 2000, 9).

Few would work in this hellish place for the miserable wages. Thousands of prisoners from the jails of Lima, Peru; La Paz, Bolivia; and Valparaíso, Chile, were conscripted to do the job. And thousands of indentured Chinese coolies were brought over under near slavery conditions to shovel and load the guano.

The Atacama also offered extensive deposits of sodium nitrate that had concentrated for centuries in vast dried-out saltpans created by the scant runoff from the snowy Andes. Unlike the guano, these nitrate minerals were often well below the surface. Prospectors, mining equipment, and substantial capital investments were necessary to bring the resource to market. By 1856, with the guano boom still under way, new mining towns and camps began to extract and process sodium nitrate, in great demand in Europe as a fertilizer and the ingredient in the manufacture of explosives such as the recently invented TNT. Thousands of landless and unemployed Chilean peasants comprised the workforce of the nitrate mines along the Peruvian and Bolivian littoral.

nitrate exports from the conquered regions reached nearly 3 billion pesos.

On the eve of the war, corruption in Peru and Bolivia and the economic crisis in Chile had diminished the military preparedness of all three future belligerents. Chile, nevertheless, was relatively more prepared. For several decades Chile had been locked in a fierce military and commercial rivalry with Peru and had competed fiercely over control of the western seacoast. Now, Peru, like Bolivia, was virtually bankrupt, in political chaos on the eve of the war, and outclassed militarily by Chile. War decided this rivalry and assured Chilean hegemony on the Pacific coast.

Legacy of Disputed Territorial Claims

The dissolution of the great Spanish colonial empire left in its wake conflicting and ambiguous territorial claims that incited long-standing disputes and border wars. Perhaps none was as intractable as Bolivia's contested coastal boundary with Chile and subsequent loss of its access to the sea. Bolivia's fundamental claim to the Atacama province was based on a legal rule dating from 1810.

According to this principle of international law, colonial boundaries became international boundaries. In other words, the territory that had been within the jurisdiction of the Audiencia of Charcas devolved directly to the independent country of Bolivia. Moreover, Bolivia's 1825 Declaration of Independence specifically incorporated within its national territory the province of Potosí, whose southern boundary included the disputed Atacama Desert. In contrast, the Chileans never explicitly dealt with the boundary issue until the discovery of guano.

Especially important in terms of Bolivia's access to Pacific ports, this boundary confirmed that the seaports of colonial Bolivia belonged to the independent nation. In 1825, Bolivia's first president, Simón Bolívar, had designated the small port of Cobija, founded in 1587 and located between the Loa River in the north and the Salado River in the south, as Bolivia's Pacific seaport. Slightly south of Cobija, Bolivia also maintained the small port of Mejillones, which later served as the main transport point for the guano and nitrates.

Although Cobija was the port closest to Potosí and the silver mines, it proved wholly inadequate, since the trek to Cobija from Potosí demanded a month of rigorous hauling by mule train. In 1840, only little more than half of Cobija's total population of 550 was Bolivian, and

The Bay of Cobija, the original site of Bolivia's Pacific seaport. Today, the port is defunct and the area belongs to Chile, lost by Bolivia after the War of the Pacific. (Martin Glassner photo)

the port town's water and food had to be brought in from Chile. Most of Bolivia's silver exports, as a result, were packed out to the larger port of Arica in southern Peru.

Part of the Audiencia of Charcas, Arica was originally part of Peru. Later it was placed under the Viceroyalty of Río de la Plata, which rebelled in 1810 and became the Province of Río de la Plata. Bolivia, or Upper Peru, then seceded and joined Lower Peru. Bolívar argued that Upper Peru belonged to Lower Peru, and when in 1821 Peru secured independence, Peru claimed Arica and land down to Chile's Copiapó. After 1825, numerous attempts were made to get the Peruvian port of Arica ceded to Bolivia. In the Treaty of 1826, the Peruvian government agreed to transfer to Bolivia a segment of the Pacific coastal territory, including the port of Arica, but Peru's congress would not ratify the treaty. In 1841, a frustrated Bolivian government briefly occupied Arica and offered to purchase it outright. (This hope remains alive. For historical and geographical reasons Arica is the most logical seaport for Bolivia.)

Only after 1840, when the discovery of guano proved wildly profitable, did Chile seriously challenge Bolivian sovereignty in the Atacama Desert. According to legal documents of 1842, boundaries of the two nations directly overlapped: Chile claimed coastal territory as far north as the 23rd parallel south latitude; Bolivia claimed land as far south as the 27th parallel. This disputed possession drove the two countries to the brink of war in 1857. That year, the Chileans attempted to seize the guano-rich Mejillones region but failed. Six years later, Chilean forces finally occupied the coastal headland. The Bolivian government nervously brandished a declaration of war, but both sides backed down in the end, and negotiations temporarily defused the crisis. Their outcome, unfortunately, depended on the incompetent diplomacy of Bolivia's blatantly pro-Chilean dictator Mariano Melgarejo.

The injudicious Melgarejo signed the infamous Treaty of 1866. By the terms of the agreement, both sides renounced their previous territorial claims. The treaty fixed the Chilean-Bolivian coastal boundary at the 24th parallel south latitude and established a shared zone of exploitation between the 23rd and 25th parallels. In effect, Bolivia gave up all claims south of the 25th parallel.

MISSED OPPORTUNITIES

Bolivian presidents and diplomats squandered several opportunities to resolve the territorial dispute with Chile. After 1840, the Chileans generally turned a cold shoulder to Bolivia's frantic diplomatic missions to the capital of Santiago and its protests over Chilean encroachments. In 1863, Chile's conflict with Spain and threatened hostilities with Argentina handed Bolivian diplomacy a unique negotiating edge.

That year, Chile occupied the Bolivian port of Mejillones. The Bolivian Congress authorized a declaration of war if "all conciliatory and diplomatic means being exhausted, no return of the usurped territory or a peaceful solution compatible with national dignity can be achieved." At this tense moment the Spanish flotilla attacked Peru's guano-producing region, and the Peruvians and Chileans allied against Spain.

Bolivia remained neutral but allowed Spanish warships access to the port of Cobija. Fearful of the outcome of the hostilities, Chile sent an envoy, Aniceto Vergara Albano, to La Paz in March 1866. Historian Bruce Farcau writes that allegedly Vergara was instructed to offer the Bolivian's virtual carte blanche in drawing the border with Chile. But Melgarejo, who was president at the time, had already canceled Bolivia's neutrality and closed its ports to Spain. Flattered and distracted by Vergara, Melgarejo refused to discuss the boundary dispute until the Spanish had sailed home. With the Spanish threat removed, and buoyed by their naval victories against Spain's superior force, Chile lacked incentive to be magnanimous. The result was the despised Treaty of 1866.

The ambiguities in this last provision proved to be especially perilous and guaranteed future clashes. For example, the treaty failed to specify precisely which resources other than guano were to be included within the 50-50 split. In 1871, when a massive silver vein was discovered near the small town of Caracoles, just south and east of the 23rd parallel, the dispute intensified. Bolivia claimed the mines, but the Chileans provided all the working capital and 10,000 miners to the operations.

Not surprisingly, Bolivians widely condemned this rash agreement as a sellout of their national patrimony. The treaty, unquestionably, was extremely disadvantageous to Bolivia, which conceded three times as much territory than Chile did by its terms. As a result, instead of resolving the territorial dispute, Bolivian resentment against the treaty's unequal demands and the heavy-handed manner of its negotiation only festered. At the same time, the quarreling over the shared exploitation zone steadily intensified. In the end, the treaty effectively drove the parties closer to war.

All attempts to amend the unequal provisions of the 1866 treaty failed abysmally. The Bolivians sent a mission in 1872 to revise the boundary, but the Chileans rebuffed it. Finally, in 1873, when it became obvious that negotiations were fruitless, Bolivia's president-elect, Adolfo Ballivián, signed a secret defense treaty with Peru. Historians believe, however, that the Chileans knew of this vague agreement from the outset but reserved the knowledge until the most opportune moment. Indeed, Chile later produced this secret alliance as the official rationale for the military occupation of Lima and all of Peru's rich nitrate operations.

In 1874, another treaty was ratified between Chile and Bolivia that terminated the zones of shared economic exploitation, but once again fixed the territorial boundary at the 24th parallel and at the crest of the Andes on the east. Shared export duties, unspecified in the earlier treaty, applied only to nitrates. A final clause in the agreement granted Chilean companies operating in Bolivia's Atacama fields a 25-year exemption from all new taxes. When Bolivia rashly ignored this provision, Chile precipitated all-out hostilities; thus, the 1874 treaty provided the immediate catalyst of war.

The Ten Centavos War

The War of the Pacific was popularly dubbed the "Ten Centavos (cents) War." In 1877, after a devastating tidal wave destroyed much of the port of Antofagasta, the municipal council there passed a reconstruction tax.

In 1878, President Hilarión Daza and the Bolivian Congress approved the modest 10¢ tax on every 100 pounds of nitrates exported from Bolivian territory. This law directly violated the 1874 treaty, and the Chileans and foreign investors were outraged. The British and Chilean–owned Nitrates and Railroad Company of Antofagasta refused to pay the tax, and tensions mounted.

At first, cooler heads prevailed. President Daza temporarily suspended the tax, and the company agreed to an annual voluntary contribution. But then Daza ended the moratorium and demanded that the tax be paid retroactively. Once again, the foreign company refused to comply. The Chileans responded with gunboat diplomacy, and anchored an ironclad in Antofagasta harbor and mobilized their entire fleet.

This time, President Daza refused to back down. With Bolivian sovereignty seemingly besmirched, Daza canceled the mining contract of the British-Chilean consortium. On February 14, 1879, Chile occupied Antofagasta—home to 5,000 Chileans and fewer than 600 Bolivians—and issued an ultimatum: Bolivia had 48 hours to accede to international arbitration of the dispute. President Daza ignored the deadline and insisted that the port first be liberated. He also withheld news of the Chilean landing for a week until after the conclusion of the popular carnival festivities then under way.

In no mood for more wrangling, Chile occupied Bolivia's Antofagasta province and the entire Pacific coast south of the 23rd parallel in March. On March 14, Bolivia announced a formal declaration of war, but war still might have been averted if Peru's last-minute conciliatory diplomacy had succeeded, or if Peru had not honored its defensive alliance with Bolivia. By this time, however, word of the Bolivian declaration of war had reached Santiago, and therefore, on April 5, Chile formally declared war against Bolivia and Peru.

Defeat and Loss of the Seacoast

Bolivia was totally unprepared for war, especially one so distant from its population centers and resource base, and suffered from grossly irresponsible leadership. Despite his patriotic bluster, President Daza was inept in the military campaign. On the battlefield, he proved cowardly, self-motivated, and (according to some accounts) often drunk. Daza withdrew his crack Bolivian regiments from the field and left the allied forces to be defeated by the Chileans in the Battle of San Francisco. Although the remaining allied forces were victorious days later in the indecisive Battle of Tarapacá, President Daza's desertion became a great national embarrassment to Bolivia.

Historians have argued that Daza wanted to protect his prized regiments as a hedge against coup attempts, but on December 27, 1879, in a clever and meticulously timed plot, officers at the front and Colonel Eliodoro Camacho, the chief of staff, overthrew Daza, and the ex-president fled into exile in Europe.

In January 1880, General Narciso Campero, a distinguished career officer and division commander, was appointed Bolivia's provisional president and assumed command of the allied forces in the field as by then both the Bolivian and the Peruvian presidents had effectively deserted command of their armies. Campero's Bolivian-Peruvian force was decisively defeated by the Chileans in May, and Campero and his exhausted troops retreated toward La Paz. At the head of one column of survivors, Campero was met with the news that the National Assembly had formally elected him president on May 31. As the marauding horde of desperate soldiers approached the Bolivian border, a cavalry force from La Paz intercepted and forcibly disarmed them. The government feared violence when the wounded and exhausted returnees learned that they would not receive the back pay owed them. For Bolivia, the shooting war was over, although hostilities between Peru and Chile continued for three more years while Bolivia watched from the sidelines, hoping for a favorable resolution.

On April 5, 1884, Bolivia signed the Truce of Valparaíso, which gave Chile control, but not permanent transfer, of Bolivia's coastal territory. A peace treaty was finally signed in 1904, whereby Chile formally annexed Bolivia's Atacama province (called Antofagasta today). Bolivia was guaranteed the right to import and export its goods through the ports of Arica and Antofagasta and to set up customs' stations. Duties on imports were to be divided, providing Bolivia 75 percent and Chile 25 percent.

Thus, with the stroke of a pen, Bolivia lost a fourth of its territory and became the landlocked nation that it is today. The War of the Pacific was officially over, but not Bolivia's relentless quest to regain a seacoast.

Rise of the Modern Party System

The War of the Pacific deeply divided Bolivian society and government, and the ensuing rancorous debate within the white ruling class produced two political factions. In short order, these factions coalesced into the two major political parties that would determine the destiny of Bolivia's citizens—rich or poor, white, mestizo, or Indian—for most of the next half-century. Despite minor differences and pseudo-ideological distinctions, both parties desired stability, national unity, and economic development. These did not come easily because both parties also desired to appropriate political power.

The Liberal Party was founded in 1883 and represented the political "hawks," who were determined to press on with the futile war at all costs. The founding Liberal leader was the highly respected General Eliodoro Camacho, the wartime chief of staff. Camacho and his loyalists—among them the president, General Narciso Campero (another war hero who had replaced Daza), and Fernando E. Guachalla (a noted diplomat)—rejected even the hint of a "dishonorable" peace settlement with Chile. These statesmen and army leaders insisted that for the sake of national honor, Bolivians could and must fight on. Or, in other words, the Liberals unrealistically refused to accept defeat and the inevitable loss of Bolivia's seacoast to Chile.

The Conservative Party responded to the entrepreneurial interests of the silver mining oligarchy and was headed by Mariano Baptista, a long-standing and very vocal opponent of the war and noted attorney for "Big Silver." Along with Baptista, who was Campero's foreign minister at the time, other leading "doves" of the Conservative Party included two wealthy mining barons, Vice President Aniceto Arce and Gregorio Pacheco. Because significant Chilean capital had funded the resurgence of Bolivia's silver mining operations, the Conservative Party was also perceived as pro-Chilean.

BAPTISTA'S DIPLOMACY

An able diplomat, Mariano Baptista represented Bolivia during the U.S.-brokered Arica peace talks on the American ship *Lackawanna* in October of 1880. Chile had attempted to split the Bolivian-Peruvian alliance by secretly offering Bolivia a corridor to the sea carved out of occupied Peruvian territory and the Peruvian port of Arica as the prize for abandoning its ally. Although such an offer was rejected and remained unpopular at home, Baptista had consistently supported a deal or separate peace with Chile. It may be small comfort to Bolivians today that to their country's credit, Baptista's diplomatic realism and pro-Chilean sympathies failed to win out over nationalism, idealism, and fair play.

As the 1884 elections neared, Campero's administration formed two partisan camps, split over war policy and political ideology. This schism appeared to bode ill for the upcoming elections, but they came off without violence.

In rhetoric more than in practice, the Liberals stood for the classical principles of the 19th century: liberty and secular, federalist rule. The party opposed the official status of the Roman Catholic Church as the state religion and the unitary form of government established in the existing Constitution of 1878. In their view, unitary government had contributed to *caudillismo* and chronic instability. They lost out on both of these policy reforms to the Conservatives.

Early in the presidency of the Liberal general Campero, the national convention of 1880 reaffirmed the 1878 constitution. This charter basically remained in effect until 1938—longer than any Bolivian constitution before or since. In 1883, Camacho, a noted Liberal theoretician, described his party as devoted to the sacred principle of liberty. Baptista and the Conservatives countered by attempting to discredit the party program as "socialist" and "revolutionary."

The platform of the Conservative Party reaffirmed Catholicism as the state religion and the unitary form of government. The Conservatives identified their party with peace, stability, and traditionalism. During the 15 years immediately after the war, the pro-Chilean "peace" party seemed to capitalize on an image of realism, pragmatism, and single-mindedness in power. The firmness of the party's rule, however, provoked more violence than peace.

Rule of the Conservative Oligarchy

Ideology served as a smoke screen for hard political competition among moneyed elite interests. Political leaders preferred to believe that ideology was best to differentiate their party in contested elections, but the real battles, often bloody, were actually over political power and control of the government, not ideas. Personal and ideological rivalry aside, both political parties shared conservative political agendas. To historian Herbert S. Klein, the 1884 election anticipated a novel form of civilian politics in Bolivia. It represented "a political contest between civilian capitalists instead of barracks militarists . . . wherein the influence of money replaced the praetorianism of the past" (1968, 27, author's translation).

In the 1884 election, the two leading candidates were to have been the leaders of the Liberal and Conservative Parties, Camacho and Baptista, respectively. Instead, Baptista was edged out and two silver magnates sympathetic to the Conservative Party, Gregorio Pacheco and Aniceto Arce, vied for presidential victory. Pacheco was the candidate of the small Democratic Party, which he created purely as his personal electoral vehicle. In the results, Pacheco received the most votes but not the necessary absolute majority. Arce, the candidate of the Conservative Party, came in second, and Camacho, third in the count.

Camacho's Liberal Party, however, controlled the most votes in the congress, which would decide the election. After an anxious behind-the-scenes compromise among the political parties, the Bolivian Congress elected Pacheco as president. By the terms of the agreement, Baptista would serve as the vice president, and in the next go-around, it would be Arce's turn at the highest office. According to plan, Arce received an absolute majority of the vote in the elections of May 1888; another silver millionaire became president.

The Liberals contested his election, openly rebelling in September 1888. With great force and violence, President Arce put down the Liberal revolt in October 1888. The silver baron exacted a fierce retribution against his enemies, and prominent Liberals were exiled, imprisoned, or shot. From exile in Peru, General Camacho masterminded an uprising in La Paz in May 1890 that also failed. The election of Mariano Baptista in 1892 elicited further civil violence by the Liberals, provoking a state of siege days before the handover of office. Once again, the government exiled General Camacho and cracked down on the Liberals. While this pattern of chronic instability continued, these Conservative governments developed significant reforms, explorations, and railroad and communications infrastructure, such as banks and military institutions, the vital railways from Antofagasta to La Paz and to Oruro, and internal roads connecting major cities.

Between 1884 and 1899, the Conservative Party monopolized the office of the presidency. The Liberal opponents, quite appropriately, labeled these 15 years of exclusion from power as the era of the "conservative oligarchy." Blocked from national office by means of free and open elections, the Liberals believed themselves justified in employing intrigue and civil violence. Although these measures failed, as the century drew to a close, the influence of the Conservative Party began to wane and that of the Liberals to rise. In the Liberal Party's favor was its alliance with the up-and-coming tin oligarchy, the dominant political force of the new century. A revolt ended the tenure of the archtraditionalists in 1899, and ushered in two decades of government by the Liberal Party.

The Federal Revolution and Liberal Party Rule

In 1898, the Conservative Party was the undisputed voice of Bolivia's traditional ruling classes. These consisted of the silver industrialists, the old aristocrats of Sucre and Potosí, and the great landowners of Bolivia's rich central and southern agricultural regions. Unfortunately, the agricultural sector—despite the fact that Bolivia remained 75 percent rural—was no longer a progressive and vibrant sector of the economy. Similarly, after sharp declines in the price of silver on the international market and in Bolivia's overall production, the great silver industrialists were no longer so "great." Their economic and political clout had been reduced by the new power brokers of the northern altiplano—the merchants of tin.

In this shifting power context, an incident in 1898 precipitated civil war. In November, the Conservative-dominated legislature, over the strong opposition of the representatives from the city of La Paz, approved the law that maintained Sucre as the nation's legal capital. This parliamentary act, which ironically had been nonpartisan, touched

The city of Sucre, formerly called Chuquisaca and renamed after the Bolivian independence hero Antonio José de Sucre, was reaffirmed as the nation's legal capital in 1898, setting off a brief civil war. (Peter McFarren photo)

off the bloody but brief civil war between the Conservatives and Liberals known as the Federal Revolution.

The revolution of 1899, in effect, transferred the seat of government from Sucre to the city of La Paz. In many respects, the dispute over the country's legal capital was symbolic and symptomatic of the most recent political-economic shift in oligarchic rule since the great Pacific war. Although regionalism was an incendiary issue, the ostensible principle of federalism versus unitary government represented a partial explanation, if not pretext, for the major revolt, which resulted in no constitutional alterations in Bolivia's governing structures.

The struggle was between the old power brokers, the silver-mining and landed elite of the Conservative Party, on the one hand, and the new power elite, the tin-mining industrialists, urban professionals, and export-importers of the Liberal Party, on the other. Additionally, Liberal politicians capitalized on a genuine grassroots indigenous rebellion for their limited partisan ends. In the highlands, the great Indian leader Pablo Zárate Willka turned the anti-Conservative revolt into a struggle against all whites and their encroachments on Indian lands of the northern altiplano. When Willka and his supporters massacred and cannibalized a detachment of Liberal soldiers, the white elite united to repress the indigenous uprising.

Frustrated by electoral fraud and unable to take over the presidential palace constitutionally, the Liberal revolt was an extraconstitutional route to office. The new century began for Bolivia with a new Liberal oligarchy: In 1900, General José Manuel Pando, a very popular war hero, explorer, and architect of Liberal uprisings, became the first Liberal president of the new era. The subsequent presidencies of the great Liberal statesman Ismael Montes from 1904 to 1908 and 1913 to 1917 further consolidated Liberal Party rule.

In the classical republican period that lasted through to 1920, there were two dominant political parties. These parties operated within a certain "gentleman's code" that provided the opposition party or parties limited expression and competitive representation in the legislature. By these means, Bolivian political party development achieved the legal, but rarely fair and nonviolent transmission of power among partisan competitors. Party government, as a result, could merely reduce rather than completely eliminate the violence and instability that has plagued modern Bolivian politics.

In 1900, of an estimated total population of 1.6 million, about 35,000, or about 2 percent, of citizens generally voted. Historian Herbert S. Klein has suggested that only 10 to 20 percent of the population were

THE DEEP ROOTS OF THE 1899 INDIAN REVOLT

Señor Baptista, I and those of my race demand justice, justice, nothing
else but justice; justice which you have the duty to give us.

■

Telésforo Mendoza, mayor of the Puraka Ayllu, 1893 (Platt 1987, 280).

Recent historical scholarship emphasizes the autonomous nature of the popular Indian uprising in 1899, and that the roots of indigenous rebellion can be traced back at least to the years before the War of the Pacific. Unquestionably, the mobilization of Indian communities in 1899 behind the Federal Revolution was crucial to the victory of the Liberal Party over the last Conservative government. Did the Liberals uncork the genie of Indian rebellion for their own ends? Were the Indians passive victims of manipulation? Or, were complex and independent interests behind the 1899 revolution?

Historians have proposed many theories to explain the causes of the civil war. One argument is that the rebellion was a rivalry between the "mining capitalism" of La Paz and the "feudal estates" of Sucre; another asserts that it was the underlying competition between northern tin miners and southern silver miners. A third interpretation characterizes it as a struggle between the "middle classes" (Liberals) of La Paz and the "ruling classes" (Conservatives or Constitutionalists) of Sucre; or the mestizos versus the white Creoles, respectively. But what about the Indian revolt?

Historians of the Zárate Willka uprising believe the indigenous revolt predated the founding of the oligarchic parties and represented an autonomous movement. The Indians pursued their own independent agendas—rebellion against the republic's taxation and tribute systems, liberal capitalist markets, and regressive land reforms. The indigenous alliance with mestizos and Liberals did not mean that these groups led the Indians by the nose. At best, the Liberal Party merely exploited the deeply rooted and explosive contradictions in the Andean social order.

The Liberals came to fear what they had unleashed, nonetheless. During the height of the rebellion in March 1899, war hero and later president José Manuel Pando warned Alonso: "No one can be unaware of the damage that is being done by this fratricidal war; to which may be added ... the caste war that is upon us, impelled by the Indian race itself" (Condarco Morales 1965, 295; Platt 1987, 283).

participant observers, much less formal actors, in the political process. Moreover, since independence, Spanish-speaking literacy, a voting requirement, never exceeded 25 percent of the predominantly Indian population, still slightly over 50 percent in 1900.

In great part, civil violence continued because Bolivians lacked a political culture of compromise. Also, in a country of scarce and unequally distributed resources, politicians and party loyalists, especially those not independently wealthy, relied on the easy spoils of government for personal enrichment and social advancement. Indeed, political violence may have occurred because of the party system rather than simply in spite of it. To the degree that the political parties reflected the highly competitive and dominant economic interests of the day, some political infighting was to be expected. As long as the middle, lower, and indigenous classes remained out of the political picture, this inter- and intraparty instability did not threaten the oligarchic status quo. But this chronic instability, even if not deep rooted, could not continue indefinitely without unintended consequences. One of these was the loss of Bolivia's Amazonian region.

At the height of the rubber boom, the Bolivian Amazon region of Acre produced millions of dollars' worth of crude rubber annually. Everyone had an eye on it, too—Brazilians, Peruvians, British, and Americans. At the turn of the century, Bolivians and the new Liberal government of General José Manuel Pando were confronted with the problem of how to enforce its legal sovereignty from a great distance. Distracted by internal politics, President Pando misjudged and mishandled the crisis. He sent three costly military expeditions from the altiplano to Acre.

Brazilians greatly outnumbered Bolivian settlers, and the Brazilian government coveted the zone's riches for itself. To protect its assets, in December 1901, the Bolivians formed the Bolivian Syndicate with Anglo-American investors (among them the noted U.S. industrialist J. Pierpont Morgan) to lease the Bolivian Acre for $40 million. Potential involvement by the United States especially alarmed Brazil, which opposed the concession outright.

In August 1902, revolt broke out in Acre, led by the Brazilian rubber man José Plácido de Castro. The Brazilians of Acre declared their independence from Bolivia, and after months of steady fighting, the Bolivians left the region for good in January 1903. Although the Amazon bubble and monopoly on world rubber would burst soon enough, Bolivia would never regain the 59,000 square miles of territory that it ceded to Brazil in the Treaty of Petrópolis.

The Empires of Silver and Tin

Since the Spanish conquest, mineral wealth has been the backbone of the Bolivian economy and a critical determinant of social class and political power. A king's treasure was extracted from the great mountain of silver at Potosí, and Bolivia's fantastic silver mines steadily produced valuable ore up until independence. In the 1850s, new capital, new technology, and new discoveries revived the dying silver trade. Flooded mines were reopened and worked with greater efficiency using steam engines. Foreign and domestic capital formed creative and aggressive joint ventures. And the new Bolivian governments, especially the Conservative governments, which were of, for, and by the silver barons, provided the political order and supported the economic liberalism and tax and transportation incentives necessary for expansion. The world market helped too, with a fantastic rise in demand for silver.

The decade of the 1860s marked the emergence of the famous barons of silver. The first of his kind was José Avelino Aramayo, who reopened the rich mines of Potosí to modern extraction methods and founded the Real Socavón Mining Company. Another baron, Aniceto Arce, ranked first in the overall volume of silver production. In 1865, Arce became a Bolivian millionaire from the riches of his Huanchaca Mining Company, the second-largest producer of silver in the world. Gregorio Pacheco opened the Guadalupe Mines in the 1870s, and became the second-richest and most important silver magnate of 19th-century Bolivia.

These men had money and power; however, silver is a limited resource and international markets are ever fluid and fickle. Silver prices dropped globally in 1870 and again in 1893, as the world's financial systems abandoned the silver standard. The age of silver, which had begun in 1873, was suddenly over by 1895. And with it went most of the great silver magnates, who failed to survive the transition into the next Bolivian mining bonanza— the tin empires of the 20th century.

A potosino, or resident of Potosí, wears clothing typical of the area: a decorated wool vest, a shirt called an "unku," and flannel trousers. (Kathy S. Leonard photo)

Bolivian miners at work in a tin mine. The nation's most important mining operations were established during the first decades of the 20th century. (Guillermo Delgado-P. photo)

The underlying conditions and governmental policies that had favored silver mining were especially important for Bolivia's entry into the modern era of mining. Publicly and privately sponsored infrastructure projects, like the opening of the Antofagasta-Oruro railway in 1895, facilitated the transport and export of industrial ores. Both the great silver age and the long period of civilian rule by the Conservative and Liberal oligarchy were essential in the successful transition to the mining of industrial metals, such as copper, lead, zinc, wolfram, antimony, and, of course, tin.

The period of 1900 to 1927 saw a meteoric rise in world tin prices. Most silver mine owners were displaced by an adventurous new group of Bolivian and foreign prospectors and entrepreneurs. Of the world-famous silver magnates, only Aramayo survived the transition to tin to become one of the "big three" tin barons. The Aramayo holdings accounted for 25 percent of the country's total tin production. The biggest and most important tin magnate, however, was Simón Patiño. His extensive holdings represented nearly 50 percent of all of Bolivian tin production. The third tin baron, Mauricio Hochschild, was of European descent, a Chilean-Argentine-Jewish entrepreneur.

THE GREAT TIN BARON

Simón Patiño, the richest and most powerful tin magnate, began life as a man of the people with limited means. He was a mestizo of humble origins who worked his way up in the world. He became a white-collar administrative employee in the large silver mines of Potosí. An adventurer, his risks paid off when he struck it rich in the depleted Uncía silver mine. Patiño steadily consolidated his holdings. He bought out the British Uncía Mining Company in 1910 and the Chilean Llallagua Company in 1924.

Patiño Mines became the single largest mining empire to be owned solely by Bolivian capital. As his enormous wealth increased, he ultimately acquired vast European holdings in mining-related and nonmining ventures.

Patiño was quite the cosmopolitan bon vivant. He maintained luxury suites in the best hotels in Paris and New York. The sweaty and dirty work—both in and out of the mines—he relegated to the tough, underpaid Bolivian miners and to his managers. In the name of Patiño Mines, his administrators would cavalierly dictate political and economic policy to Bolivian governments—and get away with it.

Until his death in 1940, Patiño remained Bolivia's most powerful and internationally known capitalist. He had routinely extended sizable private loans from his vast fortune to the government in return for private tax concessions and personal political favors. Few disputed the fact that Patiño had once wielded veto power over the Bolivian government.

The rise of the three great tin empires altered Bolivian history irrevocably. Economically, the new tin elite, and their investments, production, and profits became intimately linked with the movements of international capital and international markets. As a direct consequence, the tin era, which spanned more than half a century from 1900 to 1952, created a highly dependent national economy. Cash-starved Bolivian governments and the underdeveloped economy became slavishly reliant on the limited taxes that these private enterprises afforded the state. Often in Bolivian history, a major national resource has enriched a very few at the expense of the many, and this was clearly the case with tin.

The Bolivian economy—and therefore the Bolivian people—became further impoverished through a destructive syndrome of underdevelopment: the unequal and declining terms of trade. This structural condition trapped the country into living beyond its means because foreign imports were more expensive than the pesos earned by Bolivia's exports abroad. Unless international prices were exceptionally high, tin exports rarely earned sufficient revenues to offset the country's demand and need for expensive luxury items and manufactured goods. Moreover, an unequal trade structure promoted budget deficits and a growing national debt. In short, despite the great tin wealth, the Bolivian economy as a whole became more, rather than less, impoverished during the reign of the tin barons.

Bolivian governments served the tin interests as they had Big Silver earlier. The state subsidized mining exports in countless ways including infrastructure, transportation, monetary policies, and taxes. In short, the government footed the costs of economic development, yet received as little as 3 percent of annual mineral exports in taxes. With the government's revenues so intimately tied to Big Tin, national development projects in sectors that did not directly benefit this tiny clique of national and foreign capitalists fell by the wayside. Short of nationalization or revolution, the government had few alternatives—if it had wanted to exercise any, that is—to collaborating with Big Tin. Quite simply, the large tin mines were the source of the nation's only significant employment, foreign exchange, and state revenue.

The political consequences of the government's intimate relationship with the tin oligarchy popularized an appropriate and unique Bolivian term, *la rosca* (literally a "screw" or "twist"). *Rosca* referred to the tightly interwoven clique of political and economic elites that served and answered to the tin barons. The term served as a jibe against the corrupted ruling establishment that had been seduced by the power and money of the Big Three mining industrialists. Within this ruling establishment were the generals and military officers, the traditional landed aristocracy, the rising urban entrepreneurs and merchants, and the political class of politicians, lawyers, and bureaucrats.

In the decades before the Chaco War, the tin economy was a bumpy ride, and governmental stability and resources had bounced up and down with it. From price highs before the 1929 depression, tin prices and fiscal revenues plummeted. Earnings in 1932 were 17 percent of those in 1929. Tin profits had helped pay the country's bills, but by the end of the republican period, the state treasury was bankrupt. Without the tin revenue, the economic foundation of Liberal Party rule collapsed. Out of the debris emerged a new third party.

The Republican Revolution and the Chaco Crisis

Bolivia's two-party political system withstood two important changes in 1914 and 1920. The Liberal Party splintered in 1914 when an important group of leading Liberal statesmen and intellectuals became disaffected and abandoned the party. Zealous and well organized, these dissidents—among them Daniel Salamanca, Bautista Saavedra, and General José Manuel Pando—founded the Republican Party. Although this rupture created the first major third party, for a time, things settled back into the classic two-party pattern of oligarchic rule and fraudulent elections. At first, the new Republicans were no different from the old Liberals.

In July 1920, these Republican partisans revolted and deposed the last Liberal president, José Gutiérrez Guerra. Political fragmentation and abuses of presidential power in government by both the Conservatives and the Liberals were two major causes of the Republican Revolution. As noted by Herbert S. Klein, the party's founder, Salamanca, claimed that his party's goal was to guarantee fair elections. Ultimately, the seizure of power by the Republican Party did lead to the end of two-party, oligarchic rule because the party splintered almost immediately.

The Republicans divided into two personalist factions. Daniel Salamanca formed the Genuine Republican Party (the *genuinos*), and Bautista Saavedra headed the Socialist Republicans (the *saavedristas*). The Socialist Republicans introduced a new kind of populist politics that was often contradictory and dangerous. For the first time, politicians appealed to the interests of the rising urban middle classes. The political climate was changing in other ways, too. New ideas from abroad encouraged the formation of smaller, more ideological parties. This speeded the development of a less predictable and less controllable multiparty system. The instability introduced into Bolivian politics by the highly partisan climate, especially the rancor and rivalry between the leaders of the two Republican parties, later complicated the crisis, which arose in Bolivia's Chaco territory.

The new bosses of the Republican parties were fundamentally different in personality, political style, and class support. Saavedra was a populist with more ties to middle-class Liberals than to the powerful tin mining interests. He drew his class support from urban artisans, small merchants, and workers. His orientation fomented a new middle-class consciousness that threatened the traditional monopoly of power by the urban and rural upper classes. These establishment voters gravitated instead to the party faction led by one of their own, the aristocratic and intellectual Cochabamba landowner Daniel Salamanca. The personal animosity and competitiveness of the two leaders compounded the party rift and the underlying class conflict.

Saavedra became president in 1921. His first acts established progressive social and labor codes and doubled the taxes on mining. Clearly more attuned to the underprivileged than the other parties, Saavedra's populism was, nevertheless, intended to woo and manipulate voters. As a result, his policies were often inconsistent and repressive. In 1922, he repressed the first general workers' strike with brute military force. A miners' strike the following year resulted in the infamous Massacre of Uncía, in which military troops were set against the desperate miners. Saavedra also responded to a major Indian uprising in the highland village of Jesús de Machaca near Lake Titicaca with brutal repression.

Saavedra governed in difficult economic times, which undoubtedly contributed to the heightened social and political unrest. Extremely vulnerable to the fluctuations of the international tin market, the Bolivian economy seemed on a roller-coaster ride. Saavedra's response was to negotiate for millions of dollars in private loans from U.S. bankers at very disadvantageous terms for the country. His more radical critics complained of his cavalier and incautious approach to foreign capital. His government welcomed foreign investments and promoted the exploration for petroleum in Bolivia's eastern lowlands by Standard Oil of New Jersey. The Genuine Republicans and later an offshoot of the Socialist Republicans, the Nationalist Party, claimed that Saavedra had sold the country to the highest foreign bidder.

In 1925, Hernán Siles was selected as the Socialist Republican Party's candidate for president, much to Saavedra's dismay. Siles was Saavedra's main competitor and opponent within the party. Since Saavedra could not run for the presidency again, he had to come to terms with Siles. Saavedra, therefore, forced Siles to sign a pact. In it, Siles promised that he would strictly follow the party's agenda and Saavedra's counsel. Once president, however, Siles desired to be his own man and break out of Saavedra's political orbit. In January 1927, Siles duly established his own political party, the Nationalist Party.

In some respects, Siles was a progressive president; at least in comparative terms, he was no worse than most of his day. His government had sponsored enlightened university reforms in 1928, and when a crisis developed in the Chaco, his government responded forcefully but avoided war. Siles hoped that a more cautious policy might defuse the country's serious territorial dispute with Paraguay in the Chaco region. Nevertheless, during his presidency, Siles had to confront

Bolivia's serious economic crisis. His cost-cutting policies gained him few friends. In the end, he failed to discover better alternatives to new foreign loans. With the country facing immediate bankruptcy and daily demonstrations in La Paz, he was forced to borrow despite exorbitant rates of interest.

The political deed that most discredited him and ultimately brought down his government was his highly unpopular initiative to amend the constitution so that he might extend his term in office. He claimed that a national crisis, both economic and political, necessitated the amendment. His plan provoked universal opposition, especially among Bolivia's students, who had become radicalized by bad economic times and socialist and Marxist ideas. Political opponents of all stripes and mobs of students took to the streets in protest. The death of a student in an antigovernment demonstration ignited a full-scale rebellion. The unrest escalated into a bloody revolt with the army, the three main opposition parties, and the poor urban workers joining the protesters' ranks. On June 25, 1930, a revolt that had begun largely as a student demonstration, toppled the Siles government.

This Constitutionalist Revolution was a harbinger of major political changes. The immediate consequence was to affirm the constitutional prohibition against consecutive terms in presidential office. Another consequence was the rise of student radicalism and political activism. After 1930, Bolivian students continued to march in the front lines of revolutionary action against unpopular or unjust governments. Also, the upheaval demonstrated the power of mass action and street demonstrations over the classic palace coup. Finally, the overthrow of the Siles government cleared the way for Daniel Salamanca and the costly Chaco War.

After a brief military caretaker government, Daniel Salamanca, the candidate of a multiparty alliance, was elected president. His severe and rigid personality did not endear him to his associates or to the people. More important, he held no new solutions to Bolivia's deepening economic crisis; indeed, he made things worse with his massive expenditures in the Chaco. He tolerated no dissent and used his firm hand against the students, workers, and the political parties of the right and the left. Furthermore, President Salamanca became obsessed with the Chaco and the territorial dispute with Paraguay.

His critics have said that he saw in foreign adventures the solution to Bolivia's desperate political and economic crises. Despite Bolivia's lack of military preparation, Salamanca escalated Bolivia's aggressive colonization and militarization of the Chaco, an inaccessible and barren southeastern region bordering Paraguay and Argentina. As the armed clashes between Bolivian and Paraguayan troops increased, so did Salamanca's determination to show a strong hand. In 1931, Salamanca unwisely escalated a minor border incident into a full-scale war. The resulting Chaco War with Paraguay, a much weaker and smaller nation, was intended to restore Bolivian pride and confidence. Instead, like the War of the Pacific of 50 years earlier, the Chaco War achieved the opposite results, and in the process altered Bolivian society irrevocably.

6

THE CHACO WAR AND ITS AFTERMATH (1932–1951)

The Chaco War was the catalyst that started the process of undermining the traditional social system of Bolivia.

■

(Alexander 1962, 199)

The Chaco War was a pivotal event in the history of Bolivia. The turmoil of war and defeat provoked postwar reform, reaction, and civil war. These dramatic events, in turn, hastened the coming of social revolution. In the end, however, the painful lessons of the Chaco War and the ensuing revolution helped Bolivia regain both national pride and purpose.

The Gran Chaco

The Gran Chaco region encompasses more than a quarter of a million square miles and is currently shared by Argentina, Bolivia, and Paraguay. The vast territory is divided into three areas: the Chaco Boreal, the Chaco Central, and the Chaco Austral. The Chaco War was fought over the Chaco Boreal, the northern region between the Paraguay and Pilcomayo Rivers. The Chaco Central, which Bolivia ceded to Argentina, lies between the Pilcomayo and Bermejo Rivers. The Chaco Austral is the southern region between the Bermejo and Salado Rivers, and is also part of Argentina.

The great plain of the Gran Chaco is one of the more inhospitable regions in South America. Even at present, the region largely remains an enigma to many citizens of the Americas. Because of extremes in topography and climate, the Chaco has been variously described as a "green hell" and a desolate wasteland. It is not exactly a desert or a jungle, but the worst of both.

Water is critical to the Chaco. Depending on its presence or absence, the Chaco can become either an arid plain or a swampland. In the winter months there is little rain, but in the summers the rainfall can be excessive (up to 43 inches). Major rivers cut through the Chaco's rugged scrub plains, grasslands, and low-lying forests: the Bermejo and Pilcomayo Rivers drain southeastward from the foothills of the Andes into the Paraguay and Paraná Rivers, which are further fed by the great rivers of the Amazon Basin in the north. In the northern Chaco of Bolivia, the lesser Parapetí River meanders along a very inconsistent course.

The Chaco rivers frequently shift their course, leaving dry riverbeds and isolated lagoons in the deeper depressions of the clay soil during the dry season (late March through December). At this time, much of the Chaco turns into a giant dust bowl. In the wet months, the shallow depressions form streams, lagoons, and wetlands. The region's climate also varies radically, shifting from freezing southern winds in the winter to saunalike heat well above 100° Fahrenheit in the summer.

These extremes created a nightmare for the armies fighting in the Chaco War. During times of drought, desperate men searched for water and fought over the few isolated lagoons. During the spring and summer downpours, miserable Bolivian and Paraguayan soldiers contended with the heat and a water-soaked terrain. The mud sometimes came up above their boot tops, and the sucking mire "could swallow trucks and their cargoes whole" (Farcau 1996, 5).

Since pre-Columbian times, nomadic and seminomadic Indians have inhabited the Gran Chaco. These diverse and hardy peoples have survived by hunting, fishing, gathering, and seasonal agriculture. With the arrival of the Spanish conquerors and the postindependence pressures of national development, the hostile Chaco became a sanctuary for its original indigenous inhabitants and other Indian groups. Despite limited settlement by Europeans and the spread of Jesuit, Franciscan, and modern-day religious missions, the region remained relatively isolated and underpopulated well into the 20th century.

The northern Chaco was settled and occupied relatively peacefully, giving way to cane fields, timber exploitation, and large cattle ranches. Bolivian and Paraguayan forces militarily occupied this northern region by the beginning of the 20th century because of a long-standing territorial dispute. In 1927, Mennonite immigrants arrived and established agricultural communities in the area. The Indians, who provided a large labor pool for these European activities, were gradually "pacified," culturally "Westernized," and integrated into capital markets.

In the 20th century, the peoples of the Gran Chaco suffered great hardships and upheavals. In particular, the Chaco War brought disease and suffering to the indigenous groups of the region. Caught between two determined and destructive armies, the lowland Indians became pawns in their own land, denied the right to decide if Bolivia or Paraguay would govern them. Perhaps the highland Bolivian Indians conscripted into the Bolivian army fared worst: They died by the tens of thousands for a country that they hardly knew and over an alien and contested wasteland.

Conflicting Historical Claims

The boundary of the Gran Chaco had been contested since the 16th century. At independence, both Paraguay and Bolivia claimed the territory, but the claims were not pursued. The Bolivians relied on the natural boundaries established in Spanish royal decrees, which extended to the conjunction of the Pilcomayo River with the Paraguay River. The Paraguayans claimed all the land east of the Parapetí River. Fortunately, this land was sparsely inhabited, and settlements by the two new countries were great distances apart. The boundary dispute, as a result, remained dormant until the 1860s.

As with the Atacama province in the Pacific war, Bolivia based its claim to the contested Chaco on the principle that Spanish colonial territories should directly transfer to the new independent nations of Latin America. The territory that had belonged to Bolivia's colonial predecessor, the Audiencia of Charcas, therefore, now belonged to the independent nation. Paraguay, not unlike Chile in the Pacific dispute, staked its rights instead on actual exploration, settlement, and development of the Chaco. Additionally, Paraguay received unexpected diplomatic support from the United States in the Hayes Award, an arbitration judgment that strengthened Paraguay's legal position in international tribunals. A judge for the case, U.S. president Rutherford B. Hayes, had decided that the territory between the Pilcomayo River and the Verde River belonged to Paraguay. This triangular piece of land west of the Paraguay River had been part of the historic Bolivian claim. By completely ignoring Bolivian rights, the Hayes Award became the major sticking point that compounded diplomatic resolution of the dispute. Both countries stubbornly refused to amend their claims during the next 30 years when diplomatic efforts produced a series of treaties.

Unfortunately, none of these treaties was ever ratified. Indeed, Daniel Salamanca, a prominent opposition leader in 1907, heartily attacked the Pinilla-Soler Treaty, which had divided the disputed Chaco region in half between the nearest Bolivian and Paraguayan outposts. The parties were not permitted to advance beyond these established positions. Despite the failure to ratify the treaty, the Paraguayans perceived its existence as proof of a tentative status quo.

The Road to War

Is even Paraguay going to push us around? War should be an adventure for Bolivia. Let us go to the Chaco, not to conquer or die but to conquer!

■

President Daniel Salamanca (Farcau 1996, 13)

The territorial conflict, dormant for many years, was revived in the late 1920s. Three incidents heated up the conflict. In February 1927, a small Paraguayan patrol attacked Bolivia's Fort Sorpresa. The Bolivians captured them and in the process killed an officer. This brief clash recorded the first death of the Chaco conflict. The public reacted angrily in both countries, but President Siles defused the crisis by agreeing to an arbitration conference in Buenos Aires.

In August 1928, there was another Bolivian-Paraguayan clash, followed once again by the exchange of irate diplomatic notes and attempted mediation. In December 1928, Paraguayan troops attacked Bolivian Fort Vanguardia, killing several Bolivian soldiers. Bolivian public opinion exploded in rage and hawkish demonstrations. Siles ordered the Bolivian military to retake Vanguardia and seize the Paraguayan outposts of Boquerón and Mariscal López. In an escalating chain of action and reaction, both countries mobilized; however, a commission of Pan-American countries intervened and pressured the two belligerents to accept a compromise in September 1929, whereby Paraguay would reconstruct and return Vanguardia to Bolivia, and Bolivia would hand over Boquerón to Paraguay.

In his study *The Chaco War* (1996), Bruce Farcau emphasizes the irrational and political dimensions of the dispute. Although the Chaco territory was not essential to land-rich Bolivia, a huge country with only 2 million citizens at the time, even the hint of compromise provoked heated political agitation. The *políticos* of the opposition parties blatantly manipulated the Chaco dispute to their own advantage, whipping up the nationalistic fervor of the Bolivian upper and middle classes to a fever pitch. In this chauvinistic climate, many Bolivian politicians avoided public expressions of pacifism fearing that they might be perceived as traitors selling out the country to a weaker power.

While still representing the political opposition, Salamanca and his supporters promoted the macho slogan "to stomp hard in the Chaco." Salamanca excoriated President Hernán Siles for his feeble response to Paraguayan aggression in 1927 and 1928. Both countries severed diplomatic relations and ordered general mobilizations, largely to appease the angry demonstrators in the streets and as a calculated bluff. Neither side was ready for full-scale war.

Paraguayan defense preparations were barely midway along and the country had not yet received armaments ordered from Europe. Also, the system of roads and telegraphs in the Chaco was still incomplete. Bolivia was in a similar situation. Its foreign minister, Tomás Manuel Elío, observed that the arms that Bolivia had ordered from London had only begun to arrive and that "the war materials actually in the country would not permit an offensive" (Farcau 1996, 14). To gain time, both parties agreed to diplomatic arbitration. The judgment favored Bolivia and named Paraguay the aggressor. This enflamed Paraguayan nationalists and stirred up rancorous political infighting.

Between 1930 and 1931, both countries stalled in order to build up their arsenals for an inevitable war. Unlike in Bolivia, the Paraguayan government and public opinion were sharply divided over the Chaco policy. Cooler and wiser heads realized that a war with Bolivia would be devastating, whether Paraguay won or lost— and there was almost universal fear among the country's military leaders that Paraguay would lose. With an underdeveloped and impoverished economy, woefully deficient military preparedness, and a tiny population base in Paraguay, its war-making capabilities were inferior in every sense.

According to Paraguayan military experts, Bolivia had 8,000 men in arms compared to Paraguay's 2,900 in 1928. By the outbreak of war in 1932, Paraguay commanded a total manpower of only 3,300 troops with no trained reserves against a Bolivian force of 21,000 soldiers and trained reserves of 10,000 noncommissioned officers and 300,000 rank and file. To emphasize (and exaggerate) the disparity, the Paraguayan historian Luis Vittone described the war as a conflict between an armed country and an unarmed one.

Despite the deficient military preparation, Paraguayans were as nationalistic as the Bolivians and refused to surrender to La Paz's demands. Unlike Bolivia, however, most leading statesmen believed that the dispute could be postponed indefinitely, as in the past, and that Bolivia would accept a juridical solution. The majority of Paraguayans were anxious to avoid war at all costs.

In Bolivia, the Nationalist Party shouted down the radical leftist and pacifist voices and triumphed in the presidential elections of March 1931. Once in office, President Daniel Salamanca pulled all the stops to advance his Chaco policy, to the delight of his ultranationalist supporters and over the objections of his political opponents. The country faced a serious economic crisis because of the drastic drop in tin prices and production, as well as a debilitating political instability brought on by Salamanca's policies, but, obsessed with the Chaco, he virtually ignored other issues.

Herbert S. Klein suggests that Salamanca's impotence on the domestic front encouraged him to turn his energies to the Chaco crisis, a problem that he believed he could deal with. He pushed the Bolivian military into an aggressive expansion of Chaco outposts and a more offensive national policy, and he began to build up Bolivia's defenses.

"EL HOMBRE SÍMBOLO"

Bolivian historians have given Daniel Salamanca the epithet "El Hombre Símbolo" (the symbolic man). A complex and private man, Salamanca carefully cultivated his public image of fierce nationalism and scrupulous integrity. When he became president in 1932, he was 62 years old, emaciated, and in chronic pain with stomach cancer. José Fellman Velarde's description of him is graphic: "Skeletal, practically mummified, with a curved spine and fixed countenance, yellowed like ancient parchment, Salamanca viewed himself as the instrument of destiny" (1981, III: 151, author's translation).

An aristocrat, Salamanca was steeped in the rigid orthodoxy of eras past. As a younger man, he had witnessed the signing of the 1904 peace treaty with Chile, which he took as a personal disgrace, and became determined to prevent a similar national humiliation. He generally suspected diplomacy as a trick. Salamanca was convinced that only a victorious war against Paraguay could reverse Bolivia's record of international defeats and rescue the national reputation from further ignominy.

His government's massive military expenditures taxed the national budget, already strained by earlier debt and defense increases of more than 70 percent while revenues decreased by half in 1932.

A conservative and a hawk, President Salamanca opposed conciliation on both political and deeply personal levels. Claiming a leftist-communist threat, he repressed pacifist dissent and radical opposition to his policies at home. Abroad, Salamanca's aggressive foreign policy intentionally escalated the Chaco conflict. Jingoism and rumors that there were rich oil deposits in the Chaco further fed the war fever. Indeed, in July 1932, Standard Oil of New Jersey purchased petroleum concessions in southeastern Bolivia, which produced a significant quantity of oil; however, the Bolivian oil could not be exported to the world market because both Argentina and Paraguay refused transit rights.

Bolivians, especially after the war, generally held that U.S. and British corporate interests had supported Paraguay indirectly through Argentina. They believed (and most still do) that the American and British oil companies, Standard Oil and Royal Dutch Shell, respectively, were behind the Chaco War. Historians have still to uncover definitive proof to support this popular Bolivian conspiracy theory found in national history texts. There were, however, significant political and economic interests at work behind the scenes that aided Paraguay directly or indirectly. Nevertheless, although wealthy Argentine and foreign investors had lucrative stakes in the outcome of the dispute, there is no doubt that Bolivia's decision to go to war in 1932 was Salamanca's doing.

Bitter Defeat in the Chaco

War finally broke out in an unexpected way. It was preceded, as so many times in history, by a minor border incident. In the summer of 1931, one such incident pushed the parties to the brink of war, but diplomacy pulled them back again. In July, Salamanca withdrew the Bolivian ambassador from Paraguay's capital of Asunción and severed diplomatic relations with the country. The parties initiated talks for a nonaggression pact, while extending and fortifying their military outposts. A year later, another clash occurred over control of a vital and strategic source of water in the parched Chaco. This time the outcome of hostilities was very different.

In July 1932, Paraguayan forces attacked and recaptured the nominally Bolivian fort Santa Cruz near Lake Chuquisaca. Originally, this fort had been the Paraguayan fort Mariscal López, which Bolivia had seized in May. Salamanca, perhaps confused about what had actually occurred, nevertheless, denounced the counterattack on Fort Santa Cruz before the entire Bolivian nation as blatant Paraguayan "aggression." The general public and political elite rallied around their president and flag. Salamanca then ordered, over the opposition of his general staff, an immediate military assault on Paraguayan positions. The generals were fully aware that this military reprisal meant total war, for which Bolivia was unprepared. Unable to deter him, they forced Salamanca to take complete personal responsibility in writing. On July 18, 1932, Salamanca intentionally escalated a minor border incident into all-out war. But did Salamanca *really* know what he was doing?

One view is that Salamanca naively believed that if Bolivia landed a quick and heavy blow in reprisal, Paraguay would be strategically outmaneuvered and sue for peace. He therefore ordered the military to seize three vital Paraguayan forts: Boquerón, Corrales, and Toledo. By August, however, the Bolivian offensive had stalled amid the squabbling of Salamanca and his generals.

The military experts criticized Salamanca's "eye-dropper war" and limited mobilization strategy. When the war began, Bolivia had counted only 1,200 men in the Chaco. The generals had demanded 60 days to muster additional troops and reserves. In contrast, the Paraguayans, who were fighting for national survival, had called a general mobilization immediately. By September, they had 18,800 men in arms and launched a major counterattack. Disorganized, undersupplied, and undermanned on the spot, Bolivia suffered a rout at Fort Boquerón.

Herbert S. Klein writes that the shocking news of the defeat led to rioting by 20,000 antigovernment demonstrators. The rioters demanded the resignation of Salamanca and the return of the German general Hans Kundt, the former chief of staff whom Salamanca had exiled in 1930 after the revolt against Siles. In October, Bolivia suffered another serious defeat at Fort Arce, and Salamanca recalled the old German general.

Kundt, however, proved to be a terrible commander. He recklessly squandered his men in bloody frontal assaults on Paraguayan fortifications, and by the time Kundt was replaced by General Enrique Peñaranda in December 1933, the German's insane tactics had resulted in 14,000 Bolivian dead and 32,000 wounded.

The war became a string of defeats for the Bolivian forces. Forts Nanawa and Campo Vía fell in July and December 1933. In November 1934, a disaster at El Carmen left more than 2,600 Bolivian dead; most had died of agonizing thirst. The defeat triggered a showdown between the civilian and military leadership. The general command had tired of Salamanca's meddling in the conduct of the war, and the president had

had enough of the military's incompetence and insubordination. In November, Salamanca traveled to the front intent on removing General Peñaranda. Instead, an officers' coup, thinly disguised as a voluntary resignation, replaced Salamanca with Vice President José Luis Tejada Sorzano.

The war effort did not immediately improve, although Tejada Sorzano ordered a full-scale mobilization and proved a better political leader. A disaster at Picuiba in December resulted in 2,300 Bolivian dead, most of whom died because of thirst and the shameful incompetence of their officers. By spring 1935, the Paraguayans were at the foothills of the Andes and within striking distance of Bolivia's oil centers—the regions of Tarija and Santa Cruz—and the Chaco command center in Villamontes.

The Battle of Ibibobo, deep in Bolivian territory, proved an important turning point of the war. For the first time, the Paraguayans experienced the same disadvantages of long supply routes across the desolate Gran Chaco that had hampered Bolivia during the war. Even overextended and far from the Paraguay River, however, the Paraguayans proved they could win and inflicted on Bolivia its most humiliating defeat ever. Paraguay had almost total control of the Gran Chaco.

Desperate to defend the oilfields and their home territory, the Bolivians rallied and pushed the Paraguayans back toward the central Chaco. The Bolivians recaptured the precious petroleum region by May, as the war stalled. Exhausted, both parties agreed to a cease-fire on June 12, 1935. Although a final peace treaty was not signed until July 21, 1938, the three-year war was effectively over.

Why Did Bolivia Lose?

Recriminations began long before the war ended, and the finger-pointing intensified as the outraged Bolivian people demanded an accounting. All the major actors in the drama sought to escape blame and find scapegoats. The burning question that Bolivians, rich or poor, asked of their leaders remained the same: Why had their country lost the war? A laundry list of errors presented itself.

From the first day, chronic civilian-military bickering had hobbled the campaign. In only three years of war, Bolivia had shuffled through four barely capable supreme commanders of its forces. Paraguay had had but one, General José Félix Estigarriba, a military genius. Bolivian officers at the front had been cowardly, incompetent, and corrupt, seldom fighting and more often carousing behind the lines. Cruel nature had done more than its share to destroy four Bolivian armies. Brave and resilient Bolivian soldiers had considered the brutal Chaco itself as their greatest enemy, followed by their own officers and the Paraguayan soldiers, respectively. They had deserted by the tens of thousands. Most were illiterate and practically untrained highland Indians, who had been dumped into the Chaco wilderness to fight for the draft dodgers of the white and mestizo Bolivian establishment. In their eyes, the war had not been a national war of survival for Bolivia, as it had been for Paraguay, but a "foreign" war precipitated by Salamanca and his party or instigated by dark imperialist forces greedy for oil.

The wages of war were excessive for both belligerents. The human toll shocked the world: about 60,000 Bolivians and 40,000 Paraguayans had died. While the Paraguayan nation as a whole suffered, in Bolivia, the Indians suffered most for the entire nation. The economic price of war was staggering for both belligerents, and the social and political consequences of war were destabilizing and revolutionary.

Unlike the Bolivians, however, Paraguay's citizens engaged in less recrimination after the war. They had conducted themselves honorably in the military campaign, defending their homeland and greatly expanding its territory and resources, and they were the undisputed victors. Bolivian leaders, on the other hand, had precipitated another extensive and humiliating dismemberment of their country. Bolivia was the vanquished party for the third time running. The traumatic and unexpected Chaco defeat, therefore, served as a massive earthquake might to further destabilize the already shaky foundations of the traditional order.

Upward of 200,000 Bolivian soldiers, or roughly 10 percent of the population, had been mobilized for the war. The indigenous veterans who survived and returned from war were forever changed men. Many abandoned their old lives and were caught up in the postwar radicalism. The war had exposed the injustice of the old system and the corruption of the ruling class. Once it became clear that "the emperor had no clothes," only military repression could hold back the discontent.

Postwar Radicalism and Reform

The system had failed in a crucial hour, and that failure compromised it forever.

■

(Klein 1969, 203)

A radical political coalition of veterans, unionized labor, organized peasant syndicates, and student groups emerged in the postwar ferment. Colonel David Toro and Colonel Germán Busch, veterans and heroes of the Chaco War, became natural leaders in the movement. These young military reformers contemplated a new political system based on social justice and equality. Military socialism would help them get there. Vague socialist, populist, and nationalist rhetoric characterized their speeches and political program.

In practice, they hoped to increase popular participation in politics and renew citizens' national pride. At the heart of this new postwar nationalism and military socialism was anti-imperialism. The lofty goals of the reformers were to liberate the country from the control of the private economic interests and to create a strong and independent Bolivian state. In their eyes, the government had been hostage to the influence of foreign capital and the tin barons far too long. The military reformers hoped to break this stranglehold and to free the government to pursue the country's national development on its own terms.

President Germán Busch, who died tragically young by his own hand (Reproduced with permission of the General Secretariat of the Organization of American States)

As the presidency of Tejada Sorzano neared its last months, the climate became unusually tense. On May 17, 1936, a military coup d'état by Colonels Toro and Busch preempted the elections and deposed Tejada Sorzano. A coalition of two civilian political parties—the Republican Socialists and the new Socialist Party—joined the civilian-military junta. As the junta's president, Toro announced the establishment of a new system of state socialism that would defend the rights and interests of the working classes and the veterans. His government pledged to regain Bolivia's economic sovereignty and to end the widespread misery and poverty of the people.

Military intervention in civilian politics had already had a long history in Bolivia, so at first, the majority of the political parties accepted and even welcomed Toro. The mixed junta took great pains to reassure the traditional power brokers that reforms would not affect existing parties or leaders. By promising an evolutionary and socioeconomic coup rather than a political revolution, Toro struck an important balance between the conservatives and the radicals. Nevertheless, the rhetoric of the reformers included such phrases as the "radical transformation of the operative system" and the "transformation of the institutional base" of the government, which undoubtedly caused many to wonder what lay ahead.

The initial political calm did not last. The speeches about national reconstruction, social justice, economic development, and veterans' rights played well in theory, but when the government proposed a new mass party and aggressive legislation to implement these principles, the conservative parties panicked. Dissension within the junta also grew. The official Socialist Party, an offshoot of the Nationalist Party founded by Hernán Siles before the war, represented the junta's civilian ranks.

Socialism, however, was a confusing label for a party that barely served to unite incompatible personalities and ideological agendas. The postwar party lumped together three important groups: the traditional Republican Socialists of Bautista Saavedra, the old populist warhorse of the 1920s; supporters of the radical labor activist Waldo Alvarez; and young Marxists under the leadership of Ricardo Anaya and José Antonio Arze. When the more radical elements of the party turned against Saavedra, Busch and the military threatened another coup to end the civilian infighting. Intolerant of the civilians, Busch removed them from the coalition in an in-house coup in June.

This revolution from above left the government without a broad-based and organized civilian support other than labor and the Legion of Chaco War Veterans, a pseudocivilian group many thousands strong. To shore up his regime, Toro at first decided to create state-controlled "functional syndicates" that would organize and group the masses into professional unions. He also hoped that these syndicates would prevent the increasing communist agitation within the labor movement. When this attempt failed, Toro experimented with a state socialist party. As the partisan agitation continued, Toro moderated his policies and in so doing began to lose the confidence of Busch and the military reformers.

This civilian-military tension forced Toro's hand. Gambling that he could revive popular support for the regime, Toro took a drastic and unprecedented step in Bolivian and Latin American history. On March 13, 1937, he nationalized the operations of the New Jersey–based Standard Oil Company. The expropriation was truly revolutionary. No other Latin government up till then had dared to seize a North American company, especially without offering economic indemnification. (The Mexicans would do so a year later but with a generous indemnity.)

The idea of nationalization had germinated during the war and had become popular with the veterans, labor, and the postwar student radicals. The government of Tejada Sorzano had explored the legal ramifications. The actual confiscation, however, became the hallmark of the extreme economic nationalism of the military reformers. Toro and Busch repudiated the liberal free-market system that had subordinated the Bolivian state to the private interests of the tin barons. Their brand of national socialism increasingly followed a corporatist model wherein government regulation of the tin industry, imposed only as a temporary wartime emergency measure, became permanent.

Centrists in relation to the great extremes of the postwar political continuum, Toro and Busch came under attack from the right by the money and political interests known as the Rosca and from the left by the Marxists. Of the two military reformers, Toro implemented more radical economic policies, ranging from currency controls and tax reform to food rationing and subsidies. Neither leader succeeded in curbing the pervasive political and economic power of the tin-mining industrialists, although they tried. Both were constrained by the reactionary capitalists and the revolutionary labor movement. Angry strikers demanded that the government enact wage increases and price controls, while the industrialists vehemently opposed these measures.

The one radical economic act of which all Bolivians approved was Toro's bold nationalization of Standard Oil's holdings and operations. The company had become a popular symbol of foreign exploitation and economic imperialism, and many believed Standard Oil had caused the Chaco War. The company became a scapegoat for everything that was fundamentally wrong with Bolivia. The expropriation eased the people's frustrated nationalism and economic impotence, but it was a desperate act that could not prevent Toro's overthrow just a few weeks later.

Busch and the Constitution of 1938

> *The government that I head is not a government of class or of political sects. It is characterized by its absolute independence and will lead the country on a course that will ennoble it.*
>
> ■
>
> *Germán Busch, July 1937 (Morales 1977, 215)*

On July 13, 1937, Colonel Germán Busch unseated David Toro, his comrade in war and reform. Conservative interests interpreted the

Busch coup as the end of state socialism and a return to the old order. Busch cultivated this view, and his government, he said, would be based on nationalism and the harmony of capital and labor, not on class, sects, or ideology.

Busch, however, surprised everyone, because he meant and believed what he preached. He viewed himself as the champion of the May Revolution of 1936 and intended to bring to fruition the progressive policies of his predecessor. One of his first acts was to uphold the celebrated oil-company nationalization decree. He declared a national amnesty for the exiles of all political parties. Finally, Busch announced a constitutional convention to legitimize the political, economic, and social reforms of the military revolution.

National elections were held in March 1938 to elect representatives to the convention. The system of representation allotted seats according to state-recognized and -sanctioned professional or occupational organizations. The established political parties were included, although some abstained in protest. The system was cleverly designed so that majority representation fell to the organized groups most friendly to the May Revolution.

In a virtually unanimous vote on May 27, 1938, the pro-Busch majority in the constitutional assembly elected Busch the new constitutional president. Enrique Baldivieso, a prominent leader of the postwar Socialist Party and an ally of Busch, was chosen as the nation's vice president. Historian Herbert S. Klein describes the convention as "a major breakthrough in postwar political development" for the parties and organizations of the left (1969, 278).

The Busch convention stood out as a landmark of social progress and reform. The convention's first product was a remarkable new constitution, which anticipated in many ways the comprehensive legislation of the subsequent 1952 revolution. The historic 1938 constitution introduced a state-managed central economy that would offset and be able to balance the special interests of powerful foreign and domestic capitalists against the country's national development needs. Central to this economy was a new property law based on the principle of "social" ownership, which would respect an individual's private property rights as long as these fulfilled a social function. The constitution stopped short of outright land reform but granted the state the legal authority to expropriate estates that were unproductive and redistribute these to the peasantry.

The convention delegates failed to pass binding legislation that would guarantee civil and human rights of Bolivia's indigenous peoples.

Racism remained strong, and the thorny "Indian question" provoked heated controversy among the constitutional representatives. The more radical delegates proposed laws to protect Indian communities and their system of collective land ownership and to abolish the hated and humiliating system of involuntary personal servitude on the haciendas. The convention did approve a significant education reform law based on the principle of free and universal education for all of Bolivia's citizens. This impetus furthered the development of rural education centers for the highland Indians. Warisata, one indigenous school on the altiplano that received support, acquired a hemisphere-wide reputation for its progressive pedagogy.

President Busch abruptly closed down this massive experiment in constitutional reform in October 1938. The constitutional convention had generated such intense sociopolitical upheaval that the Busch government, which had initiated the process, found itself assailed on all political fronts. Busch felt unable to contain the extreme forces of revolution and reaction within the constitutional structure. Despite heroic

The movement to establish rural education centers, which were aimed primarily at the Indian population, gained strength in the 1930s. This photo shows a modern Bolivian classroom. (UN/DPI Photo by Greg Kinch)

WARISATA

Through the Office of Indigenous Education, the government of German Busch promoted Indian leaders and *indigenista* (Indianist) teachers. Elizardo Pérez headed the office. He was a teacher and radical intellectual who in 1928 had founded Warisata, the famous Indian teacher training school near Lake Titicaca. The Warisata school was imbued with *indigenismo*. This pro-Indian ideology believed in the moral value and regeneration of indigenous traditions and culture as the foundation for a holistic Bolivian identity and nationalism. The school's teachers were dedicated to improving the social and political status of the highland Indian, and their training ultimately furthered Indian consciousness and political organizing.

Not everyone in the Busch administration agreed with this approach. In 1938, Waldo Alvarez, a militant union leader and a former minister of labor, argued that the Indian problem was primarily one of land ownership and only secondarily one of education. However, schools like Warisata helped to mobilize the Indians to fight for their rights and demand land reform.

attempts to establish and conduct his government on the basis of constitutional legitimacy, Busch remained a military man at heart. And like the majority of veterans of his generation, he was deeply apolitical.

The political party system had been so categorically discredited by the Chaco War that Busch remained suspicious of all partisan activity. Despite the unprecedented growth of progressive organizations during his regime, Busch intentionally kept the civilian reformers and the leftist political parties at arm's length. At times, labor and national socialist groups were tolerated within his government. At others, he would make common cause with the conservative elements to fend off his militant critics. As Toro had done, Busch even experimented with a state socialist party.

To some extent these vacillations worked in his favor, keeping his critics off balance, but this inconstancy hurt the stability of his government. Busch's suspicion of political parties would—among other things—be his undoing. Although he had the advantage of heading an armed military regime, his was the typical lot of reformers—easy game for reactionaries and revolutionaries alike. Busch was discovering first-hand the dangerous problems that had bedeviled Toro. Without the support of the civilian reformers and parties of the political left, Busch and his following only had their guns to keep them in power.

As his stubborn strategy to largely circumvent the parties backfired, Busch resorted to direct popular rule. In April 1939, Busch proclaimed himself dictator. He claimed that the country's chronic economic, social, and moral crisis demanded this extreme step. In a radio address to the people, he blamed this national crisis on the power struggle between the forces of financial privilege that were striving, as in the past, to grab power and the extremists who were seeking the radical overthrow of institutions. Dictatorship allowed Busch to rule by decree.

A major achievement during his brief dictatorship was the Busch Labor Code of May 24, 1939. Although the constitution affirmed the right to unionize and to strike, the Labor Code provided for greatly improved working conditions. The progressive code represented a major triumph for the Bolivian labor movement. This extraordinary legislation was the result of successful political pressure and agitation by the recently organized workers. Shortly after the war, labor united into the Confederation of Bolivian Workers (Confederación Sindical de Trabajadores de Bolivia, or CSTB) and confronted postwar governments with their demands. The miners and railway workers were especially militant, launching a number of general strikes during the reform years of 1936 to 1939. The united mine workers' union even held a national congress in August 1939.

President Busch's final legacy of reform was the Mining Decree of June 7, 1939. This act, advanced for its time, nationalized the Mining Bank (Banco Minero), which facilitated mineral sales for small and medium-sized mining operations, and tightened state control over the Central Bank. With his signature, Busch advanced the most fundamental goal of the military reformers of 1936: national economic independence. He institutionalized and legitimized the state's control over the dominant tin-mining interests. After more than 100 years on the margins of fantastic resource bonanzas, the government's right to manage the nation's rich mineral wealth became permanently enshrined in the rule of law.

By law, the mining companies were required to remit foreign exchange currency from mineral exports to the Central Bank at a substantially lower, government-controlled rate. This fiscal policy alone quadrupled the government's tax revenues and increased its share of profits from mining by 25 percent. Of all the Busch reforms, this law would endure under conservative and radical regimes alike. Until 1952, according to Herbert S. Klein, the Central Bank "maintained complete control over all foreign sales of Bolivian tin, manipulating the exchange rate to generate government income in the form of indirect taxes" (1992, 208).

Despite his tremendous achievements in two brief years in office, Busch became terribly frustrated and discouraged. The "Great Captain of the Chaco," as he was known, felt personally assailed by the intractable forces of social change and reaction, reportedly lamenting,

A MARTYR OF THE REVOLUTIONARY LEFT

German Busch Becerra, born in the regional capital of Trinidad in 1903, was the son of a German medical doctor and a lowlander Bolivian woman from the department of El Beni. He became an army cadet, a valiant officer, and a decorated war veteran. Charles W. Arnade writes that Busch was "noted for his daring, physical fitness, and hot temper—characteristics that served him well in the Chaco War" (1996, 489). As a charismatic leader of the May Revolution and president of Bolivia, he implemented military socialism.

He died by his own hand when he was only 36 years of age. His tragic suicide shocked the country and made Busch a glorious martyr of the revolutionary left. Doubts about his death spawned a powerful conspiracy theory of Bolivian history. Popular belief held that the Rosca (the oligarchy and the Big Tin barons) had murdered Busch because his reforms threatened them; indeed, the tin magnate Mauricio Hochschild had been arrested for sabotaging the Mining Decree. Violation of the law carried the death penalty, and Busch had ordered Hochschild's execution. But when his cabinet balked, the order was rescinded. Busch, frustrated by the Hochschild case and the wholesale resistance to his reforms, committed suicide in front of his aides, explaining, "It is best to terminate my life" (Arnade 1996, 489).

The May Revolution and Busch's historic reforms and inspired words are his lasting legacy. An excerpt from the La Paz newspaper *El Diario* of June 11, 1939, expresses his revolutionary nationalism: "The slogan of my government is the economic emancipation of my country. ... It will be said that my government is revolutionary. Yes, citizens, I aspire to a revolution whose results will be these: that Bolivia enjoys its own riches and that these serve to develop its industries and agriculture" (Morales 1977, 277).

"I am a man accustomed to fighting in war, but this battle with invisible enemies disturbs me beyond measure" (Ayala 1980, 257). Busch increasingly feared that political polarization and outright sabotage would undermine the May Revolution and nullify his reforms, and in a fit of despair, he committed suicide on August 28, 1939.

After Busch's death, the oligarchy and conservative parties seized control; however, they had to contend with a mobilized and radicalized political system. Before the Chaco War new political groupings had arisen; after the war this activity expanded exponentially as dozens of new factions, movements, and political parties were formed. The Chaco experience had transformed the population and undermined old political allegiances, creating a crisis of political legitimacy. The experiment in military socialism and the constitutional convention had provided a critical opening for new parties, especially parties of the left.

The Rise of Revolutionary Parties

Four revolutionary political parties became significant in postwar politics. Two parties that represented the cause of nationalism were the Nationalist Revolutionary Movement (Movimiento Nacionalista Revolucionario, or MNR) and the Bolivian Socialist Falange (Falange Socialista Boliviana, or FSB). The MNR became a major actor in the 1940s and the key protagonist of the 1952 National Revolution. On the left, two Marxist parties were especially important: the Party of the Revolutionary Left (Partido de la Izquierda Revolucionaria, or PIR), and the Revolutionary Workers' Party (Partido Obrero Revolucionario, or POR).

The Nationalist Revolutionary Movement emerged in the wake of military socialism's demise and the oligarchy's regaining control. The party had arisen out of the pre- and postwar political ferment and had originally been closely associated with the official Socialist Party that collaborated with the governments of Toro and Busch. In the 1930s, many radicalized student activists, war veterans, and middle-class journalists who later became founding members of the MNR joined the socialists. Among these were Víctor Paz Estenssoro, Augusto Céspedes, Hernán Siles Zuazo, and Walter Guevara Arze. In 1936, these future MNR leaders opened the newspaper *La Calle*. Its partisan pages took a stridently nationalistic and anti-imperialistic stance and denounced the oligarchical Rosca and the Big Three mining capitalists as class enemies of the people. The newspaper's radical nationalism came later to characterize the ideological program of the MNR.

The MNR was founded on May 10, 1941, with Víctor Paz Estenssoro as its first leader. According to the official program, the party supported revolutionary nationalism, a strong and secure state, and the economic independence and sovereignty of the Bolivian people. The MNR's orientation, therefore, was a uniquely Bolivian blend of nationalism and socialism, but never outright fascism, particularly not of the European variety. At the time, the new party proposed a radical program, but not a revolutionary one.

The Bolivian Socialist Falange was founded in August 1937. The party had developed from a Bolivian student-exile movement in Chile that had exposed the outcasts to fascism. Important leaders of the Falangist movement included Carlos Puente, who founded the Bolivian Nationalist Action, and Oscar Unzaga de la Vega, who founded the FSB. After Puente's death, the two groups merged in 1940, and Oscar de la Vega reigned as undisputed FSB leader until his own death in 1959.

The country's conservative and privileged Catholic high school students, especially from Cochabamba and the country's temperate valleys and lowland regions, crowded into the party's ranks. The FSB professed a pro–Catholic Church, nationalistic ideology, much like fascist counterparts elsewhere in Latin America and Europe. The party was stridently anticommunist and antiliberal and adopted the national socialist model popular in Germany and Italy.

On the other end of the spectrum, the Party of the Revolutionary Left (PIR) became the most influential Marxist party of the 1940s. Its leading intellectuals were José Antonio Arze and Ricardo Anaya, who established the PIR in July 1940. The party had prewar roots in the Marxist student groups of 1928 and the exiled leftist organizations of the early and mid-1930s.

The PIR was a confrontational and revolutionary party that opposed the traditional political order as well as the postwar experiment in military socialism. The party's militant Marxism attracted the radical students and intellectuals of the middle class, including teachers and labor activists.

The PIR professed a Stalinist-Marxist ideology but claimed to be independent of international communism or Soviet control. The party was split into an internationalist, pro-Soviet faction and a nationalist, *indigenista* (pro-Indian) faction. Because of its fanatical opposition to the fascist parties of the 1940s, including the MNR, the leftist revolutionaries eventually allied with the reactionary parties of the oligarchy. (Leftist/Marxist parties often made alliances of convenience with the right, which only served to undermine their ideological credibility.)

More radical but less influential than the PIR was the Revolutionary Workers' Party of Tristán Marof and José Aguirre Gainsborg. Like similar parties of the period, the POR was the product of a leftist group that had been exiled because of its agitation against the Chaco War. In December 1934, a conference of leftist exiles founded the POR in Argentina. The party had developed from Bolivia's socialist left and the extensive writings of Tristán Marof (the pen name of Gustavo Adolfo Navarro, an internationally known Marxist theorist). Marof was credited with the celebrated revolutionary slogan "Land to the Indian, mines to the state." The phrase, probably first used by Marof in 1926, epitomized the goals of the leftists in the 1940s and became the rallying cry of the nationalist revolution of 1952.

The proliferation of radical and violently revolutionary political parties after the Chaco War prepared the political stage for the dramatic developments of the 1940s. Three developments in particular shifted the strategic balance of power between the old and the emerging new order. First, the revolutionary parties proved that they could generate significant popular support. Second, the extremely tiny national electorate had been gradually expanding and radicalizing. The franchise was no longer the secure preserve of the rich, famous, and reactionary. Third, it became increasingly difficult for the oligarchy to rule through the traditional party system if it could no longer guarantee, or at least contain, the outcome.

The Oligarchy Regroups

Badly shaken by military reformism and the inroads of the far left, a resurgent oligarchy moved to dismantle reforms and regroup the conservative forces. In March 1939, months before Busch's suicide, the Rosca had formed the Concordancia, an alliance of the traditional political parties. The oligarchy had also enlisted the support of the conservative sector of the military. In an attempt to hold back the radical tide and block the parties of the left from congressional participation, the Concordancia supported the governments of two distinguished war veterans, General Carlos Quintanilla and General Enrique Peñaranda.

In August 1939, the conservative general Quintanilla established a provisional government edging out Busch's constitutional successor, Vice President Enrique Baldivieso, who was a socialist and unacceptable to the oligarchy. Quintanilla scheduled new presidential elections for March 1940. The oligarchy backed the candidacy of General Peñaranda, an apolitical traditionalist, and exiled the reformist general Bernardino Bilbao Rioja, the commander in chief of the armed forces and leader of the Legion of Chaco War Veterans. The Concordancia's choice, General Peñaranda, became president without significant opposition.

The election of March 1940, nevertheless, demonstrated a fundamental shift. The incipient PIR, unlike other radical parties, did not abstain from participating in the election but rather fielded their leader, José Antonio Arze, as the presidential candidate. At the time, the franchise included less than 5 percent of the literate population. The opposition candidate, moreover, was a decorated war hero, who had the full moral and monetary support of the oligarchy and political establishment, including the Toro-Busch reformers and nationalists. Arze, a Cochabamba professor of law and sociology, received 10,000 votes out of a total 58,000 cast, or roughly 17 percent of the national vote. These results were extraordinary and indicated the widespread disaffection with the traditional system. This major protest vote shook the complacency of the establishment.

Herbert S. Klein suggests that during the postwar years the left had grown virtually unchecked and had made significant inroads among the middle class, which had previously supported the old political system. The complacency of the traditional parties, according to Klein, was disturbed even further when the moderate and radical left swept the congressional elections that year and took control of the new legislature (1992, 210–12). Although the political left had found a place in the system, the return to republican government in 1940 represented no more than a brief interlude.

To some extent the oligarchy's restoration was incomplete. Klein described this parliamentary interregnum of Peñaranda as the calm before the total collapse of the traditional system. General Peñaranda was an essentially passive figure, "a partisan of all causes, devoid of ideology or established convictions" (1968, 389). In the broader scheme of things Peñaranda's policies were basically conservative, especially in foreign affairs.

In the early 1940s, international events and World War II intruded on domestic politics. The Peñaranda government cooperated closely with the United States and was rewarded with economic and military assistance. After global war spread to the Pacific theater and the Japanese interrupted Malayan tin exports, Bolivia became strategically important to the United States as the Western Hemisphere's major tin supplier. To ensure an uninterrupted supply of strategic metals, the United States began to exert greater influence in Bolivia's internal politics, propping up friendly and amenable governments like that of Peñaranda and the oligarchy.

Peñaranda's regime contracted several controversial agreements with the United States, riling the radical nationalists and leftists. The government renewed Bolivia's repayment of the outstanding debt owed to U.S. banks since payments were suspended by the moratorium of 1931. In a major tin deal Bolivia agreed to sell the United States 1,500 tons of tin per month over five years.

Bolivia and World War II

It was no coincidence that Bolivia during Peñaranda's presidency was the strongest supporter in South America of the Allied cause. In 1942, soon after Bolivia severed diplomatic relations with the Axis powers, Sumner Welles, U.S. president Franklin D. Roosevelt's secretary of state, announced that the U.S. Export-Import Bank had approved a $5 million loan to Bolivia. Bolivia was required to apply $1.75 million, or one-third, of this loan to indemnify Standard Oil for the 1937 confiscation of its properties. In 1943, the hand of the U.S. State Department was evident again. On April 7, days after the state visit of U.S. vice president Henry Wallace to Bolivia, the Peñaranda government declared war on the Axis. A month later, President Peñaranda was welcomed in the United States with more loans and military assistance.

The countries of South America responded in different ways to the outbreak of World War II. Although there was general solidarity with the United States in the region, the expressions of cooperation by individual countries were warmer in some instances than in others. The majority of the South American countries remained neutral until 1945 and then declared war on the Axis. Brazil and Colombia declared war only on Germany and Ecuador only on Japan. Bolivia declared war on the Axis powers as a whole. Bolivia's declaration of war distinguished it as the sole South American country to take such a comprehensive position very early, demonstrating the Peñaranda government's support of the United States.

The Bolivian declaration of war also reflected the country's tumultuous internal politics during the 1940s and the tension between domestic and foreign policy. Because of their fascist proclivities, the MNR and FSB were pro-Axis. The Soviet-style but antifascist PIR favored the Allies. The declaration of war, however, was in the form of an executive decree issued by President Peñaranda. More than six months of bitter and heated wrangling were required for the Bolivian

Congress to constitutionally ratify the declaration of war. The ratification passed on December 4, 1943.

Opposition to the expanding U.S. role in Bolivian affairs dangerously strained partisan relations within Congress and with the Peñaranda regime. The MNR emerged as the key protagonist, bringing down five cabinets within three years through its vocal criticism of Peñaranda. The oligarchy desperately tried to discredit the party. In July 1941, the U.S. ambassador exposed the so-called Nazi Putsch, an alleged MNR-Nazi coup that involved the German ambassador. The government expelled the German ambassador and arrested suspected Nazis and MNR activists. In this purge, the radical newspaper *La Calle,* the voice of the MNR party, was raided and silenced.

Historians agree that the Nazi Putsch was fabricated by the United States, Peñaranda, and the oligarchy to crack down on fascist sympathizers. The Nazi scare was a convenient pretext to discredit the MNR, the loudest critic of the compensation agreement with Standard Oil. The tense climate also justified martial law and the formation of the Antifascist Democratic Front, an unlikely alliance between the oligarchy and the leftist PIR. Upon quelling the fascist threat, official repression next visited the tin miners upon whom the cheap flow of Bolivian tin to the war effort of the Allied powers depended.

The Catavi Massacre

The Catavi mining complex lies on the altiplano near the city of Oruro. In 1942, the mining center shut down in a wave of wildcat strikes. The miserable miners demanded better wages and working and living conditions. Insensitive and irresponsible, the government of General Peñaranda ordered the military to deal with the miners. The strike was broken in December only after hundreds of miners were killed or wounded in a bloody confrontation known as the Catavi Massacre.

In the aftermath of the tragedy were major investigations by the Bolivian government and the United States. In the Bolivian Congress, the MNR and other radical opposition parties demanded an official inquiry. Because of the moral and legislative support of the MNR and its congressional delegates, the miners and the party developed an important working alliance. For its part, the United States sent the Magruder Commission to investigate and issue a report of the massacre. The Magruder Report exposed the repressive and inhuman conditions that generally prevailed in the Bolivian mines at the time and recommended major reforms, few of which were actually carried out.

The Catavi strikes were symptomatic of a wider economic crisis. Production downturns in other trades promoted widespread labor unrest and major strikes by railway and postal workers and the country's teachers. Militant labor and the radical political parties discovered a common cause in their opposition to Peñaranda. Attacking on two fronts—the national assembly and the streets—the labor movement succeeded in gaining strength and steady improvement in pay and benefits.

Historians note that the Busch labor reforms had facilitated the proliferation of labor militancy and impeded official repression by Peñaranda and the Concordancia. The Catavi Massacre and the many incidents like it that did not achieve the same historical recognition became rallying points in labor's struggle for its rights. The Catavi tragedy and labor militancy in the early 1940s was especially significant in forging a new era of political party–labor cooperation.

The Revolution of the Majors

The military had never been swept clean of the nationalistic younger officers who sympathized with the Toro-Busch style of military socialism. During Peñaranda's regime, these officers, like the civilian opposition, had become increasingly frustrated with domestic and international policies. For four years, this faction of the military had tried to overthrow the government. Within his first weeks in office Peñaranda had had to quash a serious military rebellion, and several more coup attempts followed. The government had anticipated what became known as the Revolution of the Majors but failed to arrest soon enough the five junior officers who had masterminded the revolt.

Major Gualberto Villarroel and a group of radical officers overthrew the conservative government of Peñaranda on December 20, 1943. The MNR and a secret military lodge—the Reason of the Fatherland (Razón de Patria, or RADEPA) made up of a brotherhood of nationalistic, young military reformers—were behind the Villarroel coup. The secret society was the product of the Chaco War and included members of Legion of Chaco War Veterans and Busch devotees. In Paraguay's prisoner-of-war camps, lower-ranking Bolivian officers had formed an ad hoc brotherhood for protection and solidarity. Influenced by the European tradition of Masonic lodges and popular fascist ideologies, the secret military society assumed political importance in the postwar era. The military cells proved most effective for political organizing and coup plotting.

The tenure in office of the first MNR-RADEPA government was chaotic. At first the outside world, especially the United States, did not

President Gualberto Villarroel, center, who attempted radical reforms after taking power through a coup (Reproduced with the permission of the General Secretariat of the Organization of America States)

know what to make of the unusual Bolivian hybrid. With the exception of Argentina (on the verge of a similar experiment by Juan Domingo Perón), all the Latin American governments and the U.S. State Department withheld diplomatic recognition for six months until the MNR left the cabinet, as the sticking point for them was not so much the military government but the MNR members in its ranks.

The RADEPA seemed a strange animal with incongruous body parts. The military lodge housed two incompatible tendencies: a hard-core fascist right and a more pragmatic pseudofascist left intimate with the MNR. This unusual political-ideological mix generated as much confusion as did the earlier experiments in military socialism. The junta achieved international recognition once Villarroel dismissed the notorious MNR members, such as Víctor Paz Estenssoro, Augusto Céspedes, and Carlos Montenegro, from their cabinet posts (although they would be reappointed later) and promised to hold elections in the near future.

In the elections of August 1944, Villarroel became Bolivia's constitutional president. A large contingent of MNR deputies also returned to the halls of Congress. Even after the constitutional formalities, foreign and domestic opposition to the Villarroel government continued. An informal alliance of the oligarchy, the Marxist PIR, and the United States schemed openly against the radical government. They simplistically attacked the Villarroel government as Nazi.

The government did indeed profess a Bolivian-style nationalist socialism and admired European fascism as a universal doctrine, which espoused a strong and sovereign state. At a time when Bolivians of all walks of life and ideological persuasions viewed their country as economically dependent and sought to exert its national independence, this preeminently nationalist view had great political resonance. Moreover, Villarroel's government was not monolithic; it represented disparate and competing tendencies. Clearly, the RADEPA was more attracted to fascism than the Busch reformers, and members of the secret society held great antipathy toward the Marxist left, especially the PIR. RADEPA agents harassed and violently attacked PIR members. The party's leader, José Antonio Arze, was almost killed by RADEPA goons in 1944 when he ran for president against Villarroel.

The government's brutal repression of the perpetrators of a failed coup attempt in November 1944 gave it a black eye abroad and discredited it at home. The opposition used the event to dish out some damning antigovernment propaganda. All told, nine coup plotters were shot by a firing squad, but opposition versions circulated in which more than 60 dissidents had reportedly been killed, tortured, and mutilated. The shooting incident, or the Fusilamiento, as it became known, forced Arze into exile; he taught in the United States and requested U.S. humanitarian assistance and intervention to save Bolivian democracy.

The firing squad incident precipitated the rapid decline of the Villarroel regime, much as the Catavi Massacre had contributed to the fall of Peñaranda. Despite the progressive decrees that his government had issued on behalf of poor Bolivians, Villarroel soon found himself in a position similar to that of Busch near the end of his experiment in reformism—on the defensive and besieged on all sides.

Expansion of Labor and Indian Rights

Repression was not the most important legacy of the Villarroel years, however, since the MNR-Villarroel government was concerned with populist causes and the welfare of workers and peasants. One major achievement of the Villarroel administration was the expansion of labor unions, especially with the founding in June 1944 of an important union representing the country's miners. The Bolivian Mine Workers' Federation (Federación Sindical de Trabajadores Mineros de Bolivia, or FSTMB) was organized by Juan Lechín Oquendo, a Trotskyite. The miners' union would become labor's most influential and militant political force in the next half century.

Politically the FSTMB was under the wing of radical political parties, including the MNR. In the Villarroel cabinet, the MNR held the labor portfolio. Through its control of the labor ministry, the MNR fostered trade union development for unskilled workers and ushered through Congress additional labor reform laws that established provisions for voluntary retirement, job security, and workers' benefits. The MNR-Villarroel administration also passed important housing and family legislation to improve the general welfare of the poorer classes of society.

A second major achievement of the MNR-Villarroel years—the expansion of indigenous rights—was of historic significance. In May 1945, the government sponsored Bolivia's first National Indigenous Congress. During its sessions, the sensitive problems of land reform and indigenous servitude were raised. In part, the government was sympathetic to the plight of the Indian, but also Villarroel hoped to control a movement that had developed its own momentum.

Holding such a conference represented a provocative, indeed revolutionary, political move. By simply airing long-standing questions about indigenous rights, the delegates challenged the extensive feudal hacienda system, the oligarchy's last bastion of traditionalism and power. The rural fiefdoms of the oligarchy perpetuated the insidious racial prejudice and second-class status accorded Bolivia's Indian majority.

For many reasons, social reforms by previous regimes had largely ignored land and indigenous issues and had concentrated on legislation that benefited the urban and mining proletariat. Indigenous activism, nevertheless, was quietly spreading, encouraged by the Busch educational reforms, teacher training schools such as Warisata, the radical party movement, labor solidarity, and independent grassroots peasant organizing. There had been several past successes, such as the vibrant peasant cooperative movement founded at Cliza-Ucureña in the Cochabamba valley, which would later be the birthplace of the 1953 land reforms. Until the National Indigenous Congress, however, the reform governments had been content to enact symbolic measures.

126

The National Indigenous Congress, therefore, marked a departure from the past in that some tangible progress was realized—at least on paper—and the congress received official support and legitimacy. The government's main concern was labor relations, not property rights, and the congress's achievements were left incomplete because the government's reform decrees were not enforced until after the National Revolution of 1952. The National Indigenous Congress, however, abolished all remaining forms of the feudal system of involuntary servitude. With this meaningful step forward the delegates stopped short and did not push for comprehensive land reform.

The occasion, which seemed designed for public relations purposes as much as for lasting reforms, served as a valuable exercise in consciousness raising. The congress provided an opportunity for the political intelligentsia and military reformers to express their solidarity with the indigenous cause. President Villarroel's speeches focused on the important achievement of justice for all Bolivians. And the young MNR activist and future president Hernán Siles Zuazo confirmed what the more than 1,000 delegates present already knew: Bolivia's greatest challenge was the land problem. Siles declared that a main principle of the MNR party was that "the land should belong to those who work it," but this "leap" would take many years to achieve. "I believe," he added "that this Congress is the first step" (Dandler and Torrico 1987, 353).

Perhaps the greatest achievement of the indigenous congress was the national unity that it imposed on the nation's disparate indigenous groups. Across the country, indigenous communities organized for the great event in a series of massive meetings and regional congresses. Often the preliminary assemblies erupted in confrontations. The feudal bosses or landowners often instigated these incidents so that the peasants would be repressed or arrested as rural agitators. In its distorted reporting, the antigovernment press stoked the popular fears of an imminent indigenous rebellion.

The MNR, labor unions, and the PIR competed for a leading role in the indigenous movement. Villarroel had forged a bond with the indigenous peasants, and tragically, the ultimate fruits of this native awakening were the widespread indigenous persecutions of 1946–52 under the conservative rule of the mining oligarchy. Nevertheless, once unified in the struggle for the rights of campesinos (rural workers), Bolivia moved into the driver's seat, and the radical political parties and governments found themselves in for a bumpy ride. The political effervescence of the 1940s brought the "Indian problem" to culmination and resulted in civil war and finally revolution.

THE NATIONAL INDIGENOUS CONGRESS

The historical record, according to Bolivian scholars Jorge Dandler and Juan Torrico A., exposes the conflict within the government over the National Indigenous Congress. President Gualberto Villarroel's administration justified its call for a national Indian congress "as a method of channeling and 'controlling' a growing wave of rural agitation helped along by other political groups and even peasant leaders" (1987, 349). Putting this into practice, the government removed indigenous leaders such as Luis Ramos Quevedo and Antonio Alvarez Mamani under the pretext that they were not truly members of the indigenous class and instead appointed a governmental steering committee presided over by a non-Indian to direct the congress.

After numerous postponements, the National Indigenous Congress was inaugurated on May 10, 1945, at the Luna Park sports coliseum in La Paz. Francisco Chipana Ramos, representing the Aymara constituency, was elected president of a three-man directorate. The other two directorate members represented the Quechua and Oriente indigenous constituencies.

The congress opened with the pomp and solemnity of a 21-gun salute and the national army, diplomatic corps, and the cabinet in full attendance. The MNR newspaper *La Calle* wrote, "[T]he inauguration of a congress of natives must have appeared unusual and inexplicable to many people—something which denotes the upset of all that is customary and silently accepted as normal" (Dandler and Torrico 1987, 352).

President Villarroel's address was simple but moving. In the more than 100 years of the republic, he reminded them, previous governments had systematically postponed the solution to the plight of the Indian. He explained that his government wanted them to live better and to have housing, clothing, food, education, and health care. His government would end the abuses against them: "[T]he campesino is as much a son of this flag as any man of this land, and must be treated like a son by the government" (Dandler and Torrico 1987, 352).

Villarroel's Assassination

Villarroel's days were numbered once he divorced himself from his civilian base. The cooperation between the MNR and Villarroel's military officers became seriously strained because of escalating international and internal pressures, and the MNR's deputies were forced to leave the

La Paz's Plaza Murillo, named after Pedro Domingo Murillo, a hero of the 1809 revolts, was the site of a ghastly event in July 1946, when a mob broke into the official residence, killed President Gualberto Villarroel, and strung his body up from a lamppost in the square. (Peter McFarren photo)

cabinet. Like Busch earlier, Villarroel resorted to an exclusively military government, but the military itself was fragmented into two warring camps of junior versus senior officers. On June 13, 1946, Villarroel narrowly survived a coup.

Seven weeks later, Villarroel was assassinated in one of the more horrific incidents in Bolivian political history when various forces converged to bring down the government. On July 21, a mob of hundreds of striking teachers, railway and construction workers, student demonstrators, and the violent agitators of the Democratic Antifascist Front besieged the presidential palace.

Unable to save his regime, Villarroel resigned the presidency but unwisely refused to leave the official residence. The mob stormed the Palacio Quemado, killed Villarroel and his closest associates, dragged their bodies into Plaza Murillo, and hung them from lampposts.

The divided military had not intervened to rescue one of their own, and Bolivia's second major experiment in military socialism ended in tragedy. Villarroel's was a chaotic rule at a chaotic time, not only for Bolivia but also around the world, yet his government had struggled for the country's economic independence and the betterment of its dispossessed. The apparent political lesson to be drawn from these two devastating failures of reformism was that reform was insufficient. A multiclass, multi-institutional insurrection was necessary—in short, a revolution.

The Last of the Oligarchy

The death of Villarroel was followed by oligarchic rule. During the ensuing six years of social struggles and repression, known as the Sexenio, the Rosca enlisted the military and political reactionaries to violently roll back every progressive reform implemented in the decade after the Chaco War. In particular, the indigenous communities and the miners felt the severity of the repression and revenge of the oligarchy. The reaction was implemented under the guise of constitutional legitimacy and parliamentary civility.

Immediately after Villarroel's assassination, a provisional civilian-military junta was established and called for elections. With many radical parties banned and key leaders exiled, "secure" elections were held in January 1947. Two conservative candidates acceptable to the oligarchy ran for the presidency. Enrique Hertzog, the oligarchy's favorite, represented the conservative Republican Socialist Union (Partido de la Unión Republicana Socialista, PURS), a conglomerate of factions from the old Republican Party; the distinguished diplomat and statesman Tómas Manuel Elío represented the Liberal Party.

The results of the controlled elections were fairly predictable: The oligarchy regained power. But even under these carefully engineered conditions, the return of the oligarchy generated dissent. Hertzog achieved a narrow victory of 44,700 votes to an opposing 44,300, of which 13,000 votes were cast for the exiled MNR candidate, Paz Estenssoro. Nevertheless, the oligarchy was back in power and took immediate steps to stay there. The establishment formed the National Conciliation, an alliance of conservative political parties and the Marxist PIR. The unusual cooperation between a Marxist party and the oligarchy was the final nail in the PIR's coffin. Discredited, many former members of the PIR decided to found a new party, the Bolivian Communist Party (Partido Comunista Boliviano, or PCB) in January 1950. Others defected to the MNR.

The MNR continued to function in this period although its leaders were mostly in hiding or in exile. With representatives in Congress, the MNR pursued its radical agenda and verbal disruption of the government. When congressional elections were held in May 1949, the MNR reemerged as a major legislative force despite the government's relentless repression. The MNR's electoral success was partly the product of its intimate cooperation with labor, especially the miners.

The government's repression undermined its legitimacy and aided the MNR. In the eyes of the public, MNR loyalists were seen as martyrs of liberty. The twin evils of economic recession and political repression visited Bolivia in 1949. The mining centers were in a crisis. When the economy soured, Bolivia's miners were always among the first to fall into hard times, and in 1949, thousands lost their jobs. Labor strikes occurred almost daily, not only in the mines but also in all sectors of the economy. The conservative government resorted to military repression, ignoring even the few labor reforms on the books. This intransigence and the gross violence of the regime further radicalized the MNR and its labor contingent. The showdown produced another massacre.

The Thesis of Pulacayo

In November 1946, thousands of organized tin miners had held a special union conference in Pulacayo. There they had adopted a historic and revolutionary document known as the Thesis of Pulacayo. Inspired by Guillermo Lora, the militant unionist who reorganized the Revolutionary Workers' Party (POR) in the 1940s, and his Trotskyist beliefs, the document elaborated the ideology and plan of action of the Bolivian Mine Workers' Federation, the FSTMB. According to the Pulacayo document, Bolivian workers were the true and sole fighting vanguard of a socialist revolution. As such, workers were to initiate an armed class struggle and directly move to establish a workers' state. Workers were to reject any accommodation with all nonrevolutionary forces, from the oligarchic government to democratic regimes or even progressive political parties. The revolution could not be compromised and had to be launched immediately.

This agenda of militant class struggle constituted a virtual declaration of war against the oligarchy. Moreover, the plan of action of Pulacayo was also fundamentally at odds with the political program of the MNR, which rejected the doctrine of class warfare and proposed a multiclass, gradualist, and nationalist "revolution" in its place. In January 1947, the determined miners staged a walkout strike to affirm the confrontational agenda of Pulacayo. The oligarchy's labor minister, who was a Marxist belonging to the "accommodationist" faction of the PIR, ordered in the troops.

This act set into motion an escalating cycle of armed confrontations and deaths; for example, in June 1949, two U.S. technicians and 300

Bolivians died when the military repressed another major strike in the mining centers of Catavi, Llallagua, and Siglo XX. Juan Lechín, the charismatic general secretary of the FSTMB and an MNR senator in Congress, publicly condemned the government for these reprisals against the miners. Later, after the oligarchy had Lechín exiled, more blood was shed in armed clashes between the army and the miners.

Two MNR coup plots were then discovered. The government imposed a state of siege, or military rule, which limited civil liberties and freedoms. In the midst of another major strike on August 26, the MNR rebelled against the government. The MNR insurrection had the support of miners, workers, and peasants, as well as sympathetic active and retired military officers, although no major military units defected to the rebels. Nevertheless, because of the heavy resistance in some regions of the country, especially in the mining centers, the revolt touched off a brief but fierce domestic war. The premature discovery of the insurrection in La Paz and other serious mistakes by the MNR led to the civil war being crushed within 20 days.

Although the degree and extent of the resistance surprised the government, there was never a full-scale uprising of the masses. The military solidly backed the government, and the insurrectionists themselves were never really mobilized or armed to fight in the major cities. The MNR had expected to pull off a quick coup d'état, but the tenacity and brutality of the oligarchy in defense of the old order surprised the resistance as well. The brief civil uprising, however, had disrupted even the far regions of the country, with rebel forces holding out for some time in Cochabamba and Santa Cruz.

When it became clear that the uprising would not succeed, the revolutionaries raided the banks, seized planes from the Bolivian national airline, and on September 15, 1949, many of the leaders of the MNR and rebel forces flew into exile. However, a number of those who did not escape were captured and subsequently interned on the notorious penal island of Coati on Lake Titicaca.

Despite its dismal failure, the premature insurrection taught the MNR and the radical miners some important lessons about how to make a revolution. For the embattled oligarchy, even the failure of the revolt provided an ominous portent of the rapid shift in the balance of power against the status quo. First, the national uprising had revealed the growing strength of the MNR-labor-peasant alliance. Second, the civil war had demonstrated the extensive and deep-rooted national support for revolution.

By October 1949, the government had restored order in much of Bolivia. Despite President Enrique Hertzog's public statements that he detested arbitrary violence and repression, much of the time his government was under military rule. Pleading the strains of the civil crisis and his failing health, Hertzog officially resigned in October in favor of his vice president, Mamerto Urriolagoitia, who had been running the government since May in any case. Constitutionally, President Urriolagoitia's term as chief executive ended in August 1951. More decisive and repressive in office, he would be the last hope of the oligarchy.

The Election of 1951

The decade before 1952's National Revolution had been the most chaotic and critical in Bolivian history. The important changes in social-political institutions and popular attitudes that had taken root after the Chaco War achieved an unstoppable momentum in these years. Several developments were especially significant and essential to creating the conditions for the prerevolutionary crisis of 1949 to 1951.

The electorate had been progressively expanding and changing. Middle-class support for the traditional political parties had been eroded by the war, and the support of the upper-class intelligentsia had also declined. The youth of Bolivia's prosperous classes were drawn to radical political parties and to the streets in direct action. The MNR had managed to forge a multiclass bloc of voters that could and did win elections. Beginning with the extraordinary protest vote for the PIR in 1940, the MNR steadily won more and more votes in the congressional elections of 1942, 1944, 1947, and 1949. The PIR protest vote in 1940 marked a turning point for the radical agenda, showing that the oligarchy was vulnerable. In its wake the MNR also benefited, especially after it radicalized its agenda and adopted some of the POR's program.

The ideological foundation of Bolivian politics had been challenged and revolutionized, and the MNR emerged from this ideological cauldron as a multiclass party of the democratic left. Indeed, the MNR eventually discovered its political identity in the incendiary revolutionary slogan "Land to the Indian, mines to the state." By 1951 this battle cry resonated throughout the country.

Also by 1951 Bolivian society had become irrevocably polarized between the forces of revolution and reaction; there was no longer a middle course to follow. Reforms, elections, and congressional measures had all been tried repeatedly and had failed. Bolivian society seemed engulfed in a psychology of frustration intensified by a cycle of rising and declining expectations. With each series of reforms and stark reversals, the people's expectations of improvement would rise and then fall precipitously.

The MNR finally won a presidential election in 1951, but the election was stolen away from the party. Approximately 126,000 votes representing around 5 percent of the population were cast. The MNR candidate for president was Víctor Paz Estenssoro, in exile in Argentina. The oligarchy was horrified when the tally revealed that Paz had won 43 percent of the total votes cast. The magnitude of this MNR victory was clear: Despite the restricted electorate and the money and clout of the Rosca, Paz had received a five-to-three plurality over the official candidate, Gabriel Gosálvez.

How had this happened? The victory was not simply the result of Paz Estenssoro's popularity. The conservative parties had unwittingly diluted their votes. There were five conservative candidates competing against one another, as well as the single candidate of the MNR and radical parties. Had the conservatives backed a unified ticket, they could have won, but even in the last days of the old order, party factionalism and political opportunism impeded unity.

According to the Bolivian constitution, however, if no candidate receives an absolute majority or 51 percent of the vote, the election must be decided by Congress. Had the legalities been followed, the conservative candidates would probably have won in any case, but President Urriolagoitia was unwilling to take even the slightest risk of a pro-opposition outcome. He resigned and turned the government over to the chief of the army, General Ovidio Quiroga. Convinced that an MNR victory would bring communists to power, General Quiroga annulled the elections, and a military cabinet was appointed with General Hugo Ballivián as the interim president.

The military government was widely reviled and never able to consolidate its 11-month rule. The provisional junta was blatantly illegitimate, and the inconsistency of its rule, at times repressive and at others conciliatory, only intensified the constitutional crisis. Internal divisions among the oligarchy and traditional parties weakened the government needlessly. In the confused political climate, the civilian opposition, including the conservative Liberal Party, continued to attack the government.

A major economic crisis further exacerbated the last days of the traditional order. After World War II, the demand for tin and its international price had steadily declined. The U.S. government had stockpiled extensive stores of tin as an emergency measure during the war. In the late 1940s, sales from this strategic reserve created havoc with Bolivia's already depressed mining economy. In late 1951, a dispute with the United States over the price and sale of tin heightened the economic and political crisis. For once there was complete unanimity and solidarity. Even the oligarchy joined the MNR in denouncing this case of U.S. imperialism.

Little did anyone realize that in a few short months Víctor Paz Estenssoro would be in the Palacio Quemado and the nationalistic MNR would be negotiating with the United States not merely over the price of tin, but over diplomatic recognition and the survival of the MNR's National Revolution.

7

THE NATIONAL REVOLUTION
(1951–1964)

In semi-colonial countries neither the proletariat alone nor the middle class can triumph. When there is an alliance of classes, however, conditions are right for the National Revolution's triumph.

■

Víctor Paz Estenssoro, February 1953 (Mitchell 1977, 39)

Reforms in modern society have served as a prelude either to stability or to revolution. By 1952 in Bolivia, two decades of reforms
had been overturned, and the path to peaceful change, blocked by a
conservative, repressive oligarchy. The major reforms legislated by the
military socialists and the MNR had been reversed virtually overnight
in 1951. An oligarchy determined to protect its power and privileges
beat down popular dissent with military repression. Frustrated reforms,
therefore, resulted in a revolution.

Bolivia's defeat in the Chaco War and the massive political mobilization in the war's aftermath were also responsible for the social revolution
that engulfed the landlocked nation during Easter week of 1952. The dis-
gruntled war veterans and the general population had rejected the failed
political system of the republican era. The disastrous war had changed
Bolivia's men and women irrevocably and transformed its electorate.

Bolivia's citizens, in turn, transformed the country's politics and
social institutions. Citizens who had never voted in elections or who
had been systematically excluded from civic life were suddenly aware
of the promise and disappointment that politics could effect in their
personal lives. Disgusted with endemic corruption, economic inequality, and injustice, this new majority found its voice and rallied to the
cause of radical reform. The sons and daughters of the middle and
upper classes as well as the dispossessed became politically aware,

active, and militant. By 1952, the majority of Bolivians opposed a conservative restoration and were empowered by their anger. Bolivians transformed the MNR's revolt for national liberation into a people's revolution.

The MNR Revolt

The loyalists of the MNR launched the National Revolution on April 9, 1952. The revolt was the work of a vanguard of revolutionaries supported by workers, miners, and middle-class students and intellectuals. Initially, the peasantry and the indigenous communities were not on the front lines of the revolution; consequently, the insurrection was primarily a proletarian and urban-based revolution similar to the MNR's failed revolt in 1949. Unlike the 1949 civil war, however, better planning and kind fortune favored the rebels. Not until the months after victory did the rural revolutionary contingency join the MNR and radicalize its agenda.

Timing was critical in the revolution's success. The political climate immediately before and after the 1951 elections had been chaotic. The old elite parties had fractured into warring factions, and the economy had been devastated by a severe crisis in the price of tin. The conservative Liberal Party and even the Big Three tin mining interests were against the government, having excoriated it for the bankrupt economy and its "soft" treatment of labor and leftists. Indeed, the government had attempted to woo labor at the 11th hour before the vote by decreeing a one-third increase in salaries for miners. The mining companies, however, had denounced and blatantly defied the unilateral decree. In no small measure, therefore, this escalating dissension within the government and the traditional political parties exposed in the pre-electoral confusion had worked in the plotters' favor.

Initially, the military takeover by General Ballivián following the disastrous election results had offered hope for the old order. Claiming a duty to protect the country from a Nazi-communist menace (referring to the pact among the MNR and the Marxist parties), the junta had restored a brief stability. But within a few months the prostrate economy and deep political polarization had undermined the junta's efforts and civilian support.

Ballivián blustered and threatened, but other top military commanders began to aspire to the presidential office, and everyone knew that the junta would fall sooner or later. The question was who would strike the blow and reap the political victory? At this critical juncture, the MNR, political scientist James M. Malloy writes, "began plotting day and night with everyone and anyone looking for a formula to power" (1970, 156).

When it finally came, the insurrection was not a spontaneous rising; indeed, extensive planning and plotting secured its ultimate success. Two key MNR leaders, Hernán Siles and Juan Lechín, who had been instrumental in the 1949 uprising, once again played major roles. Both had learned from past mistakes. In 1949, a timid MNR had not armed the people, fearing the spread of civil war and a bloodbath. In 1952, a more desperate and radical MNR decided to risk greater violence, and they armed the opponents of the government.

The leaders of the revolt enlisted professional soldiers to their cause, but this was not an easy task. The MNR was suspicious of and ambivalent about the military, and the old days of MNR-military collaboration were long over. After the fall of Villarroel, the army had been thoroughly purged of its radical elements. As a result, the military establishment had remained loyal to the government in revolts, especially the uprising of 1949. The MNR judged it unlikely that career officers would defect to the revolutionaries' cause in 1952. Indeed, the military junta in power had outlawed the MNR, and the army's conservative chief of staff, General Humberto Torres Ortiz, was rumored to be interested in the presidency himself. Nevertheless, the MNR pursued a potential alliance with Torres and the right-wing (Bolivian Socialist Falange FSB), but at the last minute Torres backed out.

The MNR rebels then sought the assistance of the militarized national police, known as the *carabineros*. On the eve of the revolt—moved forward from April 15 to April 9 for fear of discovery—General Antonio Seleme, the minister of internal security and the chief of the national police, secretly agreed to support and arm the revolutionaries. He ordered the police force to open up the armories and distribute weapons to the MNR and the rebellious workers. The plan, according to James M. Malloy, was for General Seleme to become president in an MNR-military cabinet and for Hernán Siles, personally in charge of the revolt, to become vice president. But events soon took a different course.

On the morning of April 9, the startled citizens of La Paz woke to armed confrontations in the narrow streets and plazas of the city between the MNR loyalists and *carabineros* on one side and the army and government supporters on the other. The revolutionary forces of the MNR rapidly seized the city center, forcing the national army to regroup below the rebel positions. The government army also commanded El Alto along the rim of the altiplano heights above the city. Encircling the city, which lay in the deep bowl below, the government's well-armed and confident troops moved pincerlike to smash the rebel forces.

After the first day's fighting, the position of the revolutionaries seemed precarious. The superior forces of the loyalist army had the advantage, and General Seleme, who had armed the rebels gambling on an easy victory, now feared all was lost. In a panic, Seleme deserted his command and sought diplomatic asylum in the Chilean embassy. The police general's cowardice further panicked the insurgents, and some began to consider the possibility of compromise or surrender. But Siles and the MNR leaders refused to capitulate. The rebels fought on as the uprising spread to the major cities of Oruro and Cochabamba. Meanwhile, in La Paz, the city's factory workers and those from nearby Viacha armed themselves with captured weapons and joined in the battle.

The situation was reversed dramatically the next day. Militant miners from the Milluni mining complex, 10 miles north of La Paz, overran El Alto and seized the railroad station and the air force base located there, above the city. This decisive action intercepted a trainload of munitions and prevented the bombing of rebel positions. Converging on the army's forces along the heights above the city, the angry miners trapped the army from behind and pushed the government's forces ever closer toward the edge of the altiplano and the precipitous drop to the central city below.

Meanwhile, about 70 miles south of La Paz on the altiplano, the MNR cadres and miners of Oruro prevented the military garrison there from sending reinforcements to rescue the government's soldiers trapped on El Alto. This rearguard action proved to be a decisive move in the revolt. Had reinforcements arrived from Oruro, the Milluni miners would have been squeezed between the two armies of the government and probably wiped out. As it was, the government troops in La Paz realized that there would be no rescue from outside the city and became disheartened. According to Malloy's account of the battle, there was a final heroic but fruitless stand by the cadets of the military college before the government surrendered.

After three days of intense fighting, the historic Battle of La Paz sealed the MNR's victory. On April 11, the government general Torres Ortiz gave up and signed a truce with the revolutionaries. Most of the army's high command, including General Torres, who had defended the bankrupt oligarchy, fled into exile. The violent revolutionary takeover had been costly for both sides: The official record listed 552 dead and 787 wounded.

The structure of the revolt had not been that radically different from previous civilian-military coups. Indeed, Malloy notes that "the original plan smacked strongly of a Villarroel-type formula, that is, a rapid coup involving little civil participation, followed by a military-civil coalition government" (1970, 157). Malloy suggests that this may have been a conscious decision by some of the MNR leaders to diminish the role of the radical labor elements. A more conservative-reformist sector of the MNR wanted Siles rather than the more radical Paz Estenssoro to head the new government. In short, Malloy writes, "the in-country MNR elite was aiming at establishing a Villarroel-type reformist regime in which labor could have a secondary role, at best" (1970, 158).

But again events took a different course. The Battle of La Paz had been unexpectedly fierce and bloody, and although confined largely to the city, there was extensive citizen involvement, especially by the miners and factory workers. Without the support of these radical labor elements the revolt would most likely have fizzled out in the first 24 hours. Whether party leaders had intended it, the MNR owed the spectacular and surprising success of its revolutionary putsch to the socialist and Marxist miners and workers of La Paz. The MNR leadership could ignore the radical and revolutionary social goals of its leftist labor supporters only at great cost.

Making the Social Revolution

The MNR's triumph was due to its being a party of proletarians, of the peasantry, of the middle class and the petty bourgeoisie which sought transformations.

∎

Victor Paz Estenssoro (Mitchell 1977, 39)

Víctor Paz Estenssoro was welcomed home from exile in Argentina amid the wild jubilation of the citizens of La Paz, on April 15, 1952. The next day, Paz took the oath of office and became Bolivia's first revolutionary president. Ensconced in the Palacio Quemado, his government and the MNR directorate now faced the daunting task of bringing to fruition the first major Latin American revolution since the Mexican Revolution of 1910.

Winning the revolutionary victory proved an easier task than effecting profound social change. Making a social revolution challenged the core identity of the once-reformist and protofascist MNR. And the revolutionary agenda, as yet only theory and promise, raised important but unanswered questions: What was the MNR in 1952? Who were its

Victor Paz Estenssoro, political leader and president of Bolivia. The confettilike material on his head and shoulders is called mistura *and is scattered on people to show honor and respect.* (Peter McFarren photo)

loyalists and supporters? Which component of its "nationalist socialist revolution" would take precedence? What would be the party's program and policies?

In principle, the program of the MNR's 1952 National Revolution had been well established and publicized. The three central goals, which the MNR espoused before the revolutionary victory and which served as its revolutionary banner, were universal suffrage, nationalization of the mines, and land reform. The first two goals, although radical in the context of the times, could be reconciled with the nationalistic and reformist aspirations of the original MNR program. Without question, the third goal of land reform was the most revolutionary and provoked serious strains within the party.

Behind its radical-reformist facade, therefore, the first decade of MNR rule exposed a house divided between "reluctant" and "radical" reformers. Two key policies—expropriation of the mines and land reform—tested the party's mettle and revolutionary resolve. Most observers concluded that if Bolivia's peasantry had not acted aggressively and independently in land takeovers, the agrarian reform decree might not have been signed as early as 1953. Even the generally popular nationalization of the properties of the Big Three mining capitalists gave the MNR leaders moments of indecision.

Once the MNR's revolutionary coalition had achieved power, party leaders seemed to hesitate before enacting promised reforms. The more radical sectors and lower-class interest groups, however, were determined to fulfill the MNR's revolutionary promises. Thus, the euphoria of the revolutionary process and the constant pressure from the party's multiclass interests shaped legislation between 1952 and 1956. In the end, each major interest group attained its core goal. On this most fundamental level, the MNR's social revolution was a success:

THE THREE MNRs

The MNR was not a homogeneous party but a multiclass and multi-ideological coalition. The broad nature of the party had been the very basis of its far-reaching appeal and revolutionary victory. In its diversity, however, lay its potential strength and resilience in power as well as the future seeds of its eventual demise and disintegration as a ruling party.

There were, according to James M. Malloy, really three MNRs. The first MNR, the core of the party, represented the loyalist cells. The second was the labor left wing led by Juan Lechín, which included the miners' union (the FSTMB) and radical students. And the third MNR was the support group of Víctor Paz Estenssoro, in exile in Argentina.

Malloy describes these three MNRs as fundamentally different in their aims, style, and tactics. The first group, which was the closest to the original MNR and its middle-class base, had a moderate, even rightist, reformist tendency. The second group favored a revolutionary and socialist program. And the third exiled group proved the most pragmatic and nationalistic in approach.

The primary MNR had only a vague program based on principles of national dignity and self-determination. According to Malloy these core party faithfuls were more interested in the mystique of revolution and the seizure of power than in its exercise. In victory, these party loyalists had no clear idea of where the revolution was going or why. Thus, the first MNR administration would begin a journey in self-discovery and intrapartisan class conflict (Malloy 1970, 158–59).

The nationalists, labor left wing, and the miners' union realized the nationalization of the mines; the peasants and indigenous communities achieved the passage of land reform; and the majority of Bolivia's dispossessed experienced meaningful citizenship and full voting rights. By achieving these three sweeping social, economic, and political reforms the MNR's revolution has been "ranked as one of Latin America's most far-reaching processes of social change" (Mitchell 1977, 6).

Votes to the People

The first reform was the new electoral law that guaranteed universal adult suffrage to all Bolivian citizens of 21 years of age (or 18 years if married) and abolished the old requirements of literacy tests and discriminatory property restrictions. The political impact of the voting act was revolutionary. Literally over night, the country's total number of voters increased fivefold.

Since the early republic, Bolivia's electorate had represented as little as 2 percent and no more than 6 percent of the population. Over the decades, the gradual and modest expansion of the voting rolls had occurred only because of steady population increases. Just as important as the number of new voters, however, was the expansion in the electorate's social and racial composition. Before the revolutionary law, the indigenous population, which accounted for almost 60 percent of the total, had been denied the vote. The majority of new voters, therefore, were illiterate indigenous peasants, miners, and factory workers.

A quick review of voting statistics reveals the dramatic transformation of the traditional elite politics before the revolution into the populist mass-party politics of less than a decade later. In 1952, before the electoral reform law, the electorate consisted of approximately 200,000 eligible voters, or 6 percent of the nearly 3 million total population. In the 1951 elections, for example, only 126,000 persons voted. After the new law's passage, the electorate increased to nearly 1 million eligible voters, or more than 30 percent of the population. As a result, in the 1960 elections there were 900,000 voters, or about 25 percent of the 3.5 million Bolivians. In both the 1978 and 1979 elections, there were

The 1952 revolution brought full citizenship and voting rights to all members of Bolivian society, including campesinos like this man, near Tarabuco. (UN/DPI Photo by Greg Kinch)

approximately 2 million registered voters, or 40 percent of the country's population of 5 million.

Because of the decree for the universal vote, for the first time in the country's history, Bolivians had the opportunity to create an authentic, working democracy. The universal vote empowered them politically, but, as they would soon learn, only if it were respected and used wisely.

Mines to the State

We did not aim at making a social or a political revolution but an economic revolution.

■

Walter Guevara Arze (Malloy 1970, 170)

The nationalization of Bolivia's mineral riches represented the heart and soul of the MNR's goal of economic liberation. The momentous Act of Bolivia's Economic Independence was signed on October 31, 1952, at the infamous Catavi mining complex, the site of two bloody massacres of Bolivian miners. The radical decree nationalized the mining enterprises of the Big Three—Patiño, Aramayo, and Hochschild—and established the powerful state mining corporation Corporación Minera de Bolivia, better known as COMIBOL.

In economic terms, according to Richard S. Thorn, the nationalization transferred control over 85 percent of the country's tin production, 95 percent of its foreign exchange receipts, and about 50 percent of the central government's fiscal receipts from private hands to the state (1971, 168–69). The decree did not affect the country's medium and small mining companies, which remained in private ownership. Since passage of the Busch Mining Decree in 1939, the state Mining Bank had indirectly taxed these private mining enterprises, and the MNR government continued this policy.

Restricting nationalization to the Big Three tin producers proved critical for U.S.-Bolivian relations. Several of the medium-sized mines were U.S. owned, and the MNR had no desire to directly confront the United States. Respecting the private property of these enterprises was intended to allay U.S. suspicions concerning the MNR's intentions and ideological orientation. Nevertheless, even the targeted expropriation of Bolivia's Big Three mining capitalists proved a problem for the revolutionary government. The implementation of the decree created an early rift with the MNR's more radical labor left wing.

145

The official MNR program had promised that the big tin barons would not be compensated for the expropriation of their properties. The MNR had always charged that the Big Three were exploiters, who had stolen the national patrimony and had withheld taxes owed the state. The middle-class leaders of the MNR, however, were desperate to gain the favor of the United States, which had withheld diplomatic recognition from the revolution and would most likely continue to do so if there were no indemnification of private property. Since the early 1940s, the volatile Bolivian economy had relied increasingly on U.S. foreign aid, and the MNR government hoped to restore and increase the flow of dollars as quickly as possible before the economy collapsed completely.

MNR policymakers of the party's core vetoed the MNR's labor sector and agreed to compensate the big tin barons. No doubt the middle-class leadership rationalized the softening in policy as a necessary evil for the good of the revolution. Indeed, they feared that deteriorating economic conditions and continued diplomatic isolation by the United States could doom their revolution. This decision proved to be a miscalculation when the millions ultimately paid in compensation to the big tin interests bankrupted the treasury and aggravated the desperate postrevolutionary fiscal crisis.

Despite its shortcomings, this single reform law transformed the Bolivian economy. Unfortunately, it proved to be too little too late. By 1952 when the decree was passed, tin mining revenue was already in a free fall. Diminished resources, higher extraction costs, and decapitalization had already taken their toll and would continue to do so. Rather than buy Bolivia's economic independence, the nationalization decree ensured the country's continued economic dependence—and the inevitable day of reckoning between the core MNR and its labor-left constituents.

Land to the Tiller

The peasantry had never fully recovered from the repression that followed the murder of their hero, President Gualberto Villarroel. Their efforts both through open rebellion and litigation in the courts had failed to realize the legal guarantees that Villarroel had decreed in 1945. The landowners had ignored the laws outright or had feigned compliance, and most landowners also resorted to direct repression. Indians who had attended the National Indigenous Congress were punished with double the workload or thrown off the haciendas to become vagrants. Ostensibly, the subjugation of the campesinos had not changed.

In the spring of 1952, an independent and spontaneous indigenous land reform movement erupted near Cochabamba in the town of Ucureña. The peremptory land seizures there spread like wildfire across the altiplano and intermountain valleys forcing the MNR to speed up and radicalize its official agrarian reform policy. The Ucureña movement had deep roots in the region and prerevolutionary antecedents as far back as the 1930s. Shortly after the Chaco War in 1936, returning Indian war veterans had begun to organize independent rural unions in the high valleys of Cochabamba.

The Indian movement in Ucureña, nevertheless, was somewhat of an exception; it had been more advanced and less repressed than other peasant movements before the revolution. Generally, indigenous organizations and ties to the post-Chaco middle-class and mestizo political parties were weak or nonexistent before 1952. The MNR had remained ambivalent about the agrarian question during the 1940s, and compared to the other radical and reformist parties, the MNR's position on land reform had been ambiguous and tentative. Indeed, both the pre- and post-1952 MNR had sought to counter and control this growing indigenous autonomy.

In contrast, both the Party of the Revolutionary Left (PIR), a principal rival of the MNR and opponent of the Villarroel government, and the Revolutionary Workers' Party (POR), a frequent ally of the MNR, had formulated decisive positions on domestic Indian and agrarian issues. Indeed, the PIR had struggled to become the preeminent voice of peasant demands. Because of its aggressive and revolutionary stand on land reform, the Marxist party had made significant headway, especially in Ucureña where it controlled the peasant unions. Even the dogmatic POR, which had insisted on subordinating the indigenous-peasant movement to the proletarian vanguard, had established a stronger presence in the countryside than the MNR had before 1952.

The MNR became more serious about rural organizing immediately after the revolution (in which very few peasants had participated). The government created the Ministry of Peasant Affairs. Its primary task was the formation of MNR-based peasant unions, especially in the Cochabamba region. The Bolivian scholar Xavier Albó has noted that the MNR typically maneuvered to channel popular impulses toward its own objectives. And although the party sought new peasant participation, it wanted to remain in the driver's seat, "But in 1952, in the *valle alto* ("high valley") of Cochabamba, the MNR was forced into the passenger's seat" (1987, 383).

The peasants of Ucureña and their leader, José Rojas, who were at the heart of the indigenous union movement, joined the MNR. In return for their supporting the party, the Ucureña unionists retained their own leaders and proposed their own, more radical agrarian reform program. "In the face of governmental indecision," Albó explained, the campesinos of Ucureña started to occupy the haciendas on their own, "and thanks to these de facto actions, the MNR government ended up deciding in favor of agrarian reform" (1987, 383). The Agrarian Reform Decree of 1953 legalized the violent seizures of large haciendas in Ucureña and elsewhere around the country where the government failed to maintain control. The historic reform effected one of the most sweeping land transfers in Latin America, second only to the Mexican Revolution's agrarian reform.

If measured solely in terms of new property rights, the Bolivian agrarian reform may not have seemed very radical. The law confiscated only the largest estates and compensated the former owners with 25-year bonds based on the assessed property value. Medium-sized properties widely remained intact. The social and ethnic consequences of the decree, however, were especially significant, and the land reform decree reaffirmed many of the labor and human rights that Villarroel had granted the Indians in 1945.

Land reform was a crucial part of the National Revolution of 1952. It allowed theretofore dispossessed farmers to own and work their own land, as do these campesinos, shown here shearing a live alpaca. (UN/DPI Photo by Greg Kinch)

The 1953 law abolished the entire gamut of feudal labor practices that had oppressed the indigenous population. Foremost among these was the comprehensive system of rule by the local and regional bosses and oligarchs. The bosses and their paid underlings had kept the Indians ignorant and isolated. The corrupt system had prevented reforms decreed by the central government (such as those of Busch or Villarroel) from being disseminated and implemented in the countryside.

Further, the reform decree abolished the unpaid and involuntary personal services (that is, slavery) provided to the haciendas and the residences of the *patrones,* or landowners. The law ended the use of lands in exchange for labor and a portion of the produce to the hacienda. It abolished the practice of gratuitous transport of the hacienda's produce to urban markets by the peasant's beasts of burden solely at the peasant's expense.

The agrarian reform also restored to Indian communities the collective lands that had been seized by unscrupulous hacendados over the last 100 years. The reform's critics, however, contended that the ultimate intent of the MNR plan, not unlike previous liberal land reforms, was to incorporate the Indian into the market economy and ultimately replace the indigenous communities with agrarian freeholders. In short, the MNR intended to modernize Bolivian agriculture. To this end, the final provisions of the reform included technical assistance, rural development, and extensive exploration of the national territory in order to secure new lands for internal migration.

The MNR's agrarian reform radically altered the economic and social makeup of Bolivia. The before and after statistics are telling. Nearly 72 percent of the country's economically active population still depended on agricultural production in 1950. Most were landless campesinos; the rest, who owned small parcels or shared collective farming rights within traditional indigenous communities, were squeezed onto only a small percentage of the cultivated land. The 1953 land decree introduced major changes in these ownership patterns over the next two decades.

By June 1970, more than 30 percent of nearly 15 million acres of total agricultural land had been distributed to Bolivia's landless or land-poor. This successful transfer of property, however, came with significant setbacks; for example, the established policy of compensation to former owners often failed. Furthermore, land reform confiscated only very large properties. It took years or even decades to process transfer titles. Medium-sized holdings (1,500–12,500 hectares) were left intact. The land reform decree promised to compensate former owners by issuing bonds at 2 percent interest over 25 years. New (peasant) owners

BOLIVIA'S LAND REFORMS

Bolivia has undertaken three land reform programs in its history as an independent state. The first was in 1825, the second in 1874, and the most recent in 1953. According to Xavier Albó, all three were basically attempts to "liberalize" and modernize agriculture. Central to all three plans was the replacement of the *ayllus,* the traditional indigenous agricultural communities based on lineage, with private individual land ownership.

The history of land reform, moreover, followed two distinct but interrelated and continuous phases demarcated by the Chaco War. Albó argues that in the pre-Chaco period, the Indians primarily struggled to protect their communities from dispossession by the new white-mestizo oligarchy. The Indian uprisings of this period were desperate attempts to defend community lands. After the Chaco War, the players and the goals shifted. During the second phase of land reform, the Indians struggled for better living conditions on the haciendas and then the destruction of the oppressive system and the redistribution of the land to the tiller. They allied with progressive political parties and labor unions. In this phase the *ayllus* became irrelevant, according to Albó. The indigenous communities had been destroyed, transformed, or reduced to 22 percent of the lands.

The goal of the MNR land reform, therefore, was to sweep away the feudal system of lords and slaves and transform the Indian peasants into citizens and producers and consumers in an internal market. In this process the Indian would disappear altogether through intermarriage, the "Hispanization" of language and culture, migration, and the loss of the traditional communities (Albó 1987, 380–82).

had to pay off assessed value of their land in that time, but as soon as the title transfer was processed, many defaulted and the 25-year bonds became worthless paper.

A more serious problem was the catastrophic decline in agricultural productivity. The agrarian reform encouraged excessive parceling of the land into extremely small farms, and these mini-holdings were inefficient and often suffered from chronic capital shortages. The entire reform process was plagued by sluggish bureaucracy and irregular or delayed transfers of titles.

Despite a host of difficulties, the agrarian reform destroyed the feudal landowning system and the power of the landed oligarchy on the national and especially local and regional levels. This system had kept Bolivia's Indians enslaved and impoverished since the Spanish conquest. After the revolution in 1952, indigenous peoples, now officially known as campesinos, became citizens, voters, and property owners. The MNR was the first to realize that its major reforms had transformed both power and class relations in the new Bolivia. The MNR's desire to create a modern and economically developed country served as the major impetus for these radical transformations.

Modernization for the MNR

The MNR pursued its inherently modernizing mission through foreign aid, universal education, and economic development programs. An educational reform decree, which reaffirmed the initiatives introduced by Busch and Villarroel, was announced on January 20, 1953. The reform reestablished the right to universal education, and the revolutionary government pledged to extend this benefit to Bolivia's indigenous and rural communities. Local bosses had thwarted previous reforms, and the MNR was determined that this time Indians would benefit from the law.

Another important aspect of the MNR's modernization strategy was the exploration and development of Bolivia's vast land area. Major new roads were constructed, including a vital link between Cochabamba and Santa Cruz. At the same time, the government provided incentives to colonize and develop the country's rich tropical and subtropical regions. Consequently, the underpopulated departments of El Beni and Santa Cruz saw a population explosion over the following decades.

These development projects were ambitious. With the economy bankrupt, most could not have been realized without the infusion of extensive foreign assistance from the United States. Moderation of revolutionary and economic nationalism was the price the MNR government paid. In a very real sense, therefore, the MNR revolution came to depend on the goodwill of the United States and the wary new Republican administration of President Dwight Eisenhower.

Specifically, the MNR agreed to renew payment of Bolivia's national debt, which had been suspended in the post–Great Depression moratorium of 1931. Also, in June 1953, the government promised to compensate the Big Three tin capitalists for the expropriation of their mines the previous fall. In October 1953, Paz Estenssoro approved a new petroleum code that encouraged private foreign investments and exploration by U.S. oil interests. Consequently, Gulf Oil began operations in

1955. Nine other U.S. petroleum companies eventually followed. This petroleum code put the Bolivian State Petroleum Enterprise (YPFB, which stands for Yacimientos Petrolíferos Fiscales Bolivianos), founded in the wake of Busch's nationalization decree, at a competitive disadvantage, and the U.S. aid came with strings. If the new MNR government desired the technical skills and operating capital that the U.S. government and corporations had to offer, then the state petroleum industry would have to take second place to private and foreign interests, at least for the time being.

During the difficult economic times after the National Revolution, the U.S. government shipped large quantities of food aid to Bolivia. In 1953 alone, this aid amounted to $5 million. Bolivia also received sizable U.S. foreign assistance in 1956. These funds, however, were made contingent on implementation of a harsh stabilization plan devised by the United States and the International Monetary Fund (IMF). By 1960, Bolivia had attained a special status in its relations with the United States. That year, the revolutionary government received a staggering $100 million in U.S. assistance, making Bolivia the largest recipient of U.S. foreign aid in Latin America.

This aid dependency raised important questions concerning the fundamental character of the MNR and the revolution. Did the MNR's record of accommodation reflect survival of the revolution on U.S. terms? Or, did the MNR's pragmatism and moderation also reflect the core interests of the party's mainstream? For whatever reason, did the MNR compromise its principles and thereby undermine the party and the National Revolution? Or did this primarily middle-class party always harbor the seeds of failure within its distinct institutional structure and governing style? These intriguing questions have given rise to the ongoing debate over whether and why the MNR and the revolution ultimately failed.

Divide and Rule

Shortly after the revolutionary victory, Víctor Paz Estenssoro bluntly characterized both his personal pragmatism and that of the new government. "Different modes of action," Paz explained, "correspond to different periods. The hour of the revolutionaries has passed; this is the hour of the policy makers" (Mitchell 1977, 51). During the first four years of the revolution, the MNR lacked the resources to resist the demands of powerful interest groups within the party. By 1956, conditions were different as the party engaged in a comprehensive governing style of divide and rule.

Although remaining in power and in charge demanded popular support, especially at the polls, the party leaders had to make difficult decisions that inevitably alienated one or more groups in the MNR's multiclass constituency. From 1956 to 1964, the party employed a bag of political tricks to try to keep the opposing interests within its ranks in line or at the very least from tearing the party apart completely.

Among the MNR's various tactics were penetration and co-optation. The party employed these tactics most effectively in its organization and takeover of peasant unions, or *sindicatos*. Generally, the MNR preferred to gain the loyalty of existing associations, especially since the middle-class MNR cadres disliked the hard work of recruitment and grassroots organizing. It was easier to penetrate existing unions. Another reason was that indigenous groups remained highly suspicious of political parties, even of the MNR and its land reform decree. On the other hand, since the land reform the peasantry had become an essentially passive and even conservative political force that could be easily manipulated through its leaders. Recognizing that most peasants still identified with their rural unions rather than the party, the MNR simply co-opted the local union leaders to gain the loyalty of the peasants. After 1952, organizing the peasantry became vital to the party's political future. At the very least the MNR was determined to deny its rivals the peasant vote. Later, the peasants also became useful as the shock troops that the party could throw against the miners and the workers.

The MNR established the Ministry of Peasant Affairs, headed by Nuflo Chávez Ortiz, an effective MNR peasant and labor organizer. Chávez, working with Juan Lechín, recruited and sent out roving organizing teams into the countryside. The MNR also created and financed the first national rural union, the Bolivian National Peasant Confederation (Confederación Nacional de Trabajadores Campesinos de Bolivia, CNTCB). These efforts were largely successful. Within a few months of the revolution, there were 1,200 peasant unions in the department of Cochabamba with 200,000 members. By 1961, there were more than 7,500 rural peasant unions throughout the country affiliated with the MNR.

As a political party, the MNR's organizational presence in the countryside remained weak. Party structures were lacking below the level of the country's 98 provincial capitals. Often party and union structures were one and the same, and at the grassroots level there existed only the *sindicatos*. The CNTCB had always seemed to be a creature of the MNR and an instrument of state control over the rural workers. The national peasants' organization, according to Christopher Mitchell, tended to be

THE PEASANT *SINDICATO*

The rural unions, or *sindicatos*, that the Ministry of Peasant Affairs organized between 1952 and 1960 became all-embracing associations. Political scientist Christopher Mitchell described them in these terms:

> Originally modeled on industrial-style mining unions, the peasant organizations become multifaceted social institutions which monopolized local power. They dispensed justice, sometimes played a role in cultivation, and became the social center of peasant life. Most important, they provided a channel through which postreform peasants dealt with the central government. The often agonizingly slow process of obtaining land titles, the search for assistance from La Paz (schools, teachers, roads, water), the trading of votes for political favors—all these tasks in political linkage were handled by the sindicato (1977, 46).

a shadow organization. Moreover, Mitchell argues that the MNR's rural weakness was ultimately insignificant given the party's inherently divisive strategy. The MNR was not interested in mobilizing the peasants but in dividing and isolating them in order to neutralize their influence in national politics.

By 1960, however, the MNR's divide-and-rule strategy had unraveled for several reasons. Probably the most important was the MNR's falling out with the labor-left. Indeed, the divisiveness that the MNR intentionally sowed in order to keep the middle-class faction on top and competing class interests down fostered the decline of the party.

The MNR and Labor

The tactic of co-optation that had worked relatively well in building a coalition with the passive peasantry fell short in the party's dealings with the powerful and radical labor sector. Since labor support was critical to political success, the MNR was forced to make greater concessions in coalition building and coalition management. A key tactic in the party-government's relationship with labor was a form of direct power sharing known as *cogobierno*, or "cogovernment." This governing strategy provided labor with a virtual veto over the MNR government's policies. As James M. Malloy observes, "through the COB

[Central Obrero Boliviano, or Bolivian Labor Central], the labor-left became a government within the government" (1970, 186). By 1956, this constraint on the government's ability to maneuver became unacceptable to the MNR. Finally, as a result of the economic crisis between 1956 and 1960, the MNR-labor coalition broke down completely. Labor had historically had an independent voice in Bolivian politics; the MNR's attempt to tame the labor movement proved a frustrating and probably doomed endeavor.

Initially, the revolution further consolidated labor's influence. The COB was created in the heady days after the revolutionary triumph and was a national labor union that claimed to represent the general voice of Bolivian workers. Under the independent umbrella organization of the COB, most of the country's labor unions became affiliated with the party. The most important functional unions included the miners, the urban factory and construction workers, the railroad and transportation workers, and the white-collar workers such as the teachers and other state and public employees. Membership in the 1960s totaled nearly 145,000 unionized workers.

The largest single union within the COB was the Bolivian Mine Workers' Federation, or FSTMB, with 52,000 members in 1960. Juan Lechín, the famed 1940s labor activist and leader, served both as the executive secretary of the FSTMB and the COB after the revolution. As long as Lechín remained in the party's top leadership and dominated both unions, the MNR was able to maintain an effective handle on labor. After 1956, however, when Lechín left the cabinet as the minister of mining and the MNR imposed the U.S.-IMF stabilization plan, this cooperation disappeared.

The MNR's hold over the radical labor unions had always been incomplete and tentative, because, in part, the party's organization structure was spotty at the local level. The MNR's top echelon formed the National Political

Juan Lechín was Bolivia's foremost labor activist and union leader. He served as minister of mining following the 1952 revolution. (Peter McFarren photo)

Committee. This nine-member core group served as the central executive organ of the party. Several hundred active members also provided leadership under the direction of the executive committee. On the regional and departmental level, MNR chapters and command centers coordinated the activities of the affiliated, but largely autonomous interest groups.

In the labor sector, party leaders were either subordinate to union leaders or union and party leaders were the selfsame individuals. The union leaders responded directly to the COB and circumvented the MNR's functional command centers at the shop steward level. Especially in the miners' unions, this parallel leadership structure proved the rule. At the root of this dualism was the persistent class-struggle ideology of the labor-left. Labor radicals, including those in the COB and the FSTMB, had always rejected the MNR's multiclass program (although these class concerns were temporarily muted immediately after the revolution). The workers' unions maintained that only the proletariat and organized unionists could be trusted to fight for labor's interests—and events proved them right.

After 1956, when the MNR lost influence within the COB, the party relentlessly pitted union against union. With this divide-and-rule strategy, the MNR exploited the ideological and class divisions within the labor movement. The strategy successfully splintered and weakened the labor-left. Eventually, however, the divisiveness that was sown backfired on the MNR.

Revolutionary Governance Mexican Style

We want to make a Mexican Revolution, but without ten years of Pancho Villa.

■

Walter Guevara Arze (Malloy 1970, 235)

The MNR modeled the party's governing structure along the populist and corporatist lines of the Mexican Revolution. The ultimate goal was to create a one-party dominant state that mirrored the governing style of the Partido Revolucionario Institucional (Institutional Revolutionary Party, or PRI), which had consolidated the Mexican Revolution. The party believed that it could consolidate control over the dominant interest groups—the middle class, the military, the peasant associations, and the labor unions—within its broad populist coalition.

To this end, MNR organizing cadres established a number of functional associations, such as unions or party cells, within these groups. Also, all major interest groups were linked to the party either directly or indirectly in a hierarchical fashion. But from the start this scheme presented difficulties that in Mexico's case, were handled with the threat or use of force. (Indeed, every Mexican president in the first two decades after the revolution had been a general with armies under his command.) Thus, under this system, from the beginning the MNR was split internally between the intractable forces of the party's right and left. On January 6, 1953—before the revolution was even a year old—the party's right wing had attempted a coup against the Paz presidency, which they saw as too leftist and in league with the COB communists.

Only the extremely adept political maneuvering of Paz and the centrist leadership kept a lid on the situation, at first by playing off the right against the left and later reversing the process. Perhaps this divide-and-rule strategy kept the MNR in power for as long as it did; nevertheless, the MNR has been severely criticized for its controlling, divisive, and manipulative governing style. Leading scholars have viewed the divide-and-rule strategy as the primary cause of the party's disintegration and downfall.

In peasant affairs, the critics argued that the MNR's approach varied little from the traditional patrimonial control and patronage politics of the past. The party simply replaced the old landlords and corrupt *políticos* with the MNR's co-opted local leaders, party men, or government-sponsored syndicates. The MNR's top-down governing style, moreover, did not encourage democratic development.

Another critical cause of the party's demise was the chronic leadership crisis within the party and its major interest groups. Rather than diffuse these leadership conflicts, the MNR crassly manipulated them to the party's advantage. This devious behavior was especially apparent in the case between the MNR and the peasant movement. The degree to which the MNR's divisive policies were the cause or the consequence of an inherent tendency toward interest group fragmentation remains unclear and debatable, but it is clear that the MNR actively exploited and exacerbated existing tensions. Christopher Mitchell and other critics of the MNR have concluded that divisiveness was endemic to the MNR's multiple personalities and schizophrenic populism.

The voter reform law also complicated the party's attempts to consolidate and institutionalize one-party hegemony. With thousands of additional voters, especially ones easily manipulated, governing majorities were hard to come by. The explosion in political participation and interest group mobilization that characterized the new mass politics proved extremely difficult to manage. It seemed that everyone had a vote and a demand. The MNR's populist strategy and bag of tricks did not always work.

Despite clever governing techniques, the MNR failed to become a cohesive party. Mitchell has concluded that the MNR "simply supplied a party label which legitimized interest-group claims to fragments of governmental power" (1977, 7). With so few inducements, the MNR could not sustain a national party, Mitchell has further argued. The party lacked ideology or military force to induce compliance. Instead, the MNR relied on patronage and rewards, but in an underdeveloped and poor country, there are insufficient rewards for everyone. In the end, carving up its power meant fragmenting the party.

If the MNR had established a cohesive party out of its tenuous coalition of factions, perhaps the revolution might have developed differently. But severely divided both personally and structurally, the party's leaders were unable to contain their own opportunism and the growing chaos. In important respects, Bolivia proved to be unlike Mexico and the MNR unlike the PRI.

Fragmentation of the MNR

In the months before and after the revolution, the MNR had been infiltrated with thousands of defectors from both the right and the left of the political spectrum as the traditional party system disintegrated. The party received a particularly large infusion of leftist adherents who had defected from the PIR or been brought in through the MNR's aggressive mobilization of labor. As a result, the MNR's major tendencies reflected three competing ideological visions and policy agendas: those of the conservative right, the pragmatic center, and the radical left.

The party also mirrored the contrasting personalities of four key leaders. The conservative right identified with Hernán Siles Zuazo and Walter Guevara Arze. The pragmatic but activist reformers of the center admired Víctor Paz Estenssoro. And the labor-left idolized the charismatic Juan Lechín. In an attempt to create party solidarity, a governing pact promised each leader the opportunity to run as the MNR's candidate for president. Paz Estenssoro and Siles Zuazo headed the first two MNR administrations from 1952 to 1960, after which the gentleman's agreement broke down.

It was understood originally that Guevara Arze would be nominated as the MNR candidate in 1960 and Juan Lechín in 1964. The increasing fragmentation of the party, ideologies, and strong personal egos intervened, however. Instead, Paz agreed to serve and was elected as president both in 1960 and 1964. To curtail the intraparty feuding and resolve the stalemate between the far right and far left of the party, a majority of the party temporized with Paz's continuation in office. This decision, which required a constitutional amendment, eventually led to an irrevocable split in the party.

Perhaps the biggest problem for the MNR and the revolution was the economy. By 1956, inflation held the MNR hostage. In four years, the cost of living had increased more than 20 times. The party's middle-class supporters, as well as labor, suffered. Internal domestic and party pressures and external pressure by the IMF and the Eisenhower administration convinced the MNR's more conservative and pragmatic sectors that without economic and political stabilization the revolution would fail.

Before President Paz left office in August 1956, he established a Monetary Stabilization Commission. The U.S. government sent the U.S. banker George Jackson Eder to advise the commission. The Eder mission and the IMF designed an austerity program that drastically reduced government spending and stabilized the currency. Within two years these measures had significantly reduced Bolivia's inflation.

The economic stabilization, however, was a bitter pill for the MNR's labor constituency to swallow. Reductions in government spending ended social welfare benefits and food subsidies. The free-market economic plan also froze wages and trimmed bureaucracy by firing thousands of workers in the public sector, including the mines. All state controls on pricing and monetary policy were removed and the market was allowed to dictate the value of goods, services, and foreign currency.

Although an economic success in large terms, the stabilization plan cost the party heavily. Critics of the austerity argued that instead of saving the revolution and the party, the stabilization destroyed both. Its supporters countered that without the stabilization plan and the $25 million provided by the United States to help ease the pain, a rightist coup by the Bolivian Socialist Falange (FSB) in 1956 might have overthrown the MNR and ended the revolution. At the same time, an additional cost of the survival of the MNR and the revolution was greater U.S. involvement in Bolivian affairs.

The MNR's presidential candidate in the elections of June 1956 was Hernán Siles Zuazo. The sober Siles agreed to implement the unpopular economic plan, although voters did not know this at the time. Three other parties that fielded candidates included the FSB, the Bolivian

Communist Party (PCB), and the Revolutionary Workers' Party (POR). Although the MNR won easily, the party's victory was less than expected. With 17 percent of the vote, the FSB emerged as Bolivia's second-largest political party.

The MNR swept the elections with 83 percent of the total, or 790,000 votes. The party had been especially strong among urban and middle-class whites, and this support increased over the next four years because of Siles's efforts. The economic stabilization primarily benefited the middle class, and they proved grateful. The MNR competed fiercely for the middle-class vote, and in the process, the MNR consciously distanced itself from its labor allies. Siles ended the cogovernment agreement with labor and turned the party's administration over to his middle-class loyalists. His government, moreover, directly attacked labor.

In July 1957, Lechín and the COB attempted a general strike to protest the stabilization plan that had been implemented in January. President Siles, however, succeeded in splitting the labor movement and aborting the strike. Progovernment unions were induced to violate Lechín's strike order. The strategy briefly helped the government and weakened Lechín's influence within the COB. The workers' union, which became polarized into radical and conservative unions, was also weakened. Lechín's ineffectiveness angered the factions within the COB, and they tried to unseat him.

The MNR government's tactics were not always noncoercive. At first, Siles tried to defuse the miners' strikes with his own hunger strikes or threats of resignation. Ultimately, he called in the army against both the miners and the peasants in 1959 and 1960. The economic crisis and the more conservative administration of Siles had encouraged the worst in the MNR's divisive policies. The party began to disintegrate.

Two new MNR factions were formed in 1957. One was the conservative Action in Defense of the MNR (Acción de Defensa del MNR). The second was the National Left of the MNR (Izquierda Nacional del MNR), a radical group that opposed Lechín. Then, in 1958, Lechín organized the Leftist Sector of the MNR (Sector Izquierda del MNR) to serve as militant labor's opposition voice in the Bolivian Congress.

As the 1960 elections approached, the MNR fragmented further. The party leadership violated its own agreed-on line of presidential succession. Guevara Arze was denied the party's presidential nomination, so he split with the MNR, forming his own MNR faction, the MNR Auténtico (MNRA), and running as a candidate in the election. (Afterward he split with the MNR completely and formed the Authentic

Revolutionary Party [Partido Revolucionario Auténtico, or PRA].) The MNR majority, however, compromised on a Paz-Lechín ticket in 1960. The bulk of the party believed that only Paz could reunify the party and maintain U.S. support. Lechín was appointed his running mate in order to guarantee labor peace or at least some leverage with the workers.

During Paz's second term, the MNR's disintegration continued. Despite the fact that Lechín was vice president and a prominent labor leader, the new government imposed further economic austerity measures. Among these was a multinational plan for the fiscal reform of the mines, known as the Triangular Plan. The ultimate showdown between Paz and Lechín over the plan mirrored the MNR's confrontation with labor. The crisis, according to James M. Malloy, also proved to be "the swan song of the labor left" (1970, 301).

The Triangular Plan's fiscal rationalization and restructuring of the state mining corporation, COMIBOL, provoked terrible conflict in the mines and forced Lechín to break with the government. The Bolivian mines had been losing money and according to foreign experts were mismanaged and draining the treasury. As the Triangular Plan unleashed market forces on the mining sector, wages were cut and jobs were lost. Labor was harshly "disciplined" while Paz was promised $30 million in aid from the United States, Germany, and the Inter-American Development Bank once his government implemented the plan.

It is easy to imagine that the financial incentives appealed to the economist in Paz. He had planned to refinance the revolution and stimulate economic development with $205 million in U.S. economic assistance promised over the next three years. He had also hoped that a bigger economic pie and a new breed of MNR technocrats would rescue the MNR and the revolution. Instead, the mines erupted in violence, and the MNR's political opposition hit the streets in protest. The Paz government imposed a state of martial law and cracked down on the dissent.

Factionalism increased before and after the 1964 elections, and Paz Estenssoro organized his personal lobby to promote his reelection. In 1961, a constitutional amendment permitting two consecutive presidential terms had been passed. Paz's reelection, however, violated the MNR's electoral pact for a second time. Lechín was next in line to run for president, but the United States and the conservative wing of the MNR opposed him. In addition, the MNR feared another coup attempt by the rightist FSB if Lechín were elected.

In the final showdown, the political ambition of Paz won out. Having been passed over, Lechín founded the Revolutionary Party of the

THE HOSTAGE CRISIS

In fall 1963, the government of Víctor Paz Estenssoro fired more than 1,000 miners in the Catavi–Siglo XX mining complex. In December, before the miners could launch a violent protest, the government arrested two leaders. In retaliation, the miners seized 17 hostages, three of them citizens of the United States.

James M. Malloy recounts that the miners threatened to execute the hostages and march on La Paz if the government did not improve conditions in the mines. Juan Lechín, "once the second most powerful man of the revolution and at that time vice president of the nation, was powerless to avert the crisis or to negotiate a settlement favorable to the embattled miners" (1970, 301).

President Paz ordered in the military and peasant unions from Cochabamba. On December 15, Lechín and the miners were forced to surrender unconditionally. The power of labor had been definitively broken.

Nationalist Left (Partido Revolucionario de la Izquierda Nacionalista, PRIN). Siles was not pleased by the turn of events either and also deserted the MNR's fold. He organized his own anti-Paz faction, the Bloc for the Defense of the Revolution. Both Siles and Lechín—representing the party's right and left—boycotted the 1964 elections.

By 1964, the MNR had facilitated the military's reentry into politics. The party had destroyed its mass base among the workers, alienated its conservative and middle-class supporters by its divisiveness, and rehabilitated and elevated the military to a new position of legitimacy and prominence. Therefore, when Paz found himself rejected by two-thirds of the party, he agreed to a military man as his running mate, the leader of the MNR's military cell, air force general René Barrientos Ortuño.

8

THE MILITARY AND COUNTERREVOLUTION (1964–1982)

We do not vacillate in pointing out that weapons in the fists of proletarians constitute the greatest guarantee of democracy.

■

Bolivian Workers' Central (Mitchell 1977, 111)

By 1964, the National Revolution and the MNR were in an advanced stage of disintegration. The forces of counterrevolution took over, and militarism ravaged the country during most of the next 18 years. Although this brutal period of military rule appeared to descend precipitously and inadvertently, appearances were deceptive. The MNR's shifting relationships with the labor-left, the United States, and the Bolivian armed forces greatly influenced this unfortunate turning point in the revolution.

The challenge of consolidating the revolution had proven to be a huge task—certainly more complex than the destruction of the old regime and social order had been. Indeed, this was the ultimate test for the staying power of the MNR. Although great reforms had been realized, much remained undone when the return of military rule stalled and reversed the course of the revolution politically, socially, and economically.

Perhaps, as experts observed, the MNR's modernizing revolution never had more than a slight chance. James M. Malloy concluded more than three decades ago that the Bolivian case demonstrates the overwhelming difficulties that poor and underdeveloped countries confront in "completing a development-oriented revolution" (1970, 341). Malloy held that the MNR's efforts had fallen short and that the

National Revolution of 1952 remained an "uncompleted revolution." In great part, the rise of militarism not only interrupted the process but also ensured the revolution's failure.

The "New" Military

From the outset, the victorious MNR leaders had remained suspicious of the old military, and there was heated debate and intraparty dissension concerning the future role of the armed forces in postrevolutionary society. The radical left believed that the armed forces should be dismantled permanently and replaced by revolutionary worker and peasant militias. During the long revolutionary struggle, these popular militias had arisen almost spontaneously, been placed under nominal MNR control, and been loyal to the MNR revolution. Moreover, only a truly people's army, the left argued, would reflect the will of the people and protect the revolution in difficult times.

The conservative and pragmatic sectors of the MNR, however, believed that the military establishment was necessary to national development and defense and could and should be rehabilitated. A "new" military, pruned of its reactionary officers and integrated into the party's structure and patronage system, they insisted, could protect both the country and the revolution. Although the solution to the problem was basically a compromise, the conservatives and moderates won: The traditional military was reformed.

At the same time that President Paz Estenssoro reorganized the old army, he set about to weaken the military's autonomous power and subordinate the institution to the MNR and civilian authority. To this end, Paz maintained and strengthened the coercive resources that peasant and worker militias held. He intended to hold these revolutionary militias in reserve as the MNR's shock troops should the party need to offset the military.

The army's size was greatly diminished, and the ranks of existing officers were trimmed by 20 percent. The rank and file was cut by 75 percent, falling from the high of 20,000 men in uniform to 5,000. The oligarchy had forced the pro-MNR officers who had supported Villarroel and RADEPA into early retirement in 1947, but Paz reinstated these sympathetic officers to active duty.

The military's institutional mission was reassessed, as well. For the first time Bolivia's armed forces were expected to actively assist in national development. Indeed, modernization and development were to become the military's primary function. In June 1952, when the military's new role was elaborated publicly, the stated goal was to create a "productive army" that contributed to the country's progress and welfare. The military was given the tasks of constructing new roads and exploring and colonizing remote territories. The military cleared land, built schools, and distributed food around the country. Troops served as roving labor brigades to boost agricultural production. As James M. Malloy noted, the new Bolivian army became one of the first "civic action" and "modernizing" militaries in Latin America.

The revamped military also contributed to civic education in the countryside. An important part of the military's new role was to help incorporate the mass of indigenous people into citizenship and national life. This civic and educational outreach became a more natural task as the social composition of the armed forces became more diversified. After the old military academy was shut down in the wake of the revolution, the Instituto Coronel Villarroel opened. "As part of the new approach," James M. Malloy explains, the new academy welcomed "lower-class mestizos and educated Indians" (1970, 181).

The MNR, well aware that a hostile army had kept them from power between 1947 and 1952, recruited heavily within the new army. The MNR organized party cells and openly promoted officers sympathetic to the MNR. Such was the party's confidence that Paz and Siles also permitted the size of the army to steadily increase after 1956. The MNR still had ties to the native and civilian militias; however, after 1964, these militias often were not under the control of the party. Many militias, especially in the peasant sector, became linked directly to the military and repressive military governments. As a result, popular militias became highly politicized and manipulated. They fought against popular causes and, ultimately, their own best interests. Feuds and confrontations among the militias allied with the government and those in opposition were prevalent and destabilizing.

After 1956, the Bolivian military's civic action functions were supported with extensive U.S. military training and foreign assistance. The new U.S. administrations, especially that of John F. Kennedy, favored the civic action model of civilian-military relations in Latin America. The United States viewed the rehabilitated military as an unassailable nationalistic bulwark against communist subversion in the hemisphere. As the careful research of Christopher Mitchell has discovered, the Kennedy/Johnson administrations assisted in the reorganization and training of the new Bolivian armed forces to the tune of $12.4 million in military assistance from 1960 to 1965 (1977, 91).

All U.S. military funding was in the form of grants or gifts to the Bolivian government. Beginning with small grants in 1958, U.S. military aid jumped to more than $3 million in 1967. Overall assistance approximated $19 million over this period (Mitchell 1977, 91). Critics suggest that beefing up the Bolivian armed forces, albeit as peacekeepers and road builders, was a mistake. The training and assistance restored the military's confidence and transformed the recently humbled institution into a powerful adversary of civilian governments. Moreover, despite the unconditional support that the U.S. ambassador Douglas Henderson accorded President Paz, some analysts suggest that the U.S. military mission in Bolivia might have given a military coup the green light. In any case, historical events proved that the military was discontented with its new role as peacekeeper and civic do-gooder. Some senior officers clearly had the presidency in their sights.

The Restorative Revolution

Although social and political chaos ostensibly provoked the coup against President Paz, he had unwittingly facilitated his own downfall. Paz's reelection to a third term had been widely unpopular in the country and had fragmented his party. With the MNR and civilian parties weakened, the military had pressured Paz to appoint a military man as his vice president. After the elections, the diffuse but extensive opposition to the MNR focused on Paz himself. Many viewed the rump MNR as corrupt and Paz as a dictator. General René Barrientos Ortuño, chief of the air force and now vice president, was a Trojan horse within the government.

Strikes and demonstrations in late October 1964 brought the popular discontent to a head. On October 29, President Paz ordered the army to crush a strike by the miners of the large Huanuni-Catavi mining complex. The government also forcefully repressed the striking teachers and the students of San Andrés University, in La Paz, who marched in solidarity with the teachers. With the opposition political parties stirring up social discontent, the political atmosphere, according to Mitchell, was one of "national crisis" (1977, 95).

The moment was opportune for General Alfredo Ovando Candía, commander in chief of the army, and Vice President Barrientos to act. The Cochabamba army garrison rebelled, and in rapid succession, major army units around the country joined the rebellion. President Paz quickly realized that unless he called out the MNR's popular militias, he would not survive in office. But rather than risk the certain bloodbath, Paz resigned on November 4. He flew into exile, first to Lima, Peru, and later to the United States.

The political parties had been cleverly courted by the coup plotters and expected the military to establish a transitional government and quickly return the country to civilian rule. In particular, the disaffected MNR faction leaders Siles Zuazo and Guevara Arze on the right and Lechín on the left had supported the military takeover as an expedient way to rid the party of Paz. The majority of the MNR leadership was thus terribly disillusioned. Only one MNR faction survived the coup: the MNRA of Walter Guevara Arze, transformed almost immediately into the PRA, became the official representative of the MNR party under the new military government. With this PRA/MNRA alliance, Barrientos was able to drape the mantle of revolutionary legitimacy around his shoulders and at the same time exile the three top MNR leaders, Lechín, Siles, and Paz, who might threaten his regime.

Generals Barrientos and Ovando announced that the new government constituted a "restorative revolution." The coup leaders characterized the military's action as a necessary and valiant rescue mission that had saved the revolution from the MNR's feuding and corruption. The military leaders also justified the coup in the face of increasing danger of a communist takeover by the striking workers and Marxist left. Barrientos portrayed himself and the military as the authentic guardians of the revolution.

The new government became known as the Second Republic. Barrientos and Ovando formed an all-military cabinet on November 5, 1964. Two junior members of the cabinet were Colonel Juan José Torres and Colonel Hugo Banzer Suárez. Both men became prominent leaders of disaffected military factions in the decades ahead. The military junta, headed by Barrientos and Ovando, ruled de facto until the presidential elections of July 1966. In these controlled elections, Barrientos emerged as Bolivia's constitutionally elected president.

The Barrientos government was both loved and hated. While his harsh repression of the miners and political left generated a much-deserved opprobrium, the president's charismatic and populist leadership style endeared him to the peasant masses. A native of Cochabamba and fluent in Quechua, Barrientos spoke to the peasants in their language literally and politically. He seemed to understand their concerns and promised them governmental support. Barrientos assiduously cultivated the large peasant political bloc. He flew around the country in his helicopter from one remote village to the other wooing powerful Indian caciques and their followers. Not surprisingly, Barrientos became known as the "peasant president."

THE GENERAL OF THE PEOPLE

The flamboyant president René Barrientos Ortuño earned the glowing epithet "General of the People" from his many supporters, especially among the Bolivian peasantry. He was born in Tarata near the city of Cochabamba on May 30, 1919. Barrientos entered the military academy but was expelled as a supporter of Colonel Germán Busch. Later readmitted, he graduated as a second lieutenant in 1943 and was among the younger officers who backed the reformist military coup of Major Gualberto Villarroel that year. He trained in Bolivia's Military College of Aviation and in the United States, earning his wings in 1945. He also participated in the first National Indigenous Congress that year.

An MNR loyalist, Barrientos was cashiered from the military in 1949 but was reassigned as a captain after the National Revolution of 1952. A daring pilot, he flew critical missions for the revolutionary cause, surviving one nearly fatal crash. He was considered a true *MNRista* and rapidly rose in the esteem of the party and military to become a general of the air force. Although he headed the MNR's military cell and was elected vice president in 1964, Barrientos turned against Juan Lechín and Víctor Paz Estenssoro and the radical sectors of the party.

Barrientos believed that his mission was to continue the military reforms of Busch and Villarroel and to effect a responsible revolution "equidistant from the oligarchy and demagoguery" of the left (Morales 1988, 40–41). Whatever his intentions, Barrientos presided over a counterrevolution that entrenched a new oligarchy of mining industrialists, urban merchants, and agribusiness interests. Through systematic military repression, he temporarily controlled labor activism; nevertheless, his hold on power became shaky by 1968. Historians speculate that had he not died in a helicopter crash on April 27, 1969, Barrientos would have been overthrown.

The personal alliances that Barrientos formed with the indigenous bloc paid off handsomely for his government and ultimately severed many of the MNR's organizational links with Indian communities. The president substituted his charisma and military populism for the party's weak populist rhetoric. The peasants' personal loyalties to Barrientos formed the basis of a long-term military-peasant cooperation. In 1966, Barrientos institutionalized these new political ties in the Military-Campesino Pact. This formal agreement allied the country's two powerful and basically conservative political forces.

A family of street vendors, selling their homemade pottery (Kathy S. Leonard photo)

The military-peasant alliance served not only as the populist foundation for the Barrientos government but for future military rulers. It was necessary for Barrientos and subsequent military presidents to carefully nourish and manage this conservative coalition. The peasantry was the only social force in the country large enough and potentially powerful enough to challenge the army itself. The loyalty of both interest groups had to be bought with special privileges and promises. Barrientos assured the loyalty of the military's officers with generous defense spending, showering them with new weapons, training, and advancement opportunities. He won over the campesinos with lavish local celebrations and well-orchestrated land distribution ceremonies in dozens of rural communities across the country.

In addition to the government's political interests, the Military-Peasant Pact furthered the military's aggressive national security policy. Through the pact, the peasantry pledged to loyally support and defend the military against leftist subversion. The campesinos were naturals for this countersubversive role. From the outset, the primary concern of the indigenous peasantry had been agrarian reform and land titles. Once these central goals had been achieved, the peasant bloc became politically conservative and malleable. As long as Barrientos and the military protected, or professed to protect, the agrarian reform, the indigenous leaders and communities remained loyal to the government.

The National Confederation of Peasant Workers of Bolivia (Confederación Nacional de Trabajadores Campesinos de Bolivia, or CNTCB), founded in 1953, had aggregated the interests of numerous autonomous and competitive indigenous organizations. The MNR had crassly manipulated this force and turned peasant militias against angry miners. In March 1959, for example, the MNR government employed 800 armed peasants to beat down the miners' strike near Oruro. Indeed, the MNR's urban politicians were the first to break up the potent miner-peasant-student coalition, which had contributed to the success of the party and the revolution.

Barrientos continued this pattern of peasant co-optation, control, and mobilization, but with a new twist. As with the MNR, the pact permitted the Barrientos government to launch the organized peasantry against the regime's political opponents. The critical difference was that the local indigenous caciques pledged personal loyalty directly to Barrientos and to the military. The Indian leaders formally recognized Barrientos as the sole "maximum leader" of the country's peasantry. Moreover, Barrientos pitted the countryside, from where his power emanated, against the cities, the stronghold of the MNR's middle-class base. In this manner, the peasantry served as a populist, militant force that backed Barrientos and the military against the miners, leftist parties, and urban social and labor activists.

Despite his conservative tendencies, Barrientos refused to ally with like-minded political parties, especially the ultraconservative FSB. His political coalition, moreover, excluded labor and the bulk of the MNR. As a result, his rule suffered from a major institutional weakness. He attempted to remedy the organizational vacuum by founding his own political party; however, his Popular Christian Movement (Movimiento Popular Cristiano, or MPC) was mainly a personal electoral vehicle. As a party, it lacked a clear ideology, program, or organizational structure.

In the run-up to the 1966 elections, the MPC expanded into the Bolivian Revolutionary Front (Frente de la Revolución Boliviana, or FRB) and drew various political groups within its fold. The FRB's electoral slate represented the peasant confederation and various political parties, including the PRA, the PIR, and the Social Democratic Party (Partido Social Demócrata, or PSD). The FRB candidate for the vice presidency was Luis Siles Salinas, half-brother of Hernán Siles Zuazo and leader of the PSD.

The FRB coalition swept the elections with 54 percent of the 1.2 million votes cast. The peasantry represented the largest voting bloc for Barrientos. His FRB drew only 16 percent of the urban vote. No other party or coalition drew a sizable slice of the electorate in opposition. The Falangist coalition polled only 11 percent of the vote, and two factions of the MNR received 12 percent between them. In protest, the rest of the MNR abstained, and key parties of the left cast blank ballots. In even worse shape, the political remnants of the prerevolutionary parties of the oligarchy, represented by the PURS and the Liberals, failed to generate even token representation.

The electoral success of the FRB proved ephemeral, however. A controlling military man, Barrientos quickly became frustrated by the instability of the multiparty system and the vagaries of civilian politics. In 1968, a determined Barrientos followed the path of his military reformer predecessors Busch and Villarroel. He formed an official state party, the Partido Unico, but by the end of the year, as discontent continued to rise, Barrientos resorted to outright military rule.

Critics of his regime blamed Barrientos for the rise of a new Rosca, or oppressive oligarchy intimately associated with the United States. Barrientos had allied himself with an up-and-coming economic elite, which included urban industrialists and merchants and agribusiness promoters. This alliance had been conditioned on keeping labor in its place by whatever means. Also, the Barrientos government had passed the controversial 1964 investment code, which provided privileges and protections to foreign investors such as Gulf Oil and United States Steel. In the eyes of the revolutionary nationalists and radical left, this act compromised the economic independence that had been the central aspiration of the revolution.

Barrientos was also criticized for his aggressive implementation of the later stages of the controversial Triangular Plan. The multinational plan for economic reorganization

César Lora was a leftist union leader and miner who was killed in a clash between miners and government military forces in May 1965. (Photo from Palabra Encendida, 1996, by Víctor Montoya)

forced the mines to become profitable by severely trimming the bureaucracy, workers, and salaries and benefits. As unrest escalated in opposition to these draconian policies, the military took over direct management of the nationalized mining industry. In 1966, COMIBOL realized a profit for the first time since nationalization, but the social and political costs were extremely high.

This strict economic rationalization of the mines pitted the government's military force against the organized opposition of the miners' unions and armed militias. In March, May, June, and September of 1965 there were increasingly violent clashes, and the number of deaths mounted with each encounter. In May, after scores of miners had been fired by COMIBOL, at least 48 died and hundreds were wounded. Leftist union leaders, like Juan Lechín, were jailed or exiled, and at least one, César Lora, was killed. Sources vary on the true count, but the death toll in June ranged from 30 to 200.

Che Guevara and His *Foco* Strategy

Bolivia will sacrifice itself so that revolutionary conditions can be created in neighboring countries.

■

Ernesto "Che" Guevara (Anderson 1997, 703)

When the charismatic Argentine revolutionary Ernesto "Che" Guevara targeted Bolivia in his continental guerrilla offensive, he believed Bolivia would become the strategic center, or *foco,* for anti-imperialist revolutions throughout Latin America. In his revolutionary writings, this hero of the Cuban Revolution declared that Latin America would become "another Vietnam" with its center in Bolivia. He expected the United States to overreact and respond to a guerrilla insurgency there with full military force. Furthermore, he believed that the United States, once engaged, would become mired in a protracted war of national liberation against a more determined indigenous foe. Just as he believed U.S. defeat in Vietnam was imminent, he predicted as much in Latin America too.

Che Guevara detailed his guerrilla strategy in his famous treatise *Guerrilla Warfare,* which he based on the successful revolutionary insurgency of Fidel Castro in Cuba, where Guevara had cut his teeth in 1959. As Castro's chief lieutenant, he had fought bravely with the Cuban guerrilla army in the hills of the Sierra Maestra. In the early 1960s, Guevara distilled the lessons of the Cuban Revolution and applied them to all of

Latin America. He believed that the lofty Andes would become the Sierra Maestra of South America and that revolution there would first come to Bolivia. From Bolivia's location in the heart of the continent, Guevara believed that insurrection would spread like a raging contagion to every country in the hemisphere. Eventually, overwhelmed and overextended, the forces of U.S. imperialism would be decisively defeated.

In Bolivia, Guevara miscalculated terribly and paid with his life, becoming a martyr to radicals and revolutionaries the world over. What went wrong? A better question might be what had not gone wrong. Guevara selected Bolivia almost incidentally, because of geography, but ironically, the geographical location and topography of the guerrillas' zone of operations facilitated their defeat. The guerrillas first established their main base

THE REVOLUTIONARY

Ernesto "Che" Guevara, the legendary revolutionary, was born in Argentina on June 14, 1928. He studied to become a medical doctor and after graduation, began his exploration of the Americas. He arrived in Bolivia shortly after the revolution in 1953 and was impressed by the popular fervor. In 1954, he witnessed the overthrow of Jacobo Arbenz Guzmán and Guatemala's revolutionary government in a coup orchestrated by the Central Intelligence Agency (CIA). In Mexico City in 1955, he met Fidel Castro, and in December 1956, Guevara returned with the exiled lawyer and leader to Cuba to become one of the original guerrillas who overthrew the dictatorship of Fulgencio Batista and brought Castro to power in 1959.

After victory, Guevara remained Castro's right-hand man. Castro appointed him to important economic posts and diplomatic missions for the revolutionary government. As the minister of industry, Guevara shaped Cuba's socialist economic policy. Above all, Guevara attempted to create a "new socialist man" dedicated to the ideals of the revolution, but when the Cuban economy faltered, a restive Guevara resigned from the government.

In early 1965, Guevara set out on a personal mission to bring revolution to underdeveloped countries. A roving revolutionary, he participated in national liberation movements across Africa. He returned to South America and Bolivia in 1966 to lead the guerrilla movement that he hoped would spark a continental revolution against imperialism. His life was dedicated to one central purpose: the defeat of colonial and imperialist oppression and the victory of socialism.

in the isolated and wild southeastern region near the Ñancahuazú River and later moved north into the barren and rugged Vallegrande region near the Río Grande basin. The terrain was so hostile that maintaining the constant mobility demanded of rural guerrilla warfare was near impossible. To a great extent, this harsh environment of raging rivers and steep and dense jungle canyons defeated Guevara's hapless band.

The political and social conditions were also inhospitable. The indigenous people of this region spoke Guaraní, and the guerrillas—even the Bolivian recruits—had difficulty in communicating with some of them. The local people were very suspicious of the guerrillas, many of whom spoke a foreign-accented Spanish, and alerted the authorities immediately of their presence. None of the local peasantry joined the insurgency. The peasants of the region supported the Barrientos regime, and most had had their land aspirations fulfilled by the 1952 revolution. Guevara and his men might as well have been appealing to the deaf for all the resonance that their revolutionary message had with the local people; indeed, Guevara wrote in his diary that the region's inhabitants were "as impenetrable as rocks."

The attitudes of the general Bolivian population toward the guerrillas ranged from cautious and critical to fearful and antagonistic. The guerrilla force numbered only around 40 to 50 combatants, and the fact that nearly half were Cuban or non-Bolivian worked against them. The Barrientos government effectively appealed to Bolivian nationalism, further isolating the guerrillas from the people. In his writings, Guevara had repeatedly cautioned that the support of the people is "an indispensable condition" for success. Nevertheless, not only did the guerrillas lack the assistance of the rural people of the region, but also they were denied any popular support from the cities.

Guevara and the *foco* strategy were abandoned and betrayed by the pro-Soviet faction of the Bolivian Communist Party, and the revolutionaries mistakenly never established reliable links with other potentially sympathetic political groups. For example, there was strong urban opposition to Barrientos among the labor-left, and the miners were in open rebellion. The military government, in fact, claimed that the miners were coordinating with the guerrillas and publicized these false claims to justify the terrible repression in the mines. Except for a handful of mine workers, Communist Party members, and students who had joined the guerrilla band initially, however, Guevara had never connected with the authentic sources of discontent in the country.

In the midst of the guerrilla threat from Guevara in the southeast of the country, a major strike erupted at the Catavi–Siglo XX mining complex in June 1967. A panicked Barrientos ordered the army to repress the protesters with brute military force. This deadly reprisal in which nearly 90 people died, including women and children, became known as the San Juan Massacre. Barrientos may have been unduly alarmed and overreacted because of the revolutionary insurgency. Guevara, for his part, when he heard of the massacre, issued a communiqué that was never received expressing solidarity with the miners.

Barrientos aggressively targeted the miners and the labor-left as communist agitators and enemies of Bolivia. Imbued with U.S. anti-communist doctrine and counterinsurgency training, the armed forces interpreted political opposition of any kind as outright communist subversion. To stem the potential Marxist threat, Barrientos instituted an offensive policy of military intervention into the labor movement after 1965. The goal was to subordinate labor by destroying its leadership and autonomy. The two major unions, the FSTMB and the COB, were placed under the military's administrative control. By 1967, the real fear was that unrest in the mines could spark general opposition to the government; however, as Guevara discovered, "the elements in Bolivia that could threaten public order—guerrillas, miners, students and leftist political groups—had failed to coalesce" (Ryan 1998, 98).

The Bolivian army's counterinsurgency campaign might not have been successful without extensive U.S. economic and military assistance. Guevara had selected Bolivia for his first guerrilla *foco* in part because Bolivia's military was considered one of the weakest in the region. Although the army had been rebuilt and strengthened after the revolution and the defense budget doubled by Barrientos, it was not prepared to handle a guerrilla threat. As soon as news of Guevara's and his guerrillas' presence reached him, Barrientos lobbied hard for high-tech U.S. military training and aid. The U.S. government and U.S. ambassador Douglas Henderson feared that Barrientos would overreact and play into the guerrillas' hands. The United States consciously sought to avoid the mistakes of Vietnam.

Instead of pushing the panic button when the guerrilla operation was first confirmed, Richard L. Harris explains, "[T]he Washington policy makers responded to the situation in a very uncharacteristic manner for the times—they played it cool" (2000, 214). Although various Bolivian sources and journalistic accounts have portrayed the U.S. role in the campaign against Guevara in Bolivia as primary and decisive, Harris concludes "that *direct* American involvement in the entire episode was minimal" (2000, 214). He dismisses all claims of how the

THE BOLIVIAN DIARY

After Che Guevara was captured, his intimate diary fell into the hands of the Bolivian military and the CIA. When the existence of the diary was announced on October 10, 1967, publishers, anxious to make a deal for exclusive rights to its publication, descended on Bolivia. Reportedly, General Alfredo Ovando wanted to sell it to the highest bidder, and at first, some offers approached $500,000; however, as excerpts became public and copyright protection became suspect, the big bidders dropped out.

In Cuba, Fidel Castro claimed to have a copy, which Bolivian president Barrientos irately disputed. But it was revealed a year later that Antonio Arguedas, the Bolivian minister of government and both a CIA agent in the Barrientos government and a Castro sympathizer, had sent a clandestine copy to Fidel Castro after Guevara's capture. The Cubans published and released the diary to the world in July 1968, distributing hundreds of thousands of free copies.

The diary became an international sensation. Chronicling the grueling 11-month guerrilla struggle, its pages revealed Che the revolutionary and Che the man. The guerrillas endured incredible deprivations, especially near the end. Finding food and water became an interminable struggle. On one occasion, desperately thirsty and already fainting from dehydration, men drank their own urine. Severe diarrhea and cramps afflicted them afterward. Unkempt and malnourished, they suffered from scurvy, parasites, and malaria. During the last months, Guevara was nearly incapacitated by severe asthma. In early August he had exhausted his supply of antiasthma injections and resorted to an intravenous novocaine injection to get through an attack.

Central Intelligence Agency (CIA) captured Guevara as without factual foundation.

The counterinsurgency campaign against the guerrilla *foco,* however, indisputably necessitated intimate cooperation among the Bolivian military, the U.S. Department of Defense, and the CIA. U.S. military assistance and training, already extensive after 1962, increased significantly with the guerrilla threat. Early in April 1967, according to Harris, the first installment of U.S. military equipment of light arms, ammunition, sophisticated communications equipment, and helicopters arrived in Santa Cruz. More important, the United States set up a special camp,

Confessing that physically he was "a real mess" and had "lost control," Guevara, nevertheless, rallied his men on August 8, with prophetic words: "Whoever feels unable to withstand it should say so. We have reached a moment when great decisions are called for. This type of struggle provides us the opportunity to become revolutionaries, the highest level of the human species" (1994, 250). Conditions and Guevara's health continued to deteriorate.

On August 13, Guevara wrote, "Since yesterday my asthma has been getting worse; I now take three tablets a day. My foot [which had developed an oozing abscess on the heel] is almost all better." The entry the next day reveals Guevara's extreme physical and mental anguish after the army discovered his cache of medicines and supplies. "A black day. . . . Now I am doomed to suffer asthma for an indefinite time" (1994, 252–53).

On August 28, there was another despondent entry: "A dreary and somewhat troubled day. ... We finally slaughtered the little mare, after she had accompanied us for two difficult months. I did all I could to save her, but our hunger was getting worse. Now, at least, the only thing we suffer from is thirst. It appears we will not reach water tomorrow either" (1994, 260).

The last entry held little indication that the end was near. "Today marks eleven months since our guerrilla inauguration. The day went by without complications, bucolically, until 12:30 P.M., when an old woman, tending her goats, entered the canyon where we were camped and had to be taken prisoner" (1994, 295). All that the guerrillas learned from the old woman was that they were not far from La Higuera. The next day, October 8, 1967, they were ambushed.

La Esperanza, in the area to train a crack regiment of 640 Bolivian Rangers in counterinsurgency warfare.

Wearing green berets and smart uniforms, the well-equipped and trained Bolivian Rangers, known as the Second Manchego Ranger Battalion, were ready to engage the guerrillas by mid-September; however, the regular Bolivian army had already handed Guevara one of his worst defeats on August 31. Ten guerrillas under the leadership of the Cuban recruit Joaquín had been ambushed and killed in an attempt to cross the rain-swollen Masicurí River and rejoin the main guerrilla force. The victims included the celebrated East German agent Haydée

Tamara Bunke, known as "Tania," who had helped establish the *foco* and had briefly visited the guerrilla camp.

In early October, with expert intelligence provided by Hispanic CIA advisers (primarily Cuban exiles) and the aid of the local people, the Rangers cornered and captured Guevara and his comrades in a steep canyon near the tiny adobe settlement of La Higuera. A wounded Guevara was interrogated by the CIA operative Félix Rodríguez (an anti-Castro Bay of Pigs survivor) and then executed by the Bolivians. Guevara's body was wrapped in tarp and strapped to the landing skid of a helicopter, then flown to the Eighth Army Division's forward command post in the town of Vallegrande. There his death was officially revealed to the world.

WHO KILLED CHE GUEVARA?

Popular opinion in Latin America and among international leftists held that the CIA had ordered the death of Ernesto "Che" Guevara. The excellent study by Henry Butterfield Ryan concludes otherwise: "Contrary to widespread opinion, the CIA did not kill Guevara, but neither did it nor any other branch of the U.S. government try to save him, despite subsequent claims by some officials that Washington wanted him alive" (1998, 10).

Although eyewitness accounts conflict to this day, unclassified documents have resolved some mysteries surrounding Guevara's death and exposed the fabrications that President Barrientos and the Bolivian military concocted to hide his execution. Intervention by the U.S. ambassador in La Paz might have saved the revolutionary's life, but Ambassador Douglas Henderson claimed that he only learned of Guevara's capture after the guerrilla fighter had been killed. Ryan insists that U.S. officials knew of Guevara's capture by evening of the day before his execution. American officials could have intervened and saved Guevara had they acted expeditiously and decisively.

Félix Rodríguez, the CIA agent at La Higuera, argued that his instructions had been to keep Guevara alive, but that the Bolivian commander had received an order from army chief General Ovando to execute Guevara immediately. The Bolivian military feared that Guevara would become another international cause célèbre like Régis Debray. A French Marxist and theoretician of guerrilla warfare, Debray had been caught leaving the guerrilla *foco* in April and was being prosecuted as an insurgent in a Bolivian court.

Over the next months, the Bolivian Rangers continued to hunt down the handful of remaining guerrillas. Five of the 17 ambushed had escaped immediate capture. Three Cubans made it back to the Caribbean island in March 1968, and two Bolivians were killed in 1969. The Bolivian army, exuding its newfound pride and confidence, had defeated the legendary Che Guevara and discredited the Cuban model of revolution. In his eulogy for El Che on October 18, Castro instead insisted that "they who sing victory are mistaken." This "lucky blow" that eliminated Guevara's physical life, he proclaimed, did not represent "the defeat of his ideas, the defeat of his tactics, the defeat of his guerrilla concepts" (Kornbluh n.d.). Nevertheless, after Guevara's untimely death at 39 years of age, Castro abandoned the strategy of exporting his revolution.

Ryan speculates that the United States played the role of Pontius Pilate and left Guevara's fate to the Bolivians. He reports that according to the CIA station chief in La Paz, the United States feared that an imprisoned Guevara would become a potent rallying cry for revolutionaries everywhere. Consequently, upon orders delivered at 1:10 P.M. on October 9, 1967, a Bolivian sergeant (accounts vary as to whether reluctantly or willingly) entered the one-room schoolhouse where the army had been holding Guevara and shot and killed him. Reportedly, Guevara's last words were "Know this now, you are killing a man" (Ryan 1998, 154).

Barrientos and the Bolivians put out several misleading and premature reports informing reporters that Guevara had been killed in battle before the execution order had actually been carried out. A declassified memo to U.S. president Lyndon Johnson on October 9, from Walt Rostow, the national security adviser, confirmed this and noted: "President Barrientos at 10:00 A.M., October 9, told a group of newsmen, but not for publication until further notice, that Che Guevara is dead." The Bolivians kept to this story publicly and insisted that the national army alone had caught Guevara. On October 13, Barrientos affirmed that the successful counterinsurgency operation had been an exclusively Bolivian victory, which had been achieved without special foreign assistance.

Back in Washington, D.C., Rostow wrapped up the affair in a memo to Johnson dated October 11, stating, "CIA tells us that the latest information is that Guevara was taken alive. After a short interrogation to establish his identity, General Ovando—Chief of the Bolivian Armed Forces—ordered him shot. I regard this as stupid, but it is understandable from a Bolivian standpoint" (Kornbluh n.d.; Ryan 1998, 139).

Also after Guevara's death, Barrientos's hold on the government and the military weakened. A scandal sparked by Guevara's diary provoked violent demonstrations and a major political crisis in July and August 1968. By 1969, many found the social and political costs of Barrientos's rule unacceptable. With U.S. diplomatic and military support, repression had intensified. Furthermore, obsessed with anti-communism and internal security, the U.S. government had approved the deployment of U.S.-supported military units in the mines and had applauded Barrientos's no-nonsense response to social unrest. Despite steady growth on the economic front, the increase in foreign debt and the unregulated foreign exploitation of the country's natural resources had severely compromised economic nationalism.

Although Guevara's defeat was a feather in the cap of Barrientos, the victory also strengthened the role of the armed forces. In an internal memo of October 1967, Thomas L. Hughes, the Cuban specialist in the State Department's Bureau of Intelligence and Research, predicted the military's political activism. He feared that "victory could also stir political ambitions among army officers who were directly involved in the anti-guerrilla campaign and who may now see themselves as the saviors of the republic" (Kornbluh n.d.). The reformist military and especially Barrientos's original coconspirator in the 1964 coup, General Alfredo Ovando Candía, had become restless. And some of the younger officers were ambivalent and concerned about the increased U.S. influence in the country. Only the sudden death of Barrientos in a helicopter crash on April 27, 1969, delayed the military's response.

Revolution from Above

After Barrientos's demise, Vice President Siles Salinas briefly headed an interim civilian government; however, with street demonstrations and renewed partisan bickering between the MNR and the FSB, the political climate continued to deteriorate. Elections were planned and everyone hoped to win. The impatient General Alfredo Ovando Candía refused to tolerate civilian chaos, especially after it became clear that the odds of being elected president were against him. Claiming the need for "national pacification," on September 26, 1969, he overthrew Siles. As commander of the Bolivian armed forces, General Ovando remained the undisputed power behind the presidents. If anyone had entertained doubts, the coup demonstrated that as long as the military and the government remained unified, the government in power would stay in power.

An enigmatic and nationalistic reformer, General Ovando proved to be the antithesis of Barrientos. He adopted the Peruvian military's leftist strategy of "revolution from above," stating that, although countries and problems differed, "fundamentally our revolution is the same as Peru's" (Mitchell 1977, 110). Ovando's civilian-military government of the "national left" ended the repression and created a democratic opening. Once again labor unions could organize freely and exiled union leaders such as Juan Lechín could return home. Ovando terminated military occupation of the mines. COMIBOL rehired thousands of miners fired in 1965 and restored higher wages. Ovando's most popular move, however, was the expropriation of the Bolivian subsidiary of Gulf Oil.

There had been continuous opposition to the generous foreign concessions since 1955, when the Paz government had passed a new petroleum code. The goal of the cash-strapped government had been to attract foreign investment into the department of Santa Cruz and to develop Bolivia's oil resources there. Over the next 15 years, Bolivia received less than half of the profits from oil and subsequent natural gas exports, even after production increased significantly. Although generally popular in Bolivia, the nationalization stirred up significant opposition abroad and even in some sectors at home. According to James M. Malloy and Eduardo Gamarra, the Ovando government did not enhance its image by the maneuver, which "had been poorly thought out and in the short run was costly" (1988, 51).

Both the U.S. government and Gulf Oil retaliated. The United States cut aid to Bolivia by 75 percent, and the company imposed a boycott. The Bolivian treasury nearly drowned in its oil as the government lost close to $15 million in revenues. The nationalization also stirred up strong regional animosity in Santa Cruz. The department's economy, which had received 11 percent of the oil royalties, was severely hurt and its long-term regional development was threatened. Special interests—the private sector, departmental authorities, and oil workers—opposed the nationalization. Even worse, the Ovando government caved in to the combined foreign and domestic pressure. In September 1970, Ovando promised Gulf Oil a generous $78 million compensation.

Ovando's populist policies sparked serious internal tensions, which his fragile governing coalition could not handle. His government could rely on only tentative support from the labor-left, political parties, and the military. With its civilian and the military supporters split, Ovando's government teetered on a very narrow political base. The young civilian reformers in his cabinet, among them the radical reformer Marcelo

Quiroga Santa Cruz, who served as the minister of mines, lacked political standing and were too leftist for the military.

The military remained highly suspicious of these civilians and forced many, such as Quiroga, out of the government. The root of the problem was that the military itself was split into opposing factions of conservatives and progressives. The latter favored national populism and backed Ovando and the up-and-coming general Juan José Torres. The conservative military sector was associated with General Rogelio Miranda. The rightist officers opposed the labor-left and believed that Ovando's populism was irresponsible and dangerous.

Marxist union leaders also criticized the Ovando government as "bourgeois" and not radical enough. At best, they argued, Ovando's policies could achieve a form of state capitalism, but never state socialism; thus, labor's plan was to agitate and push the government ever closer toward full socialism. Because of these opposing agendas, the civilian-military rift widened steadily. Ovando attempted to mediate between the labor-left and the conservative military faction. But without a reliable or independent political base, Ovando's government depended more and more on the military, which forced him to tone down his populism and shift to the right.

The increasing opposition to Ovando climaxed in July 1970 with a series of crises and scandals. Rumors of corruption in high places had been circulating, which compromised Ovando's reputation. One rumor even implicated Ovando in the death of Barrientos. A more credible one involved Gulf Oil. Reportedly, Gulf Oil had bribed the previous military government with extravagant kickbacks. Although the evidence was sketchy at the time, later a 1975 U.S. Senate investigation would confirm that in 1966 Barrientos had used some of this foreign money to acquire a new helicopter. Overall payoffs to top Bolivian officials in the Barrientos-Ovando government were later estimated to be around $1.8 million.

Yet another crisis and scandal developed over an insurgency in the Teoponte district. This guerrilla activity, so soon after the Guevara attempt, further destabilized Ovando's government. A group of radical students of diverse ideological tendencies had formed a guerrilla *foco* at Teoponte, a region northeast of La Paz near the U.S.-owned gold mining company South American Placers. The members of this guerrilla band were largely leftist students from the University of San Andrés in La Paz. Because of extensive student unrest, the police had invaded the university in May and confiscated pamphlets on guerrilla insurgency. The students began agitating in defense of university autonomy, and some took more drastic action.

A small number, many of whom were members of the National Liberation Army (Ejército de Liberación Nacional, ELN) that had been linked to Guevara's guerrilla operation, staged an action at Teoponte. On July 20, 1970, the Teoponte guerrillas seized hostages working for the mining company. The precipitous action was doomed from the outset, and in late October, the incident came to a head. Exhausted rebels accepted the government's offer of amnesty and surrendered, but the local military commanders ignored the stated policies of Ovando and his successor and ordered the guerrillas shot. According to Christopher Mitchell, nearly 70 of the 80 university students were killed (1977, 113).

The deaths of other political opponents, journalists, and politicians of varied political orientations indicated that Ovando was unable to control the divided military and that his orders were flagrantly disobeyed. The events of early October 1970 confirmed the military's disintegration. On October 4, General Rogelio Miranda attempted but failed to overthrow Ovando. In the resulting confusion and threat of violence, however, Ovando resigned, and General Juan José Torres emerged as the new president on October 7.

Under the short 10-month rule of Torres, the tensions within the military-led revolution from above increased. General Torres advanced closer, either willingly or by default, toward a radical and socialist model of development. By this time, however, Bolivian society had become dangerously polarized over the future direction of the revolution. Should the revolution continue to be radicalized and the U.S. role drastically reduced? Or, should the revolution pursue the moderate path of state capitalist development and maintain intimate U.S.-Bolivian ties?

Despite strong opposition in some quarters, the Torres government chose the first option and moved to the left. He declared that his government was supported by four pillars—the peasants, the workers, the university students, and the revolutionary military. He pledged to further economic nationalism, agrarian reform, industrialization, labor autonomy, and an independent foreign policy. Defying the United States, Torres established relations with the socialist bloc, and defying military and middle-class conservatives, in April 1971, he pardoned communist guerrilla Régis Debray and the survivors of the Teoponte uprising. Torres also nationalized the US.-owned Matilda zinc mine.

Torres is most remembered for the controversial Popular Assembly, or Asamblea del Pueblo. On May 1, 1971, a gala parade of more than 50,000 demonstrators participated in its opening ceremonies. With 222 delegates representing labor and peasant syndicates and radical political parties, the assembly began its deliberations on June 24, and ended them on

Representation of Major Parties and Groups in the Popular Assembly

Party	Percent	Ideological Tendency	Important Leader(s)
Revolutionary Workers' Party (POR)	4	Trotskyite (syndicalist left)	Guillermo Lora Filemón Escóbar
Bolivian Communist Party (PCB), pro-Moscow wing		Soviet Marxist line (ideological left)	Mario Monje Simón Reyes Jorge Kolle Cueto
Bolivian Communist Party (PCB), pro-Peking wing (also known as Communist Marxist-Leninist Party [PCML])	7	Chinese Marxist (Maoist) line (ideological left)	Oscar Zamora Medinacelli
Revolutionary Party of the Nationalist Left (PRIN)	13	Socialist workers' syndicalism (syndicalist left)	Juan Lechín Oquendo
Nationalist Revolutionary Movement (MNR), Siles-Paz splinter group (unofficially represented)	24	Moderate national reformist (center left)	Hernán Siles Zuazo Víctor Paz Estenssoro
Revolutionary Christian Democratic Party (PDCR)	N/A	Progressive Christian democracy (center left)	Jorge Ríos Dalenz
Leftist Revolutionary Movement (MIR)	6	Leftist radical reformers and splinter of the PDCR (ideological left)	Jaime Paz Zamora
Socialist Party (PS)	N/A	Radical socialist and national liberationist or anti-imperialist (ideological left)	Marcelo Quiroga Santa Cruz
Bolivian Socialist Falange (FSB)	3	Conservative and right wing	Mario Gutiérrez Gutiérrez

Source: Based on Malloy and Gamarra (1988, 62)

July 2. The Set of Statutes approved by the assembly stated, "the Popular Assembly is constituted as the leadership and unifying centre of the anti-imperialist movement, and its fundamental objective lies in the achievement of national liberation and the installing of socialism in Bolivia. It is an anti-imperialist front directed by the proletariat" (Dunkerley 1984, 194). From the outset this workers-students-peasants' parliament seemed a wild, democratic free-for-all. All the forces of the left, which had been stifled during the reactionary decade of the 1960s and partially mobilized by Ovando, now vied for the political limelight.

Despite the diverse ideological tendencies represented in the Popular Assembly, the labor-left and Marxist groups dominated the assembly's sessions. Juan Lechín, the country's main labor leader and the executive secretary of the Bolivian Labor Central (COB), was elected president of the assembly. He attempted to moderate the ideological extremes and advance labor's core agenda, although he was not always successful. The people's assembly, nevertheless, did adopt the socialist program of the Revolutionary Workers' Party (POR), while the peasantry remained largely neglected, with only minor representation. James M. Malloy and Eduardo Gamarra indicate that the ideological left had a tendency to denigrate the peasantry as a political force. Despite the advances of the revolution, the rural Indian population's weak representation also reflected their continued subordinate status in relation to the middle class.

In the June plenary session, the assembly passed radical measures, including the rearming of popular militias, the nationalization of middle-sized and small mining companies, the establishment of worker

Class Makeup and Political Affiliation of Delegates to the Popular Assembly	
Class	Percent of Representation
Labor and trade unions	60
Middle-class organizations	24
Peasants	10
Official leftist parties	6
Delegates claiming party affiliation	76
Independent or nonaligned delegates	24
Source: Malloy and Gamarra (1988, 61)	

control, or cogovernment, in the mines, and the expulsion of Peace Corps missions in Bolivia. At the same time that the Popular Assembly debated policy during the 10 days it was in session, workers' groups resorted to direct action. Miners took over private mines, and in Santa Cruz, a radical peasant group seized haciendas and hostages. Christopher Mitchell notes that local and regional groups took advantage of the leftist and democratic opening to aggressively push their own agendas and extract concessions from the government. Santa Cruz was an important regional center of politicization and anti-Torres sentiment. The regional and rightist military commanders there finally decided to move against Torres.

The conservative military interpreted the direction of the new government as Marxist or communist inspired. They not only feared but also opposed Torres's populist mobilization of the left and his dependence on the Marxist political parties and radical unions. At all costs they wanted to forestall the reopening of the Popular Assembly in September. Despite the frustration and idealism of reformers and the strident demands by radicals to further the revolution, more than anything the failure of Torres's leftist experiment proved that the heady days of the Popular Assembly and national revolution were definitely over. It was time for "peace, order, and work" (Dunkerley 1984, 203).

Banzer's Revolt of the Right

> Soldier: destiny has changed you from a man of war, to a guardian of social peace. Serve peace, then, with your arms!
>
> ■
>
> General Hugo Banzer Suárez (Mitchell 1977, 124)

In January 1971, Hugo Banzer Suárez, former commandant of the Bolivian army's military college, staged a coup in Santa Cruz. When the revolt fizzled, Torres swiftly exiled Banzer to Argentina, but the banished colonel stole back into Santa Cruz—the center of anti-Torres plotting. This time, a broad antigovernment coalition that included supporters of the FSB, the Siles-Paz sectors of the MNR, and the anti-Torres military formed. When a second insurgency erupted in Santa Cruz in August 1971, these antigovernment forces in the country joined Banzer's rebellion. On August 22, Banzer came to power and remained there for seven years, the longest term in presidential office since Barrientos.

Banzer based his rule on the authoritarian governing model of the Brazilian military. In the early 1970s, Latin American countries were strongly influenced by the modernizing military models of Peru and Brazil. Although both militaries pursued rapid national development, the Brazilian military was more conservative and repressive than the Peruvian armed forces. The Peruvian "developmentalist" experiment, which emphasized a more radical populism and economic nationalism, came into conflict with the United States. The Brazilian model remained more directly aligned with U.S. interests and free-market policies.

Hugo Banzer Suárez became president and then dictator of Bolivia from 1971 to 1978 after masterminding a coup d'état. He was president again from 1997 to 2001 after winning democratic elections. (Peter McFarren photo)

Left-leaning Bolivian presidents Ovando and Torres had copied the Peruvian military model. The conservative colonel (later general) Banzer shifted direction and cast his eyes toward Brazil. His recipe of repressive stability and generous foreign borrowing generated unprecedented economic growth and prosperity. Basically, Banzer reintroduced the conservative policies of the Barrientos period, and his government favored the entrepreneur class, which had invested heavily in mining, hydrocarbons, and eastern agribusiness enterprises. At the same time, his government sought to demobilize and control the popular sectors. If nonviolent efforts failed, Banzer resorted to authoritarian and repressive measures to quash the slightest militancy from the worker, peasant, or student sector.

Banzer's rule reflected the values of the die-hard military traditionalists. This very conservative sector of the armed forces became known as the "institutionalists" because of their fierce desire to protect the integrity and unity of the military institution and to avoid politicization of the armed forces. The Banzer government also aligned its policies closely with those of the United States and Brazil, standing firm against all leftist and radical movements in Bolivia. Nationalist and populist critics charged that Banzer had sold the country to these foreign interests.

With few exceptions, his rightist military government rejected the uncertainties of party politics and democratic competition. In the beginning, the Popular Nationalist Front (Frente Popular Nacionalista, or FPN), a coalition of the MNR faction loyal to Víctor Paz and the FSB of Mario Gutiérrez, had lent political support to the Banzer government, but the civilian-military alliance did not last. Despising the petty partisan feuding and chaos of everyday politics, in November 1974, Banzer decided to limit political activity altogether and impose dictatorial rule. Typical of dictators the world over, Banzer believed that social stability at any cost was necessary for Bolivia's economic progress.

The government's economic policies benefited only a narrow sector of the population, however. While key sectors of the middle and upper classes prospered, workers and peasants experienced the darker side of the economic boom. The massive devaluation of the Bolivian peso in October 1972, for example, fell heavily and inequitably on Bolivia's marginal classes. Banzer's free-market strategy further aggravated existing socioeconomic inequalities: The government repeatedly froze workers' wages yet refused to regulate the skyrocketing costs of basic necessities.

On the other hand, Banzer's single-minded pursuit of free-market development was hugely popular among the prosperous new bourgeoisie. The country's private sector and regional interests, especially in the department and city of Santa Cruz, welcomed Banzer's no-nonsense capitalism. In Santa Cruz, an agribusiness elite had already grown fat on rice, sugar, and cotton profits, and increased oil and gas sales further elevated the region's political and economic significance.

The rightist government also rolled out the welcome mat to foreign investors with a slew of beneficial investment laws. Banzer's petroleum code, for example, encouraged 15 U.S. oil companies to sponsor new explorations in eastern Bolivia, and in 1974, the government awarded Brazil a generous natural gas contract. Pleased with the government's responsible economic and fiscal management and the probusiness investment climate, foreign banks were eager to extend generous loans to the Banzer government. Bolivia's conservative and stable politics and capitalist development model also encouraged the United States to double and then triple its military and economic assistance to the country.

As long as the economy grew, the majority of middle-class Bolivians tolerated Banzer's authoritarian rule, and its oppression of labor and indigenous groups, which were often in open opposition to the rightist policies. The government blocked all union organizing by the FSTMB and the COB and declared strikes illegal. In January 1974, 100 peasant syndicates blocked Cochabamba's main artery to protest the doubling of food prices. The military was ordered in to end the demonstrations, and a bloody clash ensued that became known as the Massacre of Tolata. According to Christopher Mitchell, the military killed more than 100 peasants in the confrontation (1977, 127).

The Cochabamba crisis ended the complacency of the Banzer government toward the indigenous farmers. Indeed, the Tolata massacre, according to Herbert S. Klein, was the first major bloody encounter between the peasantry and the military since 1952. Banzer recognized, however, that once aroused, the campesinos would remain a formidable challenge to the military. Thus, on February 12, 1974, the government hastened to renew the Military-Peasant Pact that Barrientos had formulated a decade earlier. Banzer reasserted his personal leadership over the peasant syndicates, removed troublesome and independent leaders, and appointed progovernment caciques to keep the peasants in line.

Political life had become severely circumscribed. Only conservative parties such as the military's Popular Nationalist Front (FPN), MNR, and FSB were permitted. The FPN served to provide the military government a modicum of civilian party backing without circumscribing its decision making. Both the MNR and the FSB were so fragmented that each party zealously guarded its bureaucratic spoils. The FSB eventually splintered into personalist factions. Key MNR leaders, who refused to go along with Banzer's policies, abandoned the coalition. In 1972, Hernán Siles was exiled and founded the MNR-Left (MNR-lzquierda, or MNRI). Víctor Paz also broke with Banzer and was exiled once again in early 1974.

Although some of the MNR and FSB continued to back Banzer, the semblance of party democracy was becoming more difficult to maintain. The military was also split and restive. On June 4, 1974, a predawn coup in the capital La Paz failed. A second coup on November 7 also failed. In a "self-coup" on November 9, Banzer reasserted control, purged the military, and banned all party activity.

After the "self-coup," the Banzer government dispensed with democratic niceties and resorted to naked military rule. On November 11, textile and mine workers went on strike in protest. The military occupied the factories and mines and departed only with Banzer's ouster in 1978. Banzer enacted a civil service law that permitted him to remove elected union officials and replace them with his own "coordinators." Strikes and unapproved union activity were banned, and Bolivian labor seemed effectively cowed. The miners, however, resisted military intervention and retained their elected labor leaders. Military occupation did not prevent miners from striking from 1975 to 1977.

By 1977, both the economy and political repression had worsened, and the pressure for the restoration of democracy was increasing. The middle class joined the disaffected popular classes against the Banzer government. Ambitious military commanders sensed an opportunity for direct advancement through a coup d'état. Indeed, if the armed forces had not been so divided, Banzer might have been overthrown much earlier.

In Washington, D.C., the administration of newly elected president Jimmy Carter focused on human rights in Latin America and criticized Banzer's antidemocratic rule. Moreover, after his foreign policy initiative failed to regain Bolivia's sovereign access to the Pacific lost in 1879, Banzer could no longer rely on Bolivian nationalism over the seacoast dispute with Chile to generate support for his regime. Nevertheless, Banzer attempted to stall his opponents with a partial political amnesty in 1977 and promises of elections in 1980. Facing the threat of an immediate coup, however, Banzer was forced to advance this timetable. He promised to retire at the end of 1977 and to hold elections in 1978.

Partially reversing himself again in December, Banzer backed his official presidential candidate, General Juan Pereda Asbún. These maneuvers fanned the opposition, and in late December, a handful of miners' wives and children began a hunger strike in La Paz's main cathedral. Intimidated by the national support for the miners, in January 1978, the government granted unconditional amnesty to political dissidents and unionists. As the exiled and imprisoned leaders reentered political life, a frenzy of activity preceded the July presidential elections.

Frustrated Democracy

The 1978 elections were especially significant because there had been no democratic elections since 1966. On July 9, 20 political parties fielded seven presidential candidates. Only two candidates, however, had any real chance of winning: Juan Pereda Asbún representing a conservative coalition called the People's Nationalist Union, was the official candidate; the other was Hernán Siles Zuazo, representing the Democratic and Popular Unity Front, a coalition of political moderates and populists. The elections, however, were marred by widespread fraud.

When Pereda won, the public was scandalized. Everyone, including the winner (probably to save face), demanded that the electoral court annul the results. General Pereda, however, was not about to squander this opportunity to become president on another uncertain election. On

Results of the 1978 Presidential Election (Major Parties and Coalitions)		
Candidate	Party or Coalition	Total Votes Received
Hernán Siles Zuazo	Democratic and Popular Unity Front	484,383
Juan Pereda Asbún	People's Nationalist Union	987,140
Víctor Paz Estenssoro	Nationalist Revolutionary Movement (MNR)	213,622
Total Votes Cast		1,971,968
Source: Morales (1992, 95)		

July 21, he led a coup from Santa Cruz, the base of his electoral support. When Pereda promised new elections in six months but then reneged, his tenure in the presidential palace was cut short by General David Padilla, who seized power in November.

Padilla's motivation and that of the younger officers in his cabinet centered on preserving the integrity of the military. The majority of the civilian demonstrators, including all the parties of the left, assumed a wait-and-see attitude. Only a faction of the FSB and the COB attacked the military's transitional regime. Despite several failed coups, the caretaker government held the scheduled 1979 elections.

Results of the 1979 Presidential Election (Major Parties and Coalitions)		
Candidate	Party or Coalition	Total Votes Received
Hernán Siles Zuazo	Democratic and Popular Unity (UDP)	528,696
Víctor Paz Estenssoro	MNR Alliance (AMNR)	527,184
Hugo Banzer Suárez	Nationalist Democratic Action (ADN)	218,587
Total Votes Cast		approx. 1,600,000
Source: Morales (1992, 96)		

Another chaotic, but also violent election season ensued. Nevertheless, after significant electoral reforms, approximately 1.6 million voters participated in the country's first truly democratic elections in 15 years. Although 57 political groups originally registered, only eight candidates participated on polling day. Of these, only three were possible victors—Siles, Paz, and Banzer—however, no single candidate received an absolute majority as required under the constitution. The Bolivian Congress would have to break the impasse.

An MNR majority controlled Congress, but observers expected either a Siles or Paz victory. Congress, however, was unable to find a majority (73 deputies of 144) to elect a president. The electoral impasse proved internationally embarrassing as foreign dignitaries arrived to celebrate Bolivia's return to democracy. On August 8, 1979, the legislators finally reached a compromise. Walter Guevara Arze, who had aspired to the country's highest office for nearly two decades, would serve as interim president for one year. The highly respected politician was the leader of the Authentic Revolutionary Party (PRA) and the president of the Senate.

But it seems that no one had consulted with the armed forces in this decision. After a mere three months, Guevara, the first civilian president Bolivia had had in more than 10 years, was ousted. Colonel Alberto Natusch Busch perpetrated the violent and bloody coup. Upwards of 200 people died in the military action of November 1, which was followed by 15 days of repression known as the "Massacre of All Saints." The procoup faction of the military had brutally vetoed the wishes of the people. General Padilla, who had headed the anticoup faction, was cashiered, whereupon he appealed to civilians to resist.

Bolivia's angry civilians needed little encouragement. Thousands of demonstrators from all sectors of society crowded the streets, and the national labor union paralyzed the country with a general strike. Perhaps the most serious blow to the coup supporters was the suspension of $27.5 million in aid by U.S. president Jimmy Carter. The coup collapsed, and the problem was again thrown into the legislature. On November 16, the Bolivian Congress selected Lydia Gueiler Tejada as interim president. Then serving as the president of the Congress, Gueiler became the first Bolivian woman to be elected president.

President Gueiler's difficult task was to preserve what remained of the democratic opening and to shepherd the country through the next presidential election. Bolivia was mired in a severe economic as well as political crisis. The peso had to be devalued a second time, and civilian-military relations fell to an all-time low. There were constant coup rumblings right up to the elections. Gueiler's own cousin, General Luis García Meza, headed a dangerous procoup faction. Despite Gueiler's attempts to restrict García Meza's insidious influence, in April she was forced to acquiesce to his appointment as commander of the army. There was an assassination attempt on President Gueiler in early June and a coup attempt several weeks later.

General Luis García Meza ruthlessly used military force to seize power and ruled as president in 1980 and 1981. (Peter McFarren photo)

The conservative sector of the military feared constitutional elections and the return to democracy. García Meza manipulated the armed forces' mistrust and resentment of prying civilians. He stoked the anticommunist fervor of military hardliners and the reactionary security apparatus. He also took advantage of fears that civilian rule would likely lead to an investigation into charges of army corruption and drug involvement. The army faction loyal to García Meza had received training from the repressive, reactionary Argentine military and had developed a cozy relationship with Bolivia's drug lords.

Miraculously, however, the election went forward on June 29, 1980. Voter turnout was one of the highest ever. One-and-a-half million Bolivians went to the polls. Unfortunately, once again no single candidate

Results of the 1980 Presidential Election (Major Parties and Coalitions)		
Candidate	Party or Coalition	Total Votes Received
Hernán Siles Zuazo	Democratic and Popular Unity (UDP)	507,173
Víctor Paz Estenssoro	MNR Alliance (AMNR)	263,706
Hugo Banzer Suárez	Nationalist Democratic Action (ADN)	220,309
Marcelo Quiroga Santa Cruz	Socialist Party-One (PS-1)	113,309
Total Votes Cast		approx. 1,500,000

Source: Morales (1992, 97)

had an absolute majority. This time around Siles and Paz, who had received the most votes, joined forces, and their supporters in Congress were instructed to vote for Siles. Fearing the victory of civilian reformers, García Meza and the military hard-liners intervened.

Rise and Decline of the Cocaine Mafia

On July 17, 1980, García Meza unleashed his paramilitary against civilians. The rampage continued over the next year as García Meza's forces ruthlessly killed, tortured, imprisoned, and exiled opponents. The military attacked the Bolivian Workers' Central and killed labor leaders. The military bombed the mines, intimidated the Catholic Church, and censored the press. García Meza boldly compared his expurgatory role to that of Chilean president Augusto Pinochet, who had burned the "Marxist cancer" out of his country's body politic during the 1970s.

Because of human rights abuses and blatant drug connections, the regime became an international pariah denied recognition by the Carter administration and the government of Ronald Reagan, as well as Latin American and European governments. Consequently, most foreign aid dried up. The Bolivian human rights assembly claimed that 300 people had been killed by the García Meza regime. Meanwhile, President García Meza and his interior minister, Colonel Luis Arce Gómez, were implicated in cocaine trafficking. Top military officers, embarrassed by Bolivia's tattered international reputation and suffering economy, decided to force out García Meza's cocaine mafia.

In August 1981, Generals Celso Torrelio Villa and Guido Vildoso Calderón seized power. But after 14 months, the most they achieved was a tepid normalization of Bolivia's foreign relations with the United States and the international community. The generals could not restore civilian respect for or trust in the government. Civilians were not fooled by the unimaginative musical chairs; the corrupt face of the generals was one and the same in their minds.

When General Vildoso, who had taken over in July 1982, announced that the next elections would be held in 1983, he was greeted with a hail of protest. Civil society wanted elections and constitutional legitimacy immediately. There were daily strikes and protest marches in La Paz and across the country. A demonstration by 50,000 angry civilians in early September finally convinced Vildoso that the military had to leave. On September 17, he resigned. The Bolivian Congress revalidated the results of the 1980 elections, and on October 5, more than two-thirds of the legislators elected Hernán Siles Zuazo president. By one count, more than 100,000 demonstrators cheered Siles on his return to La Paz three days later. On October 10, he was formally sworn in as Bolivia's president. Siles had made history. After 18 years of military rule, he became the country's first civilian president to be legally elected. In 1982, democracy had gained an important foothold, but because of the legacy of militarism, Bolivia's democratic transition would not be smooth.

9

THE CHALLENGE
OF DEMOCRACY
(1982–2002)

*Any regime, democratic or otherwise, will face problems border-
ing on the insoluble.*

■

Robert J. Alexander (1985, 73)

After almost two decades of military rule, Bolivians were anxious for the restoration of civilian government and constitutional normalcy. With such high expectations for the future, however, there was bound to be widespread disappointment. As the first civilian president following a long authoritarian hiatus, Hernán Siles Zuazo confronted the monumental challenge of reestablishing and institutionalizing democratic rule. Virtually every socioeconomic and political sector of Bolivian society demanded special favors and immediate results from the first civilian government. Despite improvements in human rights and social welfare, Siles's populist democracy failed to contain economic collapse and political instability.

Not surprisingly, the civilian rulers proved unable to resolve the pressures and demands placed on them without resorting to force to a greater or lesser degree. To the credit of Bolivia's citizens and political establishment, however, civilian rule was sustained despite major governing and economic crises. During most of the first decade of renewed civilian government, Bolivian presidents of diverse ideological and partisan persuasions struggled to overcome economic collapse and renewed social unrest and violence.

In June 1985, Víctor Paz Estenssoro was elected to his fourth term in office as Bolivia's president. The 1985 election represented a historic transition: It marked the first time since Bolivian independence that there had been a peaceful transfer of power between opposition political parties. The election also represented the first peaceful transfer of office between two constitutionally elected civilian presidents since 1960, when Paz Estenssoro had been elected president for the second time.

From the following 1989 election into the new century, the pattern of constitutional succession continued, beginning with the presidency of Jaime Paz Zamora, and followed by Gonzalo Sánchez de Lozada and Hugo Banzer, respectively. Bolivia appeared to have turned a corner in the permanence of civilian and democratic rule. Each of these governments, however, faced one or more national crises. Each responded with varying degrees of authority and pragmatism. The tension between democracy and authoritarianism was endemic. Although all political actors appropriated the mantle of 1952's National Revolution, the civilian presidents with the exception of Siles generally abandoned the populist policies and ideology of the revolution for solutions that would ameliorate Bolivia's overriding problems.

Three critical problems complicated the difficult transition to democracy. First, Bolivia's military governments had contracted massive national debts during the 1970s, a legacy of fiscal and economic irresponsibility that plagued the new civilian presidents. Second, the political and economic order of the hemisphere and the world had also been altered significantly by the early 1980s. Globalization and liberalizing market forces had created new difficulties, challenges, and opportunities for developing nations such as Bolivia, and Bolivia's civilian presidents were required to come to terms with the new global economic order. Finally, Bolivia became mired in a full-blown drug problem. During the 1980s and 1990s, every civilian government committed its resources to fighting the hemispheric drug war and drastically reducing Bolivia's role as a coca/cocaine supplier.

Considered in isolation, any one of the three crises of debt, globalization, and drugs would have proven daunting for Bolivia's fledgling democracy. At times, tackling all three problems simultaneously seemed nearly impossible. More often than not, Bolivian democracy suffered in the process. By the end of the 20th century, the consolidation of civilian rule and democratic legitimacy had become a tortuous and difficult journey and certainly one that remained an ongoing struggle in the century ahead.

The Crisis of Democratic Populism

The Siles government retained office by giving in to whatever current demand was pressed upon it.

■

(Malloy and Gamara 1988, 191)

Hernán Siles Zuazo assumed office in October 1982 fully expecting to complete his four-year term as specified in the constitution, but the Siles government barely survived three tumultuous years. During that time, there were incessant rumors and serious threats of military coups. These came to nothing, partly because of external pressures and partly because Siles stepped down a year early. Despite the harsh criticisms leveled against his administration, the United States seemed as anxious as the Bolivian electorate to preserve the fragile democratic opening that Siles had provided. To a large extent, the Siles presidency became undone less by its incompetence than by the irreconcilable demands of democracy and debt.

During the period of 1982 to 1985, Bolivia's staggering indebtedness to foreign banks and multinational organizations precipitated a major national crisis. The country owed the impossible sum of $5 billion, and there simply was no way to pay. The bulk of this massive foreign debt was in short-term loans and had been contracted by and inherited from the military, especially the Banzer and García Meza governments. Service on the debt approximated more than half of the total value of exports. To partially meet its obligations, the government was compelled to print more banknotes. By mid-1985, economic experts reported an inflation rate ranging from 14,000 to 25,000 percent—one of the highest ever.

In the 1980s, the chronic pattern of underdevelopment and mismanaged development that had trapped Bolivia so often in the past reasserted itself. The pattern hardly seemed to vary from one century to the next. First there would be the discovery of an unexpected resource bonanza, followed by excessive spending and reckless foreign loans. Eventually, when the resources and/or prices declined, an overextended treasury would be unable to make good on the debts, and the country would descend into extreme political and economic instability. The downward spiral of one of these destructive cycles engulfed President Siles.

This time around the new bonanza was oil. In the mid-1970s, the Santa Cruz region had experienced a boom in petroleum and natural gas development. As the profits rolled into the department's and the central government's coffers, ambitious regional and national development projects took off. Bolivia became a profitable investment, and the flush foreign lending banks courted the military governments, shopping their loans at advantageous interest rates. But the crunch eventually came. Oil and gas prices fell, and interest rates doubled virtually overnight as the global economy went into recession. Bolivia's loans came due, and every spare peso was needed to make the exorbitant interest payments. The principal remained undiminished and even grew as unpaid interest upon interest mounted. Bolivia, like many other developing countries around the world, found its economy in the grip of the debt trap.

But things would get worse before they got better. Foreign creditors and the International Monetary Fund (IMF) had a one-size-fits-all solution to Bolivia's debt crisis: a draconian economic austerity program. This so-called neoliberal economic formula intensified the common people's acute economic distress and the country's political instability. Throughout Latin America and the Third World, neoliberalism meant conservative, market-driven solutions to the debt crisis: debt reform without a human face. Very few governments, especially democratic ones, could withstand the public protest. Military regimens tended to fare better because repressive measures were implemented to maintain civil order. Thus, economic austerity directly threatened weak democracies.

Bolivian democracy proved to be no exception. In order to secure payment extensions and additional loans to discount earlier loans, the Bolivian government was forced to severely slash government spending. In effect, this meant firing thousands of public-sector employees and trimming or holding the line on wages and benefits. The government terminated all unnecessary services and subsidies on foodstuffs, fuels, and other basic necessities. Scores of public enterprises were privatized. Overtime this stabilization formula worked to tame inflation and compel the market to weed out all but the fiscally fittest. The social consequences, however, were devastating.

By 1984, 2 million Bolivians were on the verge of starvation. An IMF austerity program had compounded the misery already created by major natural disasters—drought and floods—in the early 1980s. By early 1985, for example, the average monthly take-home pay of a Bolivian worker was $10. Lending institutions imposed harsh repayment terms that undermined the attempts by the Siles government to restore civil liberties and shore up social welfare. Given the widespread economic desperation, it was virtually impossible to restrain Bolivia's militant labor unions and radical political parties and still respect democratic freedoms.

President Siles faced a crucial political choice to move to the right or to move to the left. He could impose the conservative austerity program and thereby alienate the workers and peasants who served as his base of support. Or, he could pursue a populist policy of the left and reject IMF austerity and meddling. To resolve the dangerous crisis he could no longer sit on the fence. Perhaps, as critics claimed, the fact that Siles was prevented from serving out his term suggested that he had made the wrong decision. Indeed, his failure provided a sad but instructive lesson on the difficulties inherent in reconciling debt, democracy, and stability. (His successors would learn and profit from this lesson.

Attempts to squeeze by with a populist left-of-center policy while simultaneously restraining both extreme radicalism and conservatism destroyed the Siles government. By early 1985, Siles had scrapped his sixth cabinet. In less than three years, he had dispensed with more than six dozen ministers. Political infighting and partisan feuding paralyzed his government. Opposition parties, including Paz Estenssoro's Historic Nationalist Revolutionary Movement (Movimiento Nacionalista Revolucionario Histórico, or MNRH) and Banzer's ADN, dominated Congress and stalled or opposed all the government's legislation, forcing Siles to rule by executive decree. If policies made it into law, nonetheless, the opposition would impeach cabinet ministers. Even worse, the ADN and MNRH plotted with factions of the Leftist Revolutionary Movement (MIR) and the military to effect a "constitutional coup." The strategy was to have the opposition-controlled Congress force Siles's resignation and announce new elections.

The Bolivian left, notorious for its factionalism, provided an unreliable foundation for the civilian government. Siles's multiparty coalition, Democratic and Popular Unity (UDP), acted more like the opposition than as political allies of the president. The UDP consisted of several left-of-center parties, including the left faction of the MNR, the MIR, the Bolivian Communist Party (PCB), and the Christian Democratic Party (PDC). Divided by ideology, personal ambitions, and partisan competition for power and patronage, more separated these coalition partners than united them. To buy their support, Siles followed a time-worn practice in Bolivian politics: He parceled out the government ministries among the parties of the left. As a consequence, the process of governing was bogged down by partisan wrangling.

When Siles's own party, the MNR-Left, or MNRI, fragmented, he lost all ability to govern. The country became a rudderless ship on stormy seas. Everyone defied the government. The PCB split into combative factions over the government's economic policy. The MIR and its leader, Jaime Paz Zamora, nephew of the powerful opposition leader Paz Estenssoro, deserted the governing coalition whenever policy disagreements arose.

This chronic instability of the governing coalition was a major problem in itself, but it was compounded by the fact that Paz Zamora, who was also the vice president, reportedly was conspiring with the military to take over the government. The hapless Siles found himself surrounded by enemies and disloyal "friends."

The military mirrored the social and political chaos and fragmented into numerous opposing factions. On one end of the spectrum were the "institutionalists" who wanted to preserve constitutional rule, and on the other were the hard-liners who resisted Marxist influences in the government and were prepared to unseat the president by force. Corruption and drug trafficking compounded the military's disarray. In June 1984, there was a drug-related coup attempt. A far-right military faction backed the "cocaine coup" of cashiered army colonels Faustino Rico Toro and Norberto Salomón. Both were notorious for their intimate connections to narcotics trafficking in Bolivia. When the Siles government attempted to investigate the military's drug involvement, this hard-line faction turned against the government. The rebellion almost succeeded; the elite antidrug forces, the Leopardos, even managed to kidnap Siles on June 30. The hasty intervention of the U.S. ambassador, Edwin Corr, however, secured the president's release.

THE OTAZO AFFAIR

The United States and Bolivian political opposition charged that President Hernán Siles Zuazo was soft on drugs. Some even claimed that not only had he failed to apply effective pressure on the narcotraffickers and seriously pursue coca eradication, but also he personally colluded with the drug chiefs. In August 1984, an incident known as the Otazo Affair severely damaged Siles's public image and that of his government.

As James M. Malloy and Eduardo Gamara relate the story, the head of Siles's Narcotraffic Control Council and intimate friend, Rafael Otazo, met with the infamous drug baron Roberto Suárez. During the meetings, which Otazo claimed Siles had authorized, the drug lord offered the government $2 billion toward the national debt. When Siles publicly denied everything, Otazo revealed the names of government officials, including a cabinet minister, connected with the coca/cocaine trade.

Although Siles's involvement remained unsubstantiated, in September 1984, the opposition-controlled Congress initiated proceedings to impeach the president for his alleged drug complicity (Malloy and Gamarra 1988, 178).

The labor-left, which had been the heart of the government's initial support, also had a large hand in the demise of the Siles government. Union unrest undermined the government's austerity programs between 1982 and 1985. In an attempt to reverse or moderate these economic measures, Juan Lechín turned his Bolivian Labor Central, or COB, against the government. As a result, there were hundreds of industrywide strikes in 1983 and six devastating nationwide strikes in 1984. Siles responded with vacillation, repeatedly temporizing with the union's ultimatums. James M. Malloy and Eduardo Gamarra believe that Siles pursued a conscious strategy to evade the socialist structural changes demanded by labor while appeasing them with short-term bread-and-butter issues.

One issue was especially rancorous: cogovernment. During the first revolutionary government of the MNR, a governing partnership existed briefly between labor and government. This cooperation was known as cogovernment, or the joint worker-state management of public enterprises. For a time COMIBOL, the state mining company, operated under cogovernment. Labor always insisted on this right under populist and prolabor governments. As with Siles, cogovernment had been a major sticking point in Torres's military-socialist government.

Cogovernment, however, would mean that labor could veto fiscal reforms and austerity measures, and the United States, foreign investors, and Bolivia's own private sector vigorously obstructed labor's struggle for dominance. Siles waved the promise of cogovernment like a flag of truce before labor militants; however, he only acceded to it under duress in 1983, and only in COMIBOL after the miners' union (FSTMB) occupied the state mines and dictated worker control. In 1984, a desperate Siles agreed to labor's demand to halt repayment of the national debt. And after a prolonged national strike, Siles offered labor a voice in Congress in May 1985. (The last time that the COB had achieved this singular privilege was during the Popular Assembly of 1971.) Siles proffered numerous concessions, but the COB refused them all. Their goal was to precipitate a nationwide crisis and force the government to suspend the constitution and postpone elections.

Although the majority of political observers blamed Siles for labor's recalcitrance and the governing crisis, the breakdown was structural and systemic. Siles was being pulled in opposite directions by two powerful and antagonistic class forces: unionized labor and private capitalists. The private sector had emerged as a very powerful lobby, represented by the Bolivian Confederation of Private Entrepreneurs (Confederación de Empresarios Privados de Bolivia, or CEPB). Despite incessant strikes and street demonstrations by tens of thousands of

JORNADAS DE MARZO

In March 1985, the Bolivian Labor Central (COB) trucked 10,000 miners into La Paz for a "march against hunger." Civilian servants and local unions joined in the march to the presidential palace. With the municipal band at their heels and tossing dynamite into the air, the strikers demanded Siles's immediate resignation and the establishment of labor rule.

The march turned into a 20-day siege of La Paz known as the Jornadas de Marzo, or "working days of March." As food became scarce, Siles ordered out the troops to break the strike. In the view of James M. Malloy and Eduardo Gamarra, the incident was a "sad testimony" to the political deterioration in Bolivia. Siles, the "father of a 'populist' revolution" and ally of the working class, confronted Lechín, "another father of the revolution" and leader of the disillusioned workers. A bloody clash seemed inevitable, but bishops stepped in and resolved the crisis. After achieving a few concessions, labor backed down, and the "working days of March" marked the COB's defeat (1988, 186).

workers and peasants, labor could not triumph against conservative business interests. But labor could and did seal Siles's fate. As his government swung back and forth like an erratic pendulum between anti- and prolabor policies, investors lost all confidence in the country.

Personally defeated and with the drug corruption scandal engulfing him, Siles acquiesced to early presidential elections. This move proved to be the death knell for the forces of the left. Discredited by their association with Siles's failed policies, the political parties that had formed the victorious UDP coalition fragmented and were unable to cooperate and mount a united electoral front. In the close presidential election of 1985, two parties on the right benefited from the disintegration of the left, and they were able to monopolize the popular vote between them.

Paz and Authoritarian Democracy

Bolivia is dying before our eyes.

■

Víctor Paz Estenssoro (Mesa Gisbert 2000, n.d.)

The campaign before the July presidential elections provided a field day for Bolivia's myriad "taxi" parties, political fragments so tiny that the party convention could practically assemble in a taxi. By the April registration deadline, almost 80 political groups were in the running. Despite coup threats, postponements, and irregularities, 18 political contenders remained on polling day. The two serious presidential contenders were Hugo Banzer, representing the ADN, and Víctor Paz Estenssoro of the MNRH. The parties of the left formed two fronts but had little chance of winning.

Almost all of the 2 million registered voters, accounting for a third of the country's 6 million inhabitants, went to the polls. The vote split almost equally along urban-rural lines, the urban voters deciding for Banzer and the rural peasant vote favoring Paz Estenssoro. Although Banzer emerged ahead, neither candidate had attained a majority of the popular vote necessary to win. According to electoral law, Congress, serving as a college of electors, would have to decide the final outcome.

After two rounds of balloting, a pact among the congressional delegates on the left decided the presidency. Of the 145 electors, 94 voted for Paz Estenssoro. With overwhelming U.S. and hemispheric pressure to respect the final outcome, the defeated Banzer had little choice but to accept his loss gracefully. Moreover, not only had he been promised

Results of the 1985 Presidential Election (Major Parties)			
Political Party and Candidate	Total Popular Votes Received	Percentage of the Vote	Congressional Seats Allocated
Nationalist Democratic Action (ADN), Hugo Banzer Suárez	493,735	29	51
Historical Nationalist Revolutionary Movement (MNRH), Víctor Paz Estenssoro	456,704	26	59
Leftist Revolutionary Movement (MIR), Jaime Paz Zamora	153,143	9	16
MNR-Left (MNRI), Hernán Siles Zuazo	82,418	5	8
MNR-Vanguard (MNRV)	72,197	4	6

Source: Morales (1992, 103).

PAZ ESTENSSORO'S ECONOMIC TECHNOCRATS

Behind the scenes of his new government Víctor Paz Estenssoro formed a select group of economic advisers headed by Gonzalo Sánchez de Lozada. President of the Senate and the owner of a medium-sized mine company, Sánchez de Lozada had close ties with the private sector and had served as planning minister in Paz's previous government. Paz's economic technocrats developed a stabilization and recovery program modeled on that of the Nationalist Democratic Action (ADN) working group, which had visited Harvard and consulted with Harvard economist and "shock therapy" expert Jeffrey Sachs, in the months before the elections.

"There was a great deal of cross-fertilization" between the economic teams of the ADN and the reconstituted MNR (which had unified for the election), explained James M. Malloy and Eduardo Gamarra. The MNR-ADN-Harvard plan emphasized the role of the free market and the private sector, and the "taming" of labor radicalism. Paz kept his economic plan secret even from his own cabinet and carefully timed its unveiling for August 29, 1985 (1988, 194–95).

Gonzalo Sánchez de Lozada, who served as chief economic adviser to Víctor Paz Estenssoro, became Bolivian president in 1993. (Peter McFarren photo)

a clear field next time around, but also, as a former military dictator, his future bid for the presidency depended on his continued respect for civilian rule and the constitutional process.

Paz Estenssoro was determined not to repeat Siles's mistakes, but he was fully prepared to impose orthodox economic policies and authoritarian measures to maintain order. In his inaugural speech, Paz

Estenssoro promised a "government with authority, and without anarchy" (Morales, 1992, 103). A wily and experienced politician, he made sure that he had the political clout to do what he said. Unlike Siles, who had lacked an independent mandate to rule, Paz had solid legislative, partisan, and interest-group support.

He organized his cabinet to maximize his political maneuverability and control. Pragmatism rather than ideology or populism influenced his difficult governing decisions. Since this would undoubtedly be his final presidency, the 77-year-old Paz seemed not to care what Bolivians thought of him in the short term. A realist and an astute economist, he understood that he had a difficult but historic charge—to restore Bolivia's economic viability by the only means possible: economic austerity.

After less than a month in the presidential palace, Paz Estenssoro bypassed the legislature and issued the historic and infamous executive decree Law 21060, known as the New Economic Policy (Nueva Política Económica, NPE). He prepared for and implemented the stringent austerity program like a blitzkrieg military maneuver. Caught off guard, the COB fired back with an indefinite nationwide strike in early September 1985. Ten days later, the government imposed martial law and arrested and interned hundreds of union leaders in isolated detention centers. With a rare legislative majority in his pocket, Paz Estenssoro constitutionally extended this authoritarian stratagem and kept labor at bay well into 1986.

It had been many years since a democratic president could exert such dominance over the legislature. This rare executive power was the result of a political agreement, the Pact for Democracy, between the MNR and the ADN. Signed in October, this legislative alliance guaranteed "cooperative action" between the two major parties of the right. The pact guaranteed the government the necessary legislative majority to implement its programs. Some compared the exceptional executive power that the pact provided to the "imperial presidency" in the United States. Indeed, Bolivia's new model of "pacted democracy" appeared to solve a long-standing and vexing dilemma—how to maintain a formally democratic system and still produce strong governments. The trick would be to get the balance just right.

Paz Estenssoro's "democracy with authority," however, generated criticism in many quarters. Imposing a draconian economic austerity program by military force created a number of enemies. The government's relations with labor, business, and the middle class were often strained. Paz was ineffective and not authoritarian enough in the eyes of the private sector. From the perspective of the popular classes (workers and campesinos), Paz was a dictator, ruling by executive decree and martial law.

The NPE and the government's ruthless repression of dissent hit the miners especially hard. When Paz Estenssoro reorganized the state mining company, 11 mines were closed and 23,000 miners lost their jobs. In August 1986, more than 10,000 striking miners marched on La Paz in a final attempt to save the nationalized mines. Paz Estenssoro reimposed martial law and arrested more than 150 of the leaders. Labor was severely weakened by the government's aggressive response. Symbolically, in 1987, the once indomitable labor leader, Juan Lechín, stepped down as the chief of the COB and ended his union activism of more than three decades.

The workers' desperation was such that they continued to hold out, however. Labor stoppages nearly every month disrupted economic recovery from mid-1986 to mid-1989. In March 1988, a nationwide strike of petroleum workers threatened a military coup, and unrest by students led to a police invasion of the university. Thousands of unemployed and "relocated" miners and peasants migrated to the subtropics to raise coca leaf and join the illegal drug economy. As a result, the total acreage of coca leaf cultivation tripled after 1985, and Paz Estenssoro was compelled to sign a powerful antinarcotics decree, Law 1008, in

Bolivian workers protest in 1986 against the collapse of the world tin market, an economic catastrophe for which they blamed the United States. (Guillermo Delgado-P. photo)

THE NARCO VIDEO SCANDAL

All Bolivian governments have been tarred with the drug corruption brush at one time or another. Víctor Paz Estenssoro's administration, which had created the Pact for Democracy with the Nationalist Democratic Action (ADN) Party of Hugo Banzer, was no exception. The narco video scandal that erupted in spring 1989, however, tarnished the reputations of several political figures. A year earlier, the Bolivian drug king Roberto Suárez had received a visit from ADN politicians, who had sought financing for the upcoming 1989 electoral campaign. The event was secretly taped, and to embarrass Banzer's ADN and Paz Estenssoro's MNR-ADN government—as well as the presidential hopefuls of both parties—Suárez released the video, which documented the meeting between an ADN congressman and a military officer with Suárez. Because Banzer had developed close ties with the Republican Party of the United States during his presidency and had capitalized on this relationship after he left office in 1978, the scandal reflected poorly on the U.S. Drug Enforcement Administration (DEA) and the Republican Party's victorious presidential candidate, George H. W. Bush.

Moreover, the narco video scandal also embarrassed the MNR, which had unified behind the candidacy of Gonzalo Sánchez de Lozada, as well as the Leftist Revolutionary Movement's (MIR) presidential contender, Jaime Paz Zamora, who was shown embracing a major drug trafficker. The tapes touched off a national outcry against the three major parties (ADN, MNR, and MIR) in the May election and their alleged drug connections. Congress launched an immediate investigation. The scandal, however, blew over as the congressional deputies of the three parties absolved one another of wrongdoing. Instead, they indicted those involved in leaking the videotapes, and a month later they arrested Suárez.

1988. The unpopular Law on the Regulation of Coca and Controlled Substances made the cultivation of coca leaf illegal in specified regions of the country. Paz Estenssoro also acceded to further militarization of the drug war and intervention by U.S. military advisers and special troops to accommodate Washington, D.C.

The drug trade also played a back-door role in the country's economic revitalization. At the same time that the severe austerity stimulated the rise in coca/cocaine production, the profits from increased production subsidized the difficult economic recovery. An estimated $500 million (around 20 percent of total profits) may have returned to the domestic economy from the multibillion-dollar illegal trade. The dollars generated from one-third to one-half of the country's foreign exchange. No wonder that some dubbed Paz Estenssoro's economic miracle the "cocaine stabilization."

Despite significant improvements in inflation and international credit, the New Economic Policy had its problems, some of its own making. Bolivia's tin-based economy took a dive after the crash in the tin market in 1985. Monthly strikes hurt economic recovery and risked democracy. A military coup became a real possibility during a major strike by the country's petroleum workers in 1988. The NPE exacted an unfair toll on humble workers, while the professional and urban middle classes were affected only mildly, and white-collar jobs remained plentiful despite austerity. The injustice inherent in the NPE exacerbated social inequality and conflict. A popular quip held that the economy was doing better, but the people might not survive.

One could debate whether Paz Estenssoro played the part of savior or villain. Did Paz's controversial policies reflect his "tough love" or a disguised authoritarianism? No doubt his government had its share of setbacks. The drug scandal embarrassed the party, and the MNR lost seats in 1987 mayoral elections. But one thing was clear: The octogenarian left office a very popular president. Paz Estenssoro's 70 percent popularity rating, according to Eduardo Gamarra, was "the highest ever for an outgoing Bolivian president" (1996, 330). And Herbert S. Klein has concluded, "To the surprise of both enemies and friends, this seeming relic of a past era proved to be the most dynamic and able civilian politician to rule in the last two decades" (1992, 274).

Still, party loyalists, who were already jockeying for an advantage in the next presidential elections, viewed Paz Estenssoro as a political liability. When ex-general Banzer announced in mid-1988 that he would run, the two-party governing pact between the ADN and MNR quickly unraveled, and party cooperation ended in February 1989. With the elections around the corner, it was each man (and party or faction) for himself.

Liberal Revolution and Continuity

Coca is not cocaine. Coca is good and it is ours. Cocaine is bad; it is a substance that came from elsewhere.

■

Jaime Paz Zamora ("Coca Is Banzer's First Priority" 1997, 2)

The three most promising contenders in the 1989 presidential elections were Hugo Banzer Suárez, Gonzalo Sánchez de Lozada, and

Jaime Paz Zamora. Political pundits called the trio the "three look-alikes." More appropriately, they should have been called the "three sound-alikes," because their campaign promises were practically indistinguishable. With the collapse of the economy in 1985, Bolivian politics had shifted to the right, and despite the cocaine crisis and escalating violation of human rights, Bolivians were almost single-mindedly focused on economic recovery. Therefore, so were the leading candidates.

Almost everyone expected Banzer, who was being portrayed as "a gentle, intelligent dictator," to win easily. He was the oldest (at 62 years of age) and most experienced statesman of the three, but Bolivians had long and mixed memories of his authoritarian rule. Some, like a La Paz *chola* interviewed by a *New York Times* reporter on polling day, recalled only the prosperity, while political activists on the left remembered a quite different man and promised never to be reconciled to a Banzer victory.

The MNR's candidate was Gonzalo Sánchez de Lozada, or "el Goni," who earned his political stripes as Paz Estenssoro's economic point man for the New Economic Policy. A true MNR party loyalist, he was blatantly Paz Estenssoro's favorite. The feelings were mutual, and at the party's nominating convention, Sánchez de Lozada insisted that he was not Paz Estenssoro's successor but his disciple. With his "gringo" accent that reflected his upbringing and education in the United States, Sánchez de Lozada made quite a stir in Bolivia. To many of his compatriots, the 58-year-old rising star acted more American than Bolivian. On the other hand, his technocratic and Americanized image became a part of his attraction to Bolivia's younger generation of voters.

Jaime Paz Zamora was the youngest presidential contender, and the least likely to win. Fifty years of age, the *cochabambino* had served as vice president in Siles Zuazo's UDP-coalition government. As a young man, he had studied for the priesthood in Europe but soon discovered his calling in politics instead. Paz Zamora was a longtime activist. In 1971, he had been one of the founders of the MIR, the left-of-center protest party. He had been among party members who had been imprisoned and exiled during the Banzer dictatorship. As the current leader of the somewhat moderated and social democratic MIR–Nueva Mayoría (MIR–New Majority), his candidacy appealed to the bulk of younger middle-class voters and professionals, who had become alienated from the traditional parties.

The 1989 presidential election was somewhat unusual compared to previous elections since the transition to democratic rule. In 1986, the

Paz Estenssoro government, with the support of the ADN, had passed a new electoral reform law, which prevented the electoral slate from becoming clogged with the dozens of "taxi" parties and their nominees. Consequently, nine parties were on the ballot on voting day; however, only the three most powerful and popular parties—the MNR, ADN, and MIR—could realistically attain the presidency.

The elections were well conducted. There were problems, however, with ballot irregularities and voter abstention. Six percent of the vote had to be annulled, and blank votes totaled 4 percent. Although more than 2 million voters had registered, another million citizens, who could have registered and voted, failed to do so. Nevertheless, Bolivians

Results of the 1989 Presidential Election (Major Parties)				
Candidate	Party	Percentage of Popular Vote Received	Total Votes Received	Number of Congressional Seats Apportioned
Gonzalo Sánchez de Lozada	Nationalist Revolutionary Movement (MNR)	23	363,113	49
Hugo Banzer Suárez	Nationalist Democratic Action (ADN)	23	357,298	46
Jaime Paz Zamora	Leftist Revolutionary Movement (MIR)	20	309,033	41
Carlos Palenque Avilés	Conscience of the Fatherland (CONDEPA)	11	173,459	11
Antonio Aranibar Quiroga	United Left (IU)	7	113,509	10
Other Parties		6	99,457	0
Total of Valid Votes Cast		90	1,415,869	157

Source: Morales (1992, 106)

could be rightly proud that they had conducted another peaceful democratic transfer of power.

The vote was extremely close, and no one received a majority. Once again, Congress would have to decide the final outcome. With 23 percent of the popular vote, Sánchez de Lozada stood ahead of Banzer only by a thin margin. Paz Zamora trailed with almost 20 percent. Nevertheless, in Congress, his party commanded a pivotal role. Shopping for the best political deal, he sealed a pact with Banzer. With the required absolute majority of votes in his pocket, Paz Zamora, who had trailed both Sánchez de Lozada and Banzer in the popular vote, emerged as Bolivia's next president.

The final outcome was an upset and seemed unfair when the third runner-up was elected. What was really impressive is that all the contenders respected the process nonetheless. After the 1985 elections, James M. Malloy and Eduardo Gamarra noted that, "To accept defeat and remain in the political fray according to the existing rules is one of the more crucial ethics of a democratic system" (1988, 194). This observation proved especially true in 1989.

The results shocked many, as did the new governing pact, the Patriotic Accord. After all, Banzer had had Paz Zamora imprisoned in 1974 and had repressed MIR loyalists. Paz Zamora publicly explained the alliance with his former enemy as the product of a new spirit of national consensus and dialogue. Indeed, the two parties carved up the cabinet and government between them. Banzer's ADN selected the vice president and 10 out of 18 cabinet ministers. They controlled finance and planning and overall economic policy. Although he had no cabinet position, everyone recognized that Banzer would remain an important informal power in the government.

The policies of Paz Zamora were basically similar to those of his uncle, Paz Estenssoro. His first

Jaime Paz Zamora became president of Bolivia after the 1989 elections even though he actually finished third in the popular balloting. (Peter McFarren photo)

213

test came when 80,000 protesters besieged the newly dubbed "National Unity" government in October. Teachers who had not been paid and demanded salary increases organized a nationwide hunger strike. Despite his campaign rhetoric and the populist program that had characterized the MIR in the past, Paz Zamora rejected their demands. He held firm on the harsh neoliberal austerity program instituted by his predecessor and in mid-November imposed a state of siege. A predawn military operation rounded up more than 800 protesters and ended the teachers' strike. Despite sharp criticism from the Catholic Church and human rights groups, Paz Zamora persisted in this hard line. When popular protest got out of hand, he responded with martial law.

The MIR-ADN coalition government continued the conservative policy shift begun in 1985. To justify his reorientation, Paz Zamora employed such catchphrases as "new-style politics." In his speeches he echoed Paz Estenssoro and consistently criticized the "old" political formulas, which had manipulated ideology, populism, and radicalism to sway voters. Ironically, Paz Zamora began his presidency promising to return morality to government and to govern for all, especially the poor and dispossessed. But when his term ended, his administration was considered one of the most corrupt since the return of civilian rule. Allegedly, his party and cabinet had become linked with drug trafficking.

Democratic and economic continuity was the major contribution of the Paz Zamora government. Despite the outcry against his unscrupulous and pragmatic style, Paz Zamora was not more authoritarian than Paz Estenssoro had been. One might argue further that in order to control unrest and implement policy, especially the unpopular antinarcotics control law, Paz Zamora's successors were also forced to emphasize the authoritarian component of Bolivia's unique brand of democracy.

Paz Zamora's government, like the majority of democratically elected governments after 1982, primarily sought to guarantee the political stability essential for renewed foreign investment and economic growth. There was a new political climate, and in many respects Bolivia had closed the book on the tumultuous era that had begun after 1935. The great tin mining enterprise had collapsed in 1985. Although important, mining could no longer be the lifeblood of a more diversified and modern national economy. The recalcitrant labor movement, especially the once powerful miners' union and Bolivian Labor Central, had largely been subdued.

In its place were powerful new forces. These were the grassroots organizations of the indigenous peoples and the peasantry and the national and regional unions of the militant coca growers. Connected to the coca/cocaine economy, they posed a formidable challenge to the state. How could civilian governments deal with these explosive grassroots movements and still advance democracy? The resolution of this dilemma had become critical to the consolidation of electoral democracy and its deepening respect for civil and human rights.

The drug problem and the militancy of the peasantry and coca growers has bedeviled every post-1982 civilian government. Paz Zamora responded with a new antidrug strategy. He attempted to divorce coca production from cocaine and drug trafficking and associate it with alternative development. He popularized the slogans *"Coca no es cocaína"* (Coca is not cocaine) and "Coca for development" at home and abroad. His antidrug policy ostensibly opposed—at least publicly—the "criminalization" of coca production and its forcible eradication.

This tactical shift away from the more hard-line antidrug policy of Paz Estenssoro was unpopular in the United States. Paz Zamora's government was drawn deeper, nevertheless, into the full militarization of the drug-producing Chapare region of the country. Bolivia received record amounts of antinarcotics-related assistance from 1990 to 1993, despite the fact that the minister of interior and several key officials were removed for rumored drug connections. As Bolivia's economic problems receded, the drug crisis loomed ever greater on the political horizon and colored the 1993 elections.

Ascendancy of the New MNR

The major parties and coalitions that competed in the 1993 elections included the MNR, a coalition of the MIR and ADN, and two populist parties that had emerged in the late 1980s. The first of these latter parties was the Civic Solidarity Union (Unión Cívica de la Solidaridad, or UCS) of Max Fernández, a wealthy beer entrepreneur. The second was the Conscience of the Fatherland (Conciencia de Patria, or CONDEPA), led by Carlos Palenque, owner of a popular radio station. Both of these up-and-coming parties appealed to the marginalized and working-class voters, but they pulled votes away from the mainstream candidates, making it harder for a single candidate to win a majority.

Gonzalo Sánchez de Lozada of the MNR was the victor, nevertheless, beating out Banzer for the second time. Sánchez de Lozada had lost the presidency in 1989, despite a plurality of the vote. He had become chief

RESURGENCE OF THE PEASANTRY

In the late 1970s, a new peasant union, the Confederation of Peasant Unions of Bolivia (Confederacíon Sindical Unica de Trabajadores Campesinos de Bolivia, or CSUTCB), was founded and became Bolivia's largest umbrella organization of peasant unions. Until 1988, its leader was Genaro Flores, an Aymara who headed the indigenist party Tupac Katari Revolutionary Liberation Movement (Movimiento Revolucionario Tupac Katari de Liberación, or MRTKL). Confined to a wheelchair after García Meza's paramilitary goons tried to assassinate him, Flores served as spokesman for the peasants.

The economic austerity programs imposed on the Bolivian economy pushed the country deeper into the drug crisis. Desperate miners and peasants turned to coca cultivation and the drug trade to survive. The government responded with eradication programs and militarization of the drug war. In the 1980s and 1990s, the indigenous and peasant movements coalesced to oppose the eradication and criminalization of coca production. Using direct action tactics like strategic roadblocks, hunger strikes, mass rallies with coca leaf "chew-ins," marches, and occupations, the peasants forced the government to compromise.

Both economics and the indigenous culture encourage coca production. In the tropical regions, coca is the most easily grown, harvested, and

The army discovers a Bolivian cocaine factory. (Peter McFarren photo)

marketed crop. And coca is the sacred leaf of the Aymara and the Quechua peoples, central to their religion, folklore, medicine, and social relations. The peasant majority identified coca with their unique national identity and saw the drug problem as not of their making. Federations of coca-leaf growers of the Chapare-Cochabamba, Yungas–La Paz, and Yapacaní–Santa Cruz regions turned coca cultivation into an issue over national sovereignty and the preservation of Andean culture.

Defense of coca cultivation unified the peasant movement behind the powerful regional and national Peasant Coca Growers' Union. Over the years, the popular campesino leader Juan Evo Morales Ayma has become the premier representative of these *cocaleros,* or coca-leaf growers. Since 1988, as leader of the largest Chapare coca growers federation, Morales has passionately defended the farmers' right to grow the sacred coca leaf, arguing that the *cocaleros* were not addicted to coca but to eating: They depended on the crop to survive. As their most influential spokesman, Morales charged that the plight of the growers, who had seen plenty of eradication but little development, was being ignored.

The *cocalero* unions, meanwhile, have become very influential in the CSUTCB, which in turn has come to dominate the COB, much as the miners' unions had in the past. Both the peasant and the labor movements have developed close ties to the parties of the left and the indigenous movement. In 1989, this alliance resulted in 7 percent of the national vote for the United Left (Izquierda Unida, IU) Party and gave the *cocalero* and campesino unions a voice in the National Congress. The leader of the CSUTCB, Felipe Quispe Huanca, known as "el Mallku" (eagle in Aymara), also heads the Pachakuti Indigenous Movement (Movimiento Indígena Pachakuti, MIP), a political party that competes with Morales's Movement Toward Socialism (Movimiento al Socialismo, MAS).

Since 1997, when he was overwhelmingly elected the Chapare's deputy, Morales has repeatedly attacked official drug enforcement policies in the legislature. In January 2002, majority lawmakers of the Chamber of Deputies (109 of the 130-member lower house of Congress) expelled Morales for serious ethical transgressions because of statements against the government's antidrug policy. Widespread campesino protests in support of Morales and charges of interference by the U.S. Embassy in Bolivia, however, forced Morales's reinstatement. In the 2002 elections, anti-Morales comments by the U.S. ambassador Manuel Rocha helped, rather than hurt, Morales's bid for the presidency.

The battle for the coca leaf has had a major impact on the political mobilization and ascent of the peasantry and the empowerment of the indigenous peoples. Since a resurgent peasantry represents the largest voting bloc in the country, democratic governments have had to become more accountable to this radical constituency.

of the MNR in 1990 and was a passionate critic of Paz Zamora's administration. Finally taking over the presidency, he was determined to effect major structural reforms in governance, education, and the economy. As a wealthy mine owner, Sánchez de Lozada favored the power of private enterprise and market capitalism, and his extensive privatization program eliminated many of the remaining vestiges of state capitalism, reversing to an even greater degree the legacy of the National Revolution.

A mastermind of Paz Estenssoro's economic "shock therapy," Sánchez de Lozada was committed to the NPE, and promised to continue its policies; however, he wanted to combine structural adjustments with democratic and legal reforms. To realize his goals, he allied with the UCS, the Tupac Katari Revolutionary Liberation Movement, and the leftist Free Bolivia Movement. This coalition guaranteed him a

CONSTITUTIONAL REFORM

Simón Bolívar created the first Bolivian constitution of 1826 and modeled it after his idea of Athenian democracy. This constitution was in effect for only two years before it was modified in 1831. The second constitution replaced the lifetime presidency of Bolívar's document with the more democratic four-year presidential term.

The 1831 constitution established the provision that a presidential candidate must win an absolute majority of the vote (50 percent plus one); otherwise the Congress would have to decide among the top three contenders. Given the instability of Bolivian party politics, this provision has been central in the majority of presidential contests ever since. And since the return to democracy in 1982, every president has been elected indirectly by the Bolivian Congress. This has produced tense and unexpected electoral outcomes.

In August 1994, Congress approved the Constitutional Amendments Law. Its 35 articles established direct elections for half of the members of the Chamber of Deputies from single-member districts. The term of office for presidents, members of Congress, and mayors was increased from four to five years, and the voting age was lowered to 18 years.

Reflecting changed political and global circumstances, especially the decreased role of the state apparatus, the reformed governing structure devolved more power to the regional and local levels. Article One of the constitution defined Bolivia as a multiethnic and pluricultural society. New provisions also created the office of an independent human rights ombudsperson to monitor democratic rights and liberties and Bolivia's compliance with international human rights norms.

two-thirds majority in Congress and the passage of major constitutional and administrative reforms in 1994 and 1995.

Generally, the reforms focused on expanding participation in government decision making and alleviating the suffering and inequality created by market-oriented economic policies. Especially important were reforms that addressed cultural rights and ethnic self-determination. Polling data had alerted Sánchez de Lozada to the importance and weight indigenous groups and issues had gained in Bolivian politics. Partly for this reason, he selected Víctor Hugo Cárdenas, an Aymara and leader of the indigenist Tupac Katari party, as his vice president. Once in office, Sánchez de Lozada sponsored constitutional reform, bilingual and multicultural education reforms, and several new agencies to oversee ethnic and gender issues.

The new, technocratic MNR of Sánchez de Lozada seemed to be pulling a page from the party's past in its pursuit of modernization and development. However, Sánchez's modernizing project sought to combine a cultural and political revolution with the structural and economic one. Two 1994 laws epitomized these dual, seemingly contradictory goals: the Law of Capitalization and the Law of Popular Participation. Capitalization meant the privatization of state enterprises like the YPFB, the national railroads, electricity, smelting foundries, telecommunications, and national airlines. The profits from the sales were partly slated for (and went toward) direct social investment and poverty reduction. Citing anthropological research, however, Kevin Healy and Susan Paulson question if the capitalization reforms achieved their intended consequences. The privatization program, which was to redistribute wealth to the people, actually benefited multinational corporations, "leaving little or no money in the hands of the majority of the population" (Healy and Paulson 2000, 2, 12).

Popular participation involved a major devolution of decision making and budgetary autonomy to the local level. By redistricting and multiplying local governing units, more than 300 municipalities were recognized and established. It was especially important that indigenous villages and their traditional governing units, largely unincorporated in the past, were included. This decentralization has transformed the political landscape into one where 85 percent of the municipalities have rural (and often indigenous) majorities. Based on population, the new municipalities receive 20 percent of central government remittances to manage local development needs. Towns that had received nothing or a pittance in the past and had been forced to rely solely on municipal receipts in some cases multiplied their resource base 10 times over.

Regional counterparts and developmental experts continue to disagree about whether Bolivia's neoliberal policies and innovative reforms will succeed in the long term. If they do, they have the potential to profoundly alter Bolivian politics. But critics such as Susan Paulson and Pamela Calla view Sánchez de Lozada's popular participation and privatization reforms as a shaky marriage of "apparently irreconcilable political philosophies" (2000, 124). The radical new local structures have been plagued with corruption, mismanagement, inertia, and insufficient financial support. For some time, there has been a growing consensus in Bolivia and abroad that the neoliberal policies, despite the Sánchez reforms, have actually exacerbated the social and economic inequalities that they had promised to overcome.

Once again, Bolivia provided the region with a controversial and challenging model. In 1985, the Paz Estenssoro government implemented a textbook economic stabilization, the so-called Bolivian miracle. In 1994, Sánchez de Lozada developed a strategy of political and economic restructure that has been watched carefully by the rest of Latin America. Bolivia's following president, Hugo Banzer Suárez, offered yet another Bolivian model to the region, his "zero coca" policy. This new plan pledged to end the country's drug dependence in merely five years.

Banzer's Final Presidency

Bread, Housing, Work.

■

Campaign slogan of Hugo Banzer, Nationalist Democratic Action (ADN) party presidential candidate, 1997

In 1997, Bolivians went to the polls for the fifth time since the return to formal democracy, and for the first time, the 1994 reforms of the constitution determined the electoral outcome. Newly elected candidates for president, Congress, and mayoral offices now served five years instead of four. Voters elected half the members of the Chamber of Deputies (65 of 130 deputies) in single-member districts by simple majority. A proportional representation system determined the rest. This was also the first time that Hugo Banzer won both the popular vote and actually achieved the presidency. The question is, Why did he finally win in 1997?

Bolivian voters seemed to want change. Opinion polls suggested a reaction against the privatizing trend of the Sánchez de Lozada years. In

Results of the 1997 Presidential Election (Major Parties)			
Candidate	Party	Percentage of Popular Vote Received	Number of Congressional Seats Apportioned
Hugo Banzer Suárez	Nationalist Democ-ratic Action (ADN)	22	43
Juan Carlos Durán	Nationalist Revolutionary Movement (MNR)	18	30
Jaime Paz Zamora	Leftist Revolutionary Movement (MIR)	17	30
Remedios Loza Alvarado	Conscience of the Fatherland (CONDEPA)	17	22
Ivo Kuljis	Civic Solidarity Union (UCS)	16	23
Total of Valid Votes Cast			148

Source: United States Central Intelligence Agency (2000, n.p.)

particular, the economically and politically marginalized felt alienated from the reforms and the corrupt government. With close to 70 percent of the population below the poverty line, Bolivians were most concerned about the economy, specifically unemployment, poverty, and low wages. Not surprisingly, parties of all persuasions depicted themselves to be on the side of the marginalized and promised them relief.

With 10 political parties running, why did the electorate move further to the right? Several possible reasons may explain Banzer's victory. In times of crisis, the Bolivian electorate has a strong tendency to favor conservative parties that emphasize nationalism, order, and discipline. The ADN blamed the MNR for poverty and unemployment. Claiming he would roll back political corruption, Banzer proposed the elimination of the privatization laws and contracts with foreign companies. He also pledged an expanded state role in credit, health, and housing and the total eradication of the coca/cocaine problem via alternative development.

The MNR, instead, insisted that privatization would help capitalize and regenerate the economy. Paz Zamora, the MIR candidate, was highly critical of liberal market economics and proposed a stronger state role.

In the area of drugs, he proposed alternative development and a dialogue with the coca-leaf growers. The populist CONDEPA party focused on corruption and the humble majority's fears of privatization and foreign investors. Of all the main parties competing, only CONDEPA's presidential candidate, Remedios Loza (popularly called "*la chola* Remedios"), had an indigenous, as well as populist, background. Although three of the vice presidential candidates represented populist indigenous sectors, on the whole, indigenous voices were poorly represented. This reality partly explains the general alienation of ethnic majorities from the electoral and party process and market reforms.

Bolivians saw the expensive media campaign as a "dirty war" among the three favored candidates. In televised debates and high-priced television spots, the incumbent president (although prohibited by the constitution from running himself) focused on personal attacks against Banzer and Paz Zamora rather than the issues. Banzer was characterized as an unreformed dictator and Paz Zamora as a close friend of drug dealers. Voters were also reminded of the 1989 alliance between the two by the jingo "A vote for Jaime Paz is a vote for General Banzer." Despite efforts, Banzer received a plurality of the popular vote, and after a congressional runoff election, Banzer was finally in office.

As his predecessors had done, Banzer first fashioned a powerful "mega-coalition" of the ADN with the MIR, the UCS, CONDEPA, and several smaller parties. This alliance assured his government the largest parliamentary majority since redemocratization (CONDEPA left the coalition in 1998) and still allowed him to enforce his conservative and authoritarian policies with legislative and international, especially U.S., backing.

Shortly after his election, Banzer initiated what he called a National Dialogue, in which he proposed a four-point program for his government. His administration was to rest upon four equal pillars: dignity, opportunity, equity, and institutionalization. Of these four, social equity ultimately proved impossible to attain. Although the government instituted poverty-reduction initiatives, President Banzer did not reverse the privatization policies instituted by his predecessors. He deepened market reforms and forged additional and stronger ties with private and foreign investors.

The opportunity provided through economic development was also problematic. The economy fell into another severe crisis in 1999–2000, forcing an economic reactivation program. By the end of Banzer's term in 2001 (Banzer left office a year early because of his declining health), the economy had recovered somewhat but had not achieved the goal of

COCA, ECONOMY, AND INDIGENOUS CULTURE

The coca leaf has had a central role in native economies and cultures of the Andes dating back 4,000 years to the region's earliest civilizations. In the Inca Empire cultivation of coca was protected and regulated by the royal family, and the right to chew coca leaves was reserved for the highest nobility. Historians believe that mass consumption of coca followed the Spanish conquest and accompanied extensive forced Indian labor in the silver mines of Potosí. Only by chewing coca leaves were the Indians able to support the absolute darkness, extreme temperatures, brutal work, and chronic hunger that assailed them in the mines. Coca had a sedative effect on the stomach and physical pain.

Initially, the Spaniards considered coca chewing an unhealthy, dangerous, and diabolical practice and tried to suppress its use. They eventually realized, however, that their prejudices were reducing the treasury, for without coca, the *mitayos* could not work the mines efficiently. Deprived of the vitamins that the coca leaf provided, many Indians had lost their teeth, were unable to chew, and consequently died. Coca provided an important economic as well as cultural function. Bolivia's indigenous people of today believe that it still does.

7 percent growth. Institutionalization had focused on strengthening the judicial system and democracy, and these results were mixed as well. A reformed penal code and judicial system proved very harsh and very effective in arresting and prosecuting drug offenders. The reform, however, was widely seen as a major impediment to further democratization and improved respect for human rights.

The fourth pillar, his Dignity Plan, was intended to restore the country's dignity in the international arena by means of the complete eradication of all illegal coca-leaf production in Bolivia. Banzer directed much of the renewed power of the state to realization of an active foreign policy agenda and his single-minded commitment to end the coca/cocaine scourge. His "zero coca" policy brought the government and the military into increasingly repressive and violent confrontations with the country's coca growers and the powerful Cochabamba-Chapare unions. As a result, the government's repressive tactics and violations of human rights quickly became the object of hemispheric and international criticism and threatened democratization.

Nevertheless, perhaps, as Paz Estenssoro will be remembered for his economic miracle, Banzer will be remembered for his "zero coca" policy. When he stepped down and transferred his mandate to Vice President Jorge Quiroga Ramírez in August 2001, President Banzer, like Paz Estenssoro over a decade earlier, announced to his constituency and the world, "mission accomplished." But the final word was far from in. The drug problem and the endemic violence between the military and the coca growers continued to plague Banzer's successors. If and how this seemingly intractable drug war is finally won will determine the future of Bolivian democracy and economic development. A clear example of the complex interplay was the 2002 national elections.

Elections of 2002

The powerful prococa candidate Evo Morales demonstrated incredible voter support despite U.S. meddling in the 2002 presidential election. A recession and escalating campesino-military confrontations during the latter half of 2001 that spilled over into the six months leading up to the June 30 election posed a dilemma for the 11 candidates. Leading MNR contender and former president Gonzalo Sánchez de Lozada, whom pollsters had indicated was unpopular because of his government's promarket reforms, promised jobs and a gentler hand in coca eradication. The leftist Morales, representing the Movement Toward Socialism (Movimiento al Socialismo, MAS) promised to end U.S.-led coca eradication altogether, stop payment on the national debt, and renationalize privatized enterprises. Other candidates, who also sounded populist antimarket themes, included the independent Manfred Reyes Villa, a former army captain and Cochabamba mayor and millionaire. Two popular mayors, the independent Ronald MacLean from La Paz and Santa Cruz's Johnny Fernández of the UCS, also ran, while MIR's Jaime Paz Zamora attempted a comeback.

In a country with 60 percent of the population below the poverty line and an outstanding $6 billion national debt, millions of dollars were spent on the campaign. (By one count, more that $5 million were applied to Sánchez de Lozada's and Paz Zamora's campaigns.) Furthermore, with the exception of Morales, who was called a Marxist and drug trafficker by opponents, all of the top four runners were embarrassed by corruption-related scandals during the campaign. As a result, apathy ran high; Bolivia's 4 million voters seemed turned off by

			Percentage of the Popular	Number of Congressional
Candidate	Party	Popular Vote	Vote Received	Seats Apportioned
Gonzalo Sánchez de Lozada	National Revolutionary Movement (MNR)	624,126	23	47
Evo Morales	Movement Toward Socialism (MAS)	581,884	21	35
Manfred Reyes Villa	New Republican Force (NFR)	581,163	21	27
Jaime Paz Zamora	Leftist Revolutionary Movement (MIR)	453,375	16	31
Felipe Quispe	Pachakuti Indigenist Movement (MIP)	169,239	6	6
Total Valid Vote		2,778,808	93	

Results of the 2002 Presidential Election (Major Parties)

Source: Corte Nacional Electoral (2002, n.p.)

all the usual suspects from the traditional parties, which hoped to capitalize on the need for change by enlisting popular soccer players and folksingers for congressional tickets. Meanwhile, on the altiplano, Felipe Quispe and his Pachakuti Indigenous Movement represented the frustrated indigenous vote.

With only miniscule support in the months before the election, Morales's second-place finish was the big surprise. As analysts had predicted, remarks made days before the election by U.S. ambassador Manuel Rocha that U.S. aid could be jeopardized if a certain prococa leader were to be elected popularized Morales's militant message. Indeed, none of the front runners received the necessary majority of the popular vote, so the outcome was decided in the Bolivian Congress, where a pact between the MNR and the MIR (including the UCS and ADN) made Gonzalo Sánchez de Lozada the country's next president. The irony of the outcome was that pre-electoral polls had indicated that the MNR candidate was the least favored by Bolivia's voters. But such seemed to be the way of Bolivian elections, as voters prepared for another five years of "Goni" and pacted democracy. In opposition to the ruling coalition were the antiestablishment, proindigenous, and pro-coca parties of Morales and Quispe, a polarizing and potentially ominous sign for Bolivian democracy. The presidency of Sánchez de Lozada did not survive 2003. Beginning in February, violent clashes between antigovernment and government forces over economic and coca eradication policies left more than 80 Bolivians dead and forced the president's resignation on October 17.

Widespread protest coalesced in a month-long "gas war" against the government's plan to export liquefied natural gas to the United States via Chilean ports. Strong nationalist sentiment and fears of external interference in Bolivia were key motivations behind the popular revolt. As provided by the constitution, Vice President Carlos D. Mesa Gisbert assumed the presidency and formed an emergency government. President Mesa, a journalist and noted historian, promised to hold a referendum on the gas export controversy and to call a constituent assembly to decide the future of Bolivia's fragile democracy.

10

BOLIVIA AND THE
NEW CENTURY

Political questions and the life of social institutions depend on men.

■

Guillermo Francovich (1945, n.p.)

Recent decades have witnessed major reform within Bolivia: an impressive democratic and economic resurgence, a more modern electoral system (with expensive media campaigns), and extensive technological and communications expansion. Bolivians are mobilized and wired like never before. Internet use is high among the elite and urban middle classes within the country and among the Bolivian emigrants around the world. Both the public and the private sectors have developed and nurtured impressive access to online information ranging from official and commercial to tourist interests.

The high-speed communications of the 21st century have represented a unique opportunity for this landlocked nation to connect and interact with individuals, organizations, and countries far beyond its confined geographical borders, and Bolivians have readily seized this opportunity. This powerful engine of globalization has had widespread impact on the country's politics, culture, and national and ethnic identities. And with the new opportunities of globalization have come real and potential problems—problems that Bolivia shares with developing nations everywhere, as well as problems that are unique to its own geopolitical and multicultural heritage.

What will it mean to be a Bolivian in the decades ahead? How has the country's greater political maturity impacted its centuries-long struggle for economic development and modernization? What will modernization mean for its pluricultural and multiethnic society and

227

governing structures? Are we witnessing the emergence of *Bolivia, la Nueva* (the New Bolivia) as echoed in political slogans? And what about the old problems and dilemmas that have dogged the country's past up into the present? Will they finally be resolved or merely reemerge in different forms? What progress has Bolivia seen in reducing political instability and authoritarianism, social injustice and inequality, illicit drug trafficking, and regional isolation?

Finally, what does the future hold for this "land of struggle" and its courageous and resilient people? Have Bolivians abandoned the era of revolutionary change and turmoil that began with the country's most devastating war and ended with the gradual and silent passing of a generation of heroes and villains? Have today's younger, more professional, pragmatic, and internationalized leaders the wisdom, integrity, and ability to resolve the ongoing struggles of democratization, moralization, and integration? And what lessons have they learned from the past that may guide them tomorrow?

Human Rights and Bolivian Democracy

Militarism and dictatorship in the 1970s gave birth to a vibrant human rights community in Bolivia, which has continued to struggle against current encroachments and violations by the state apparatus. Since the return to democracy in 1982, every Bolivian government has wrestled with a difficult conundrum: how to rule democratically, yet authoritatively. This means that the state not only must be committed to civil and human rights but also must be able to forge the social and political consensus, civility, and compromise necessary for internal stability.

The government's prosecution of the Andean drug war has complicated this monumental challenge and compromised Bolivian democracy. Official repression of union activists and peasant community and *sindicato* leaders, especially the coca growers (*cocaleros*) of Cochabamba and other subtropical and tropical regions of the country, has become an urgent concern. The Bolivian government has been caught between conflicting domestic and international agendas created by its aggressive antidrug and coca eradication policies on the one hand, and the democratic resurgence of civil society and popular grassroots organizations on the other. The clash of these forces has been violent and politically destabilizing.

Human rights violations have occurred since the return to democracy and became acute after 1997 when President Banzer implemented his "zero coca" policy. Forcible eradication of thousands of acres of coca crops in the Chapare region of Cochabamba by the military and militarized antidrug forces has unified peasant and indigenous groups into organized and militant resistance not seen since the spontaneous agrarian takeovers in 1953. The Banzer-Quiroga government attempted to control and negotiate with peasant organizations, sometimes to no avail. As the standoff has continued, so have violations of civil liberties and human rights.

The coca growers' federation of Evo Morales has become a powerful, aggressive, and national force in Bolivian politics. Its unprecedented influence is the result of working within the democratic process and relying on peaceful but confrontational tactics of direct action, popular resistance, and the ballot box. Major roadblocks, strikes, demonstrations, and national marches and celebrations of the coca leaf—such as the first march of the *cocaleros* from the Chapare region to La Paz in 1994 and the annual "Coca Chew-in Day" celebrated around the country—have proven especially effective protest strategies.

Popular movements and interest groups have also turned to the hallmark of democracy—electoral politics. In the 1997 elections, for example, the party of the United Left (IU), which had been stridently opposed to militarized eradication policies, swept the vote in the coca-growing Chapare. Although the leftist party achieved only 3 percent of the national vote and had no showing anywhere else in the country, it won 19 percent of the vote and all parliamentary seats for the department of Cochabamba. Four representatives, one of whom is Evo Morales, head of the coca growers' federation, have been the voice of *cocaleros* and indigenous peasants in the halls of Congress. And the pro-coca movement almost achieved control of the presidential palace in the 2002 election.

Since the passage of the Law to Regulate Coca and Controlled Substances in 1988, state repression against peasant and indigenous leaders has intensified. Drug-related arrests by special judicial prosecutors and drug police have escalated 100 percent. Despite—indeed, some critics charge because of—new judicial reforms, Bolivia's criminal justice system has resulted in unequal justice. Domestic and international human rights experts have charged that the law has unfairly penalized the poor and the little fish in the drug trafficking and production chain rather than the big drug dealers.

Influential and wealthy offenders receive kid-glove treatment and often avoid arrest altogether. The poor languish under deplorable prison conditions, while the connected inmates manage private luxury cells. There was a major scandal in 2000, for example, when a relative by marriage of President Hugo Banzer was acquitted of drug trafficking. In sum, the criminal justice system has dispensed injustice, corruption, and favoritism. These abuses pose a new and insidious problem for Bolivian democracy and the restoration of moral integrity to civic life.

Because of the marked rise in violations, the government is under intense scrutiny, and both the Bolivian Catholic Church and the nongovernmental and government organizations have monitored the state of human rights. Also, the 1994 constitutional reforms established the official Human Rights Commission of the Chamber of Deputies. These domestic human rights agencies have exposed abuses by the government; for example, in 1997, according to Amnesty International, the national president of the Bolivian Human Rights Assembly, a vocal critic of official misconduct, was abducted and tortured by the police. Such incidents have served to dramatize the importance of human rights issues within Bolivia and the regional and international community of nations.

Bolivian presidents, therefore, have had to respond to dual pressures within the country and without. They have had to practice what they preach. For example, President Banzer approved the Brasília Declaration of South American presidents in September 2000. Ironically, the joint declaration contained a "democracy clause," which would expel from their ranks a president who might seize power by undemocratic means. The high profile of democratization and human rights in Bolivia's relations with its hemispheric neighbors and the international community, unfortunately, has been partially eclipsed by the government's aggressive antidrug policies.

Ending the Andean Drug War

> The 21st century will find a dignified Bolivia, working towards development and well-being, and moving ever farther from drug-trafficking circles.
>
> ■
>
> President Hugo Banzer Suárez ("Bolivia's Coca Wipe-Out" 2000, n.p.)

Aggressive prosecution of the drug war has been central to Bolivia's domestic and foreign policy agendas. Positive international political and economic relations with the United States and global lending agencies such as the International Monetary Fund and the World Bank insisted on effective drug eradication programs. Bolivia's international reputation and reintroduction into the global community were at stake.

The country's economic collapse and the "shock therapy" implemented in 1985 caused coca production to soar. By the end of the decade, Bolivia was the second major source country for coca leaf and cocaine paste. Also in 1985, the U.S. Congress passed the annual Foreign Assistance Act, which mandated a drug certification process for all nations receiving foreign aid. By law, the administration was required to certify annually if countries receiving aid were complying with U.S. antidrug enforcement measures. If countries failed to comply they could be "decertified" and the aid cut off, which quickly became a powerful instrument of coercion in U.S.-Bolivian relations.

Not coincidentally, after Bolivia was decertified and millions in aid suspended in 1986, the Paz Estenssoro government approved militarization of the drug war and joint military maneuvers. In 1988, the Bolivian Congress passed the Coca and Controlled Substances Law, one of the strictest antinarcotics laws in Latin America. The law made coca-leaf cultivation illegal everywhere except in the Yungas of eastern La Paz department, Bolivia's traditional coca-growing region since Inca times. As a result of these measures, Bolivia was recertified in 1989 and received nearly $100 million in antinarcotics assistance.

The government of Paz Zamora attempted to forge a more independent drug policy. He orchestrated a hemispheric and international campaign to promote alternative economic development and voluntary eradication instead of forcible eradication by the military and special drug police. He joined other Andean presidents in seeking to shift the policy emphasis to more demand-side solutions, shared responsibility, and, of course, alternative development strategies. The U.S. Congress approved $2 billion in counternarcotics assistance to the region over the next five years. The emphasis, however, was militarization of the drug war.

In May 1990, Bolivia and the United States signed the Anti-Narcotics Agreement, which made the militarized drug war official, and after a storm of protest in Bolivia, the Bolivian Congress approved the agreement in 1991. President Sánchez de Lozada signed a new bilateral extradition treaty shortly after his election, and the Bolivian Congress approved it in 1995. The bilateral agreement permitted the extradition of Bolivian drug criminals to the United States for prosecution.

Sánchez de Lozada, however, personally believed that the alternative development strategy was a failure. Like Paz Zamora, he tried to divorce coca from cocaine and resisted, as have all Bolivian presidents to date, efforts by the United States and the United Nations to declare all coca cultivation illegal. But all his efforts to develop alternative commercial uses for coca leaf (a strategy similar to Paz Zamora's "Coca for Development") failed, too. There was little international interest in coca-leaf tea, food, analgesics, or cosmetics. In 1994, he gave the green light to a massive antidrug offensive in the Chapare. His program, "Option Zero," depended on substantial international aid to fuel alternative development and structural economic changes, and compensation to growers for voluntary crop eradication. The plan flopped.

With great fanfare, in 1997, President Banzer promised to end the drug war in Bolivia once and for all. His Dignity Plan promised to eradicate all illegal coca cultivation by the end of his term in 2002. He phased out economic compensation for voluntary eradication and sent in the troops and antidrug forces to burn and pull up the coca crops by force. Over three years, soldiers eradicated from 74,000 to 94,000 acres of coca plants, or 70 to 90 percent of the country's overall coca acreage. In February 2001, as he opened a two-day international conference on the illegal drug trade in Santa Cruz, Banzer, in effect, announced his mission accomplished. He claimed that all illegal coca plantations in the Chapare region had been eradicated.

This achievement (still to be qualified), however, had also created enormous problems for the country. By eradicating more than 90,000 acres of coca in four years and practically putting Bolivia out of the drug business, there was less money circulating in the country, and unemployment had begin to climb upward. The economy had fallen into another recession, and the main labor and peasant federations had shut Bolivia down several times with roadblocks, marches, work stoppages, and hunger strikes. There was violence and repression. Banzer declared several states of emergency, which restricted public protests and imposed a curfew, and most of the time the country was engulfed in a low-intensity civil war.

When Banzer resigned for health reasons, his successor, Jorge Quiroga, continued the aggressive eradication policy and fared no better. As critics had predicted, most peasants were replanting coca and opening up more jungle to new coca acreage. The economic downturn and drop in aid dollars as well as President Quiroga's new antidrug offensive further aggravated conditions. The government moved to restrict legal coca cultivation in the Yungas and to further militarize eradication in the Chapare. In September 2001, Quiroga ordered the Expeditionary Task Force, an armed unit of 1,500 ex-soldiers, who were U.S. trained and paid directly by the U.S. Embassy in La Paz, against the militant *cocalero* unions with violent results. The task force operated like riot police or shock troops and was deployed to quell demonstrations and to open up main roads blocked by *cocaleros*. Nicknamed "America's mercenaries," these reservists, the Bolivian government and U.S. Embassy insisted, were commanded by regular Bolivian army officers and not as a paramilitary force.

Dubbed the "Chapare coca war," the increasingly violent clashes between the task force and the *cocaleros* led by Evo Morales, their candidate for the presidency, provided a tense backdrop for the elections. In late December, Quiroga issued a decree outlawing the drying, transport, and sale of coca leaves in the Chapare. In January 2002, the government's attempts to shut down the local markets where coca leaves were legally sold ended in a major confrontation in Sacaba, a town near the city of Cochabamba, and the death of several soldiers. The government blamed Morales, who was ousted from Congress, touching off more demonstrations by supporters. Sympathy strikes in major cities by Felipe Quispe's CSUTCB shut down the country. The Quiroga government backed down for the time being and allowed the Sacaba market to reopen; however, in this climate of opposition to the U.S.-funded task force and the government's militarized antidrug policy, Morales's popularity with campesino voters increased. Many feared (among them the U.S. ambassador, Manuel Rocha) that Morales could win the popular vote, but in June, he came in second to Gonzalo Sánchez de Lozada.

The crisis in the Chapare and the resurgence of coca cultivation continued to be a problem for Sánchez de Lozada only days after he took office in August 2002. Although the U.S. State Department stopped funding of the Expeditionary Task Force in July and forces were being withdrawn, the coca war in the Chapare was not over. The irregular force had been heavily criticized at home and abroad for extensive human rights violations, which convinced members of the U.S. Congress that the Expeditionary Force had become a liability for U.S. antidrug policy in Bolivia. Nevertheless, the Sánchez de Lozada government favored a "zero coca" policy and, despite campaign rhetoric to the contrary, maintained a strong military presence in the Chapare in the form of the regular army and militarized antidrug police. Whether this will mean compensated or forcible eradication and more or less repression depends on many factors, especially the state of the Bolivian economy and Bolivia's relations with the United States.

Clearly the drug war has not yet been won in Bolivia, but almost everyone agrees that Bolivia's coca crop has been significantly reduced. Long-term success, however, rests on extensive economic development and massive dollars to fuel it, not just the quick fix of alternative crops. Otherwise, any success will be short lived, and the production that has been diverted to neighboring countries will return to Bolivia when the price is right and circumstances change.

Economic Development and Globalization

Now we require access to markets, to guarantee that our citizens' willingness to exchange illicit activities for legitimate ones is not frustrated.

■

President Jorge Quiroga Ramírez (Enever 2002, n.p.)

Underdevelopment and poverty explain why Bolivia has relied on the coca-cocaine economy, and forcible crop eradication has only aggravated the precarious conditions of subsistence farmers. Since the return to democracy, times have been difficult. The aid-dependent Bolivian economy has had to rely heavily on foreign assistance, adding up to perhaps more than $1 billion in the last two decades. The debt crisis—largely resolved after most of Bolivia's public and private debt was forgiven or reduced by buy-backs, debt-for-equity swaps, and loan restructuring—is back. Desperate economic times since 1998 have forced the government to borrow extensively to keep from falling off the treadmill. Designated a "highly indebted poor country" by international lending institutions, Bolivia has received some concessions but on condition that it spend more resources on alleviating the country's worsening poverty.

Bolivian economic experts realized that Bolivia could survive the end of the drug war only if the economy continued to grow and foreign investment and aid continued to flow in at a higher rate. Only then could the legitimate economy offset the reliance on the informal coca cocaine economy. Bolivia's influential private entrepreneurs and the Banzer-Quiroga government believed that the stigma of the drug economy was the cause of the country's economic crisis. Economic reactivation could only succeed after the coca-cocaine connection was severed.

To encourage both investment and aid, Bolivian governments have downed all the required austerity medicine. They have privatized and liberalized the economy, making the Bolivian economy one of the most open in the world; indeed, aid to Bolivia has increased. The U.S. Agency for International Development disbursed more than $300 million for economic and alternative development during the period of 2000 to

2002. However, these sums, although historically high, proved unable to even begin to compensate for the overall loss to the economy sustained by civil disruption, labor strikes, unemployment, and agricultural decline owing to coca eradication.

Experts have estimated that the country lost from $500 million to $1 billion annually because of coca-leaf eradication. Recent Bolivian governments had hoped that by doing the most in South America to combat the drug trade, they could achieve special bilateral access to the U.S. market. They have thus far been disappointed. Meanwhile, the economy's overall growth has bottomed out at zero. The economic crash has hit especially hard after an average 4 percent growth rate in 1990–97 and 5 percent in 1998.

In these hard economic times, even the private entrepreneurs have become leery of all that privatization, liberalization, and globalization may mean. Tariff reductions in 1997 in preparation for greater Bolivian integration into the markets of its neighbors, such as Mercosur (the South American Common Market in which Bolivia is an associate member) have resulted in record failures of national industries. Weaker Bolivian enterprises have been unable to compete with counterparts in Argentina, Chile, Paraguay, Uruguay, and Brazil, especially given the extensive currency devaluations in the region. As Bolivian industry continues to operate under 60 percent of capacity and hundreds of small and middle-sized companies fail, the government has maintained a rigid free-trade, noninterventionist policy. The private sector, which has traditionally favored market mechanisms, is now screaming for government subsidies.

Bolivian labor and the peasantry have long been antagonistic to extensive foreign investment and foreign ownership of Bolivian-owned companies and state enterprises. They have resisted the globalization trend tooth and nail; for example, privatization of the water works by the Bechtel Corporation in Cochabamba triggered more than four years of nationwide civil unrest during the Banzer-Quiroga government. Market liberalization has also greatly increased the flow of contraband products into Bolivia.

In order to be competitive in export markets, workers have been expected to work longer hours for less pay. And the currency devaluation in 2002, although intended to make Bolivian goods more competitive abroad in a "beggar thy neighbor" scheme, has actually beggared the Bolivian working and middle class. Simply to survive, thousands of Bolivians have become indebted and unable to pay their small loans. Labor unions, although weakened, have fought back. General strikes and blockages of main highways have become routine events, which result in great economic loss. As incoming President Quiroga stated at his investiture ceremony in August 2001, "We have seen five months of blockades and protest. What we need now are five months of work" (2001, n.p.).

The economic crisis in the Southern Cone—especially in Brazil and Argentina, major export markets for Bolivian gas—has demonstrated that regional economic integration can be a double-edged sword. Nevertheless, the governing elite and sectors of the middle classes see economic salvation in globalization. They believe globalization is inevitable and necessary for the revitalization and integration of the Bolivian economy into the region and the world and the country's long-term economic development. So far, their optimism and faith is not widely shared among Bolivia's popular classes.

The Struggle for the Seacoast

The solution to this nineteenth century problem should now be looked at from a twenty-first century perspective.

■

Bolivian ambassador Julio Sanjines Goytia to the United States (Gumucio 1987, 213)

Since the loss of its seacoast, Bolivia's determination to directly access the Pacific Ocean has been a constant national aspiration. Defeat in the War of the Pacific and failures of diplomacy to reverse the loss of the seacoast suggest an important lesson for future Bolivian foreign policy. Political unity and stability and economic development are essential if Bolivia is to be an effective player on the regional, much less global, stage. Over the last century, Bolivian presidents have explored all bilateral and multilateral forums to promote their cause. The results have been meager, mainly consisting of diplomatic and moral support. With the return to democracy, Bolivia has achieved greater internal stability and respect among the world's nations, both of which are very necessary for foreign policy success. Hopefully, the country's aspiration for its own seaport and national seacoast will fare better in the 21st century than it has in the past.

Bolivian governments of every stripe—military, democratic, conservative, and populist—have all failed to sustain diplomatic advances on the seacoast question. Many believed that dealing with like regimes would work; however, in 1971, initiatives between the Chilean socialist

Salvador Allende and Bolivia's social populist Juan José Torres failed, for example. Negotiations among the three conservative military presidents—Hugo Banzer, Augusto Pinochet, and Francisco Morales Bermúdez—during the years of 1974 to 1978 bore no fruit either. And the anticipated breakthrough in 1986 between Paz Estenssoro and Pinochet came to nothing; in fact, the failure of Paz's "keep all doors open" approach hurt him politically.

For a time, Chile and Bolivia were locked in rigid bargaining positions. Chilean statesmen would only entertain talks on the seacoast if Bolivia restricted its diplomacy to bilateral contexts. Bolivia conditioned the normalization of diplomatic relations with Chile, which had been broken earlier, on engagement in negotiations. Both countries completely diverged on the point of territorial compensation. The Bolivians generally rejected this condition, and the Chileans insisted on a quid pro quo.

In the late 1970s, Bolivian foreign policy broke out of its Andean isolation and abandoned the stalled bilateral strategy for an aggressive multilateral campaign in regional and international organizations. Bolivian ambassadors and delegates made the circuit of organizations from the Andean Parliament, the Organization of American States (OAS), and the United Nations (UN) to the Nonaligned Movement.

The strategy paid off. In 1978, U.S. president Jimmy Carter's personal interest in helping find a solution to Bolivia's landlocked status helped pave the way for a positive outcome at the Ninth General Assembly of the OAS a year later. The 1979 resolution affirmed Bolivia's right to a sovereign exit to the Pacific Ocean. Subsequently, the foreign policies of U.S. presidents from Ronald Reagan through George W. Bush have supported the hemispheric consensus.

Bolivia's democratic presidents have pursued this multilateral diplomacy further. Paz Zamora gained ground in summit meetings with the presidents of Peru and Chile during his term from 1989 to 1993. In an aggressive stance, he described Bolivia's landlocked status as a constrictive "geopolitical encirclement" by its neighbors. He urged the region's diplomats to seek a 21st-century resolution to the 19th-century maritime problem. His efforts produced the 1992 Ilo Convention whereby Bolivia and Peru agreed to pursue economic cooperation and regional integration. Similar bilateral talks with Chile fell through.

In 1993, Sánchez de Lozada also followed a multipronged and nontraditional approach to the landlocked status problem. He specifically framed Bolivia's geopolitical confinement within the context of globalization and the demands of regional development and integration. His

Dignidad y Realismo policy resulted in a meeting with the Chilean presidential candidate Eduardo Frei in 1993 in Santiago and with him as president in 1994.

President Banzer extended his predecessor's diplomacy. He also linked Bolivia's landlocked status and improved bilateral relations with Chile to globalization. Both countries, as a result, focused on increasing cooperative economic and commercial relations. Banzer met with the new Chilean president, Ricardo Lagos, who appeared committed to a resolution of the seacoast issue. Banzer was personally devoted to Bolivia's territorial question. Observers speculated that both presidents were retiring elder statesmen who viewed the restoration of full diplomatic relations between Chile and Bolivia and some resolution of the seacoast problem as high priorities for their administrations. Nevertheless, Bolivia's quest for a seacoast remains unresolved.

The Bolivian heads of state continue to supplement multilateral strategies with new bilateral and trilateral initiatives with Chile and Peru. They hope that an approach that emphasizes the comprehensive economic development of the Andean region in terms of the challenges of globalization will uncover new approaches and opportunities for resolution of the seacoast issue.

Bolivia in the World: Future Prospects

Bolivian presidents have envisioned their nation's place in the 21st century among the established democracies and prosperous economies of the hemisphere and the world. To attain these goals, Bolivia has pursued both regional and international forums of cooperation. The traditional focus on autonomy, national interest, and state security has expanded into a greater concern for human development and security, and ultimately a greater receptiveness to hemispheric solidarity and global interdependence.

Bolivia has pursued its common interests with its neighbors, especially in the areas of crime, corruption, money laundering, and drug trafficking. For Bolivia, the summit diplomacy of the Americas has been an important vehicle for hemispheric coordination and future cooperation. This new hemispheric regionalism has helped Bolivia counteract its historically peripheral and isolated status. As a consequence, Bolivia has advanced on the *salida al mar* (seacoast) campaign and elevated its international status and visibility.

Bolivia's new multilateralism has clearly enhanced inter- and intraregional cooperation, and it has allowed Bolivian statesmen the political space to promote their nation's interests. Bolivia has been able as a result to structure a more independent policy vis-à-vis the United States in the area of drug enforcement. On the issue of democratization and human rights, Bolivia has made significant progress. Formally, the government has embraced regional and international human rights values, and hopefully, these commitments abroad will reinforce not only formal but also substantive democratic development at home.

In the intractable area of economic growth and development, greater hemispheric and regional integration may help Bolivian presidents humanize free-market reform and economic globalization and more effectively address the critical problems of poverty and inequality. Clearly, much will depend on the economy. As the second-poorest country in the hemisphere after Haiti, a series of major natural disasters have left the people and government reeling. Flash floods, droughts, and a devastating earthquake have taken a terrible toll in human life and stymied economic recovery.

If future Bolivian statesmen can become effective domestic leaders and actors in international affairs, and all of Bolivia's people can meet them half way, together they can resolve domestic and regional problems. After a period of respectable, and even invigorating, political and economic growth in the 1990s, the country has experienced another grave economic crisis. Despite these cycles of progress and decline, Bolivia's formal democracy has persisted. Bolivians have not given up but have continued to explore constitutional and structural reforms in order to move closer to substantive democracy. Much will depend on the economy and equity of access to its resources, for few democracies can survive crushing poverty and inequality for very long.

Even in times of crisis, however, Bolivians have continued to hope and to struggle to achieve the conflicting aspirations of a multiethnic society. Bolivians are a people of struggle and of perpetual hope. And although much progress has been realized over the country's history, much more remains to be done. For now, Bolivia has regained international respect as a responsible democracy, a reliable economic partner, and a principled and effective international actor. The rest is up to the new generation.

APPENDIX 1
BASIC FACTS ABOUT BOLIVIA

Official Name
República de Bolivia (Republic of Bolivia)

Government
Under the Constitution of 1967, revised in 1994, Bolivia is a republic. There are three branches of government: the executive, the legislative, and the judicial. The executive branch, based in La Paz, consists of the president, the vice president, and a cabinet of 14 ministers. The president serves as both the head of state and the head of government. The vice president not only is a member of the president's cabinet but also serves as the president of Congress, performing an important role as the major legislative officer. Cabinet officers are appointed by the president.

The president and vice president are elected on the same ticket by direct popular vote and serve a five-year term. (The president is constitutionally barred from seeking immediate reelection.) However, to be elected, a presidential candidate must receive an absolute majority of the popular vote (50 percent plus one), rather than a plurality. Since this rarely happens, presidents are elected indirectly from among the top two or three contenders in a runoff election in Congress, where deputies of both chambers serve as electors.

The legislative branch, also based in La Paz, includes the bicameral Congreso Nacional (National Congress), with a total of 157 seats. Both legislative chambers are of equal importance but with distinct and complementary responsibilities. The lower house is the Cámara de Diputados (Chamber of Deputies), with 130 seats; the upper house is the Cámara de Senadores or Senado Nacional (Chamber of Senators or the National Senate), with 27 seats. Senators are elected by direct popular vote. There are three for each of Bolivia's nine departments, and they serve five-year terms. (The term of office for the executive and legislative branch was extended from four years to five years by the constitutional reforms of 1994.) In the lower chamber of Congress, 68 members (*uninominales*) of the 130 deputies are elected by simple majority vote from single-member districts, as established by the 1994 electoral reforms; the remaining 62 members (*plurinominales*) are elected from party lists by proportional representation.

The third branch of government is the judiciary (*poder judicial*), which primarily consists of the Corte Suprema de Justicia de la Nación (Supreme Court of Justice of the Nation) and the Tribunal Constitucional (Constitutional Tribunal). The Supreme Court is the highest court of justice and consists of 12 ministers (*ministros*), or judges, who are elected by a two-thirds vote of all 130 members of Congress. Ministers serve a 10-year term and may not be immediately reelected. The seat of the Supreme Court is in Sucre.

Major political parties include the Nationalist Democratic Alliance (ADN), Nationalist Revolutionary Movement (MNR), Leftist Revolutionary Movement (MIR), Civic Solidarity Union (UCS), Conscience of the Fatherland (CONDEPA), Bolivian Socialist Falange (FSB), Leftist Revolutionary Front (FRI), United Left (UI), and Free Bolivia Movement (MBL). Other small parties that have figured in past or recent elections include the Christian Democratic Party (PDC), Movement to Socialism (MAS), Socialist Party (PS), Liberty and Justice (LJ), Bolivian Democratic Party (PDB), and Bolivian Socialist Vanguard (VS or VSB). Also of significance are the Bolivian Communist Party (PCB), Tupac Katari Revolutionary Liberation Movement (MRTKL), Katarist Liberation Movement (MKL) or the Democratic Nationalist Katarism (KND), and the Pachakuti Axis (EJE).

Political Divisions

Capital

The constitutional capital is Sucre; the de facto capital and seat of government is La Paz.

Departments

There are nine departments, divided into 112 provinces and 316 municipalities.

Geography

Covering 1.1 million square kilometers (425,000 square miles), Bolivia is about the size of Texas and California combined. It is the sixth-largest country in South America.

Boundaries

Bolivia occupies the heart of South America between 9° 38' and 22° 53' south latitude and between meridians 57° 25' and 69° 28' longitude west of Greenwich. A landlocked nation since the War of the Pacific in 1879, Bolivia borders Brazil on the north and east, Peru and Chile on the west, and Argentina and Paraguay on the south.

Topography

Two chains of the great Andes (the Cordillera Occidental and the Cordillera Oriental, or Real) transverse the western part of the country and form a great plateau called the altiplano, which has an average altitude of 3,658 meters (12,000 feet) above sea level. Many of Bolivia's major cities (La Paz, Oruro, Potosí) and about half of its population inhabit the altiplano. The city of La Paz is the highest working capital in the world at 3,640 meters (11,910 feet) in altitude. Lake Titicaca, shared with Peru, lies at an altitude of 3,812 meters (12,507 feet) and is recognized as the world's highest commercially navigable body of water.

The vast majority of the country is in the eastern lowland region of the Oriente. Extensive grasslands, rain forests, and intermountain valleys form the northern and eastern two-thirds of Bolivia. Many of these regions comprise the coca-leaf-growing area of the country. Extensive river systems, including the Río Beni, Río Mamoré, and Río Madre de Díos, flow northward into the Amazon Basin and bisect the Oriente, but because of rapids only a few rivers are readily navigable. Via the Río Pilcomayo and the Río Bermejo, which empty into the Paraguay River in the southeast, Bolivia has access to the River Plate and Atlantic Ocean.

Highest Elevation

The Nevada Sajama, a volcanic peak that extends 6,542 meters (21,464 feet) skyward in the Cordillera Occidental of the Andes, is Bolivia's tallest point and among the highest in South America. In the Cordillera Oriental of the Andes, the peaks of Illampu at 6,421 meters (21,067 feet) and Illimani at 6,402 meters (21,005 feet), which overlooks the city of La Paz, are the two next highest mountains in Bolivia

Demographics

Population (2001 Census)

With a population of 8.3 million people, Bolivia is one of the less populous countries of South America and the world. About 65 percent of the population is urban, and 36 percent, rural. Life expectancy at birth is 63 years. The illiteracy rate is 16 percent.

Largest City

Santa Cruz, the lowland capital of the Oriente, appears to have recently overtaken La Paz, the governing capital on the Altiplano, as Bolivia's largest city, based on the preliminary results of the 2001 Census. With a population of 1.1 million Santa Cruz exceeds by a significant margin that of La Paz (792,499). The entire La Paz metropolitan area, however, comprises an estimated population of 1.5 million.

Language

Bolivia is a multiethnic, multicultural society with an indigenous population of 55 to 70 percent. Spanish, Aymara, and Quechua are Bolivia's three official languages. Spanish is spoken by more than 80 percent of the population, and 20 percent of the population may speak only Aymara and/or Quechua, or Guaraní. A majority of Bolivians speak an indigenous language, as well as Spanish. Aymara is spoken in the northern Altliplano, Quechua in the southern highland and valleys, and Guaraní in the eastern lowlands. There are also more than two dozen distinct indigenous languages and dialects in the lowlands.

Religion

Roman Catholic, 95 percent
Protestant, 5 percent

Economy

Gross Domestic Product, or GDP (2000)

$8.3 billion; 67 percent of the population lives below the poverty line.

Economic Sectors (2000)

Agriculture, 22 percent
Hydrocarbons and gas, 14 percent
Industry, 15 percent
Manufacturing, 13 percent
Services, 63 percent
Tin, 6 percent
Trade, $1.2 billion, largely with the United States
Total debt outstanding and disbursed, $6.8 Billion

Most Important Sources of Foreign Revenues

Mining: Tin, Gold, Zinc, Tungsten, Antimony, Silver, Lead, and Iron
Hydrocarbons and Natural Gas
Wood and Textile Products, Jewelry
Industry/Manufacturing: Mineral Smelting
Agricultural Products: Coffee and Soybeans

APPENDIX 2

CHRONOLOGY

Pre-Columbian Bolivia

Before 10,000 B.C.	Peopling of the Americas from Asia
c. 10,000	Development of the early cultures of the Upper Andes
900	Chavín, the first Pan-Andean civilization
100 B.C.	Early Tiwanaku and regional states
A.D. 900–1000	Classical period of the Tiwanakan civilization
c. 1100–1460	Development of the Aymara civilization
c. 1460–1500	Armies of the Inca invade and conquer the Aymara kingdoms
1470	Aymara kingdoms revolt against the Inca

Spain in South America

1532	Spanish conquerors led by Francisco Pizarro begin the conquest of the Inca Empire
1536	Rebellion of Manco Capac II
1538	Spanish conquerors colonize Upper Peru, establish the Viceroyalty of Lima, and founding the city of Chuquisaca (Sucre)
1542	Spain institutes the *repartimiento* and *encomienda* systems
1545	Cerro Rico is discovered, leading to the founding of the Villa Imperial of Potosí; silver becomes the basis of the new colonial economy
1558–59	Establishment of the Audiencia of Charcas with its seat in Chuquisaca (Sucre); founding of the city of La Paz
1570s	The *mita* labor system is instituted to ensure steady flow of Indian workers for the mines

1572–76	Spanish viceroy Francisco Toledo visits Upper Peru; forced resettlement of the Indian population is instituted; mercury amalgamation process is used to extract silver
1624	Founding of the first university in Upper Peru, the University of San Francisco Xavier of Chuquisaca
1695	Discovery of silver at the mountain of Uru-Uru, near Oruro
1730	Indigenous rebellion in Cochabamba against Spanish authorities
1767	Jesuits are expelled from the Audiencia of Charcas
1776	Establishment of the Viceroyalty of Río de la Plata, with seat in Buenos Aires, and transfer of the Audiencia of Charcas to the control of Buenos Aires
1780–82	Indian rebellion of Tupac Amaru II (José Gabriel Condorcanqui)
1782	Reorganization of the Audiencia of Charcas and the establishment of the intendancy system

Struggle for Independence

1808	Napoléon invades Spain and overthrows the royal government
1809	Rebellion of Pedro Domingo Munillo and population of La Paz on July 16
1809–25	War of Independence in Upper Peru
1825	Liberation of Upper Peru and Bolivian independence on August 6
1825–26	Simón Bolívar rules in name for only a few months after the Assembly of Notables appoints him Bolivia's first president on August 13
1826–28	Marshall Antonio José de Sucre is elected president of Bolivia's first republican government
1829–39	Rule by General Andrés de Santa Cruz
1825–26	Assembly of Notables in La Paz appoints Símon Bolívan as Bolivia's first president in 1825, and he rules for only a few months
1835	The army of Santa Cruz defeats Peruvian general Agustín Gamarra

1836–39	Santa Cruz creates the Peru-Bolivian Confederation, but Chile invades and defeats Santa Cruz
1841	Peruvian president Gamarra invades and is defeated, ending attempts to annex Bolivia and unify the two countries
1841–47	Government dominated by General José Ballivián
1848–55	Governments dominated by General Manuel Isidoro Belzú
1850s	Modern silver mining era
1850s–70s	Discoveries of guano, nitrates, and silver deposits in Bolivia's Atacama province
1864–71	Government of Mariano Melgarejo, who cedes Bolivia's Amazonian lands to Brazil
1879	War of the Pacific begins with Chile's seizure of Bolivia's coastal territory
1880	Battle of Tacna ends Bolivia's direct role in the War of the Pacific
1884	Bolivia is defeated and becomes landlocked

Era of Civilian and Republican Government

1880–99	Civilian Conservative Party rule under the silver oligarchy
1899	Revolt of Liberal Party shifts power to La Paz and the tin oligarchy; the Zárate Willka Indian uprising is put down
1899–1903	Rebellion of the Acre region, which is ultimately lost to Brazil
1899–1920	Liberal Party governments
1902	Tin supersedes silver as Bolivia's major export
1904	Peace treaty of War of the Pacific signed with Chile
1920	Rebellion by Bolivia's indigenous peoples is repressed
1923	Miners' revolt is suppressed with violence and bloodshed
1932–35	Chaco War with Paraguay results in devastating Bolivian defeat

Era of Military Socialism, Reform, and Revolution

| 1936–39 | Military reformist governments of David Toro and Germán Busch |

1937	President Toro nationalizes Standard Oil on March 15
1939	Suicide of President Busch
1940–43	Return of conservative civilian rule under President Enrique Peñaranda.
1941	Founding of the Nationalist Revolutionary Movement, MNR
1942	Catavi Massacre kills hundreds of striking miners in December
1943	Bolivia declares war on the Axis powers during World War II
1943–46	Military reformist government of Gualberto Villarroel and MNR
1944	Founding of the Bolivian Mine Workers' Federation (FSTMB)
1945	First National Indigenous Congress
1946	Overthrow and death of President Villarroel
1946–51	Conservative rule by feudal-mining oligarchy; repression of revolts of 1947 and 1949
1951	Nationwide elections are overturned and military takes over
1952	National Revolution led by the MNR takes place in April
1952–64	Civilian MNR governments of Víctor Paz Estenssoro and Hernán Siles Zuazo
1952	Establishment of the Bolivian Labor Central (COB)
1952	Universal vote extended to all Bolivians; nationalization of the mines
1953	Land Reform Decree; Educational Reform Decree
1956–57	International Monetary Fund (IMF) economic stabilization program imposed
1961–64	Reform of state mining; U.S. aid is increased

Militarism and the Postrevolutionary Era

1964	Vice President René Barrientos Ortuño overthrows President Paz Estenssoro
1964–69	Restorative Revolution of Barrientos
1966	Barrientos cements the Military-Peasant Pact
1966	Ernesto "Che" Guevara brings his guerrilla *foco* to Bolivia

1967	Military-miner confrontation turns into the San Juan Massacre at Catavi–Siglo XX mines in June; Che is captured and killed on October 7
1969	President Barrientos dies in helicopter crash; coup by General Alfredo Ovando; nationalization of Bolivian Gulf Oil Company
1970–71	Left-wing military "revolution from above" by General Juan José Torres
1971–78	Military coup and conservative rule by General Hugo Banzer Suárez
1974	Massacre of Torata during military-peasant confrontation. Banzer's "self-coup" postpones elections and represses opposition
1978–80	Cycle of coups and transitional governments; elections of 1978 are sullied by fraud and military intervention; democratic elections of 1979 are followed by another military coup
1979	"Massacre of All Saints" in November; Lydia Gueiler Tejada, Bolivia's first woman president, heads interim government
1980	Bloody cocaine coup of General Luis García Meza overturns the year's presidential election
1981–82	Generals Celso Torrelio Villa and Guido Vildoso Calderón seize control as pressure for elections grows

Return to Democracy and Growing Economic Crisis

1982	Congress revalidates the 1980 elections; Bolivia returns to democracy and presidency of Siles Zuazo in October
1982–85	Hyperinflation, economic collapse, and governing stalemate end Siles's rule a year early
1985–89	Economic stabilization by Paz Estenssoro government under governing pact with ex-dictator Banzer and his ADN party
1985	Global crash of tin prices sends economy into deep recession
1986	Major mine closings cause political unrest; U.S.-Bolivian antinarcotics operation "Blast Furnace" begins in July
1987	Antinarcotics operation "Snowcap"

1988	Narco-video scandal embarrasses Paz-Banzer coalition; antinarcotics Law 1008 criminalizes coca-leaf cultivation
1989–93	Coalition government of Jaime Paz Zamora's MIR and Banzer's ADN; "Coca for Development" and neoliberal economic policies put in place
1989	First national "Coca Chew-In Day"; García Meza is tried in absentia for drug corruption
1990	Andean Drug Summit militarizes the Bolivian drug war; indigenous peoples undertake the "March for Territory and Dignity"
1993–97	Privatization of state enterprises and constitutional reforms by government of Gonzalo Sánchez de Lozada and MNR technocrats; Víctor Hugo Cárdenas becomes the first Aymara vice president
1993–94	Bolivian Supreme Court convicts García Meza, who is extradited from Brazil to serve a 30-year prison term for drug trafficking
1997–2001	Banzer government's economic austerity and forcible coca eradication incites coca growers and worker-peasant unions
1998	Earthquake in Cochabamba region destroys three towns
1999	Bolivia ends year with the lowest growth rate in 10 years
2000–2001	Banzer claims eradication of illegal coca crops in the Chapare; floods and natural disasters; IMF and World Bank grant Bolivia $1.3 billion debt forgiveness
2000	Violent protests in Cochabamba against water hikes; government linked to corruption–drug traffic scandal
2001	Paz Estenssoro, four-time president, dies in June at 98; battling cancer, Banzer hands over government to Vice President Jorge Quiroga Ramírez; mineworkers' leader, Juan Lechín, dies at 89 in August
2001–02	President Quiroga faces social unrest as Cochabamba "Water Wars" derail water privatization by Bechtel and Evo Morales and peasant

coca-growers protest coca eradication in the Yungas and bans on the sale and transport of coca leaves in the Chapare

2002   Clashes of military, peasants, and coca growers force government to suspend eradication and controls on coca-leaf marketing; ex-president Banzer dies in May; Gonzalo Sánchez de Lozada is elected president

2003   Gonzalo Sánchez de Lozada resigns as president on October 17 after a year of violent confrontations with his government over projected gas exports (the "gas war") and coca eradication policies. Vice President Carlos D. Mesa Gisbert assumes the presidency of an interim emergency government

Appendix 3

Bibliography

Aguirre, Carlos B. "Wetlands in Bolivia: Pantanal Preservation and Sustainable Development." In *The Pantanal of Brazil, Bolivia, and Paraguay: Selected Discourses on the World's Largest Remaining Wetland System.* Ed. Frederick A. Swarts. Gouldsboro, Pa.: Hudson MacArthur Publishers for Waterland Research Institute, 2000.

Albó, Xavier. "From MNRistas to Katarists to Katari." In *Resistance, Rebellion, and Consciousness in the Andean Peasant World, 18th to 20th Centuries.* Ed. Steve J. Stern. Madison: University of Wisconsin Press, 1987.

Albro, Robert. "The Populist Chola: Cultural Mediation and the Political Imagination in Quillacollo, Bolivia." *Journal of American Anthropology* 5 (2000): 30–88.

Alexander, Robert J. *The Bolivian National Revolution.* New Brunswick, N.J.: Rutgers University Press, 1958.

———. *Bolivia: Past, Present, and Future of Its Politics.* New York: Praeger, 1982.

———. "Bolivia's Democratic Experiment." *Current History* 84 (February 1985): 73–76, 86–87.

———. *Prophets of the Revolution: Profiles of Latin American Leaders.* New York: Macmillan, 1962.

Anderson, Jon Lee. *Che Guevara: A Revolutionary Life.* New York: Grove Press, 1997.

Andreas, Peter. "Free Market Reform and Drug Market Prohibition: U.S. Policies at Cross-Purposes in Latin America." *Third World Quarterly* 16 (1995): 75–87.

Arnade, Charles W. "Busch Becerra, Germán." In *Encyclopedia of Latin American History and Culture.* Vol. 1. Ed. Barbara A. Tenenbaum. New York: Charles Scribner's Sons, 1996.

———. *The Emergence of the Republic of Bolivia.* New York: Russell & Russell, 1970.

253

Ayala Z., Alfredo. *Historia de Bolivia en cuadros sinópticos*. 2d ed. La Paz: Editorial Don Bosco, 1980.

Bader, Thomas McLeod. *A Willingness to War: A Portrait of the Republic of Chile During the Years Preceding the War of the Pacific*. Ann Arbor, Mich.: Xerox University Microfilm, 1967.

Bailey, Helen Miller, and Abraham P. Nassatir. *Latin America: The Development of Its Civilization*. 3d ed. Englewood Cliffs, N.J.: Prentice-Hall, 1973.

Bakewell, Peter. "Bolivia: The Colonial Period." In *Encyclopedia of Latin American History and Culture*. Vol. 1. Ed. Barbara A. Tenenbaum. New York: Charles Scribner's Sons, 1996.

Bethell, Leslie, ed. *The Cambridge History of Latin America*. Vols. 1–2, *Colonial Latin America*; vol. 3, *From Independence to c. 1870*. New York: Cambridge University Press, 1985.

"Bolivia: Landless Farmers Unite." Latinamerica Press. Available online at http://www.lapress.org/ArticlePrint.asp?IssCode=0&lanCode=1& artCode=2430. Downloaded August 17, 2001.

"Bolivia's Coca Wipe-Out." BBC News Online. Available online at http://news.bbc.co.uk/. Downloaded December 20, 2000.

Burkholder, Mark A., and Lyman L. Johnson. *Colonial Latin America*. 2d ed. New York: Oxford University Press, 1994.

Cardozo, Efraím. *23 de octubre; una página de historia contemporánea del Paraguay*. Buenos Aires: Editorial Guayra, 1956.

Ceaser, Mike. "Bolivia: The Shrinking Nation." *Bolivian Times*. Available online at http://www.boliviantimes.com/2001/ed02/other/ bolivia.htm. Downloaded October 7, 2001.

Chauvin, Lucien O. "Drug Eradication Effort Worsens Poverty among Bolivian Farmers." *Miami Herald*, January 25, 2001, n.p.

Chevalier, François. "The Roots of Caudillismo." In *Caudillos: Dictators in Spanish America*. Ed. Hugh M. Hamill. Norman: University of Oklahoma Press, 1992.

Cobo, Father Bernabé. *History of the Inca Empire*. Trans. and ed. Roland Hamilton. Austin: University of Texas Press, 1979.

———. *Inca Religion and Customs*. Trans. and ed. Roland Hamilton. Austin: University of Texas Press, 1990.

"Coca Is Banzer's First Priority." *Latinamerica Press* 29 (July 10, 1997):2.

Coffin, Philip. "Coca Eradication." *Foreign Policy in Focus* 6, no. 7 (March 2001): 1–4.

Cole, Jeffrey A. *The Potosí Mita, 1573–1700: Compulsory Indian Labor in the Andes*. Stanford, Calif.: Stanford University Press, 1985.

Condarco Morales, Ramiro. *Zárate, el temible Willka.* La Paz: Talleres Gráficos Bolivianos, 1965.

Cossío del Pomar, Felipe. *El mundo de los incas.* Mexico City: FCE, 1975.

Crabtree, John, Gavan Duffy, and Jenny Pearce. *The Great Tin Crash: Bolivia and the World Tin Market.* London: Latin America Bureau, 1987.

Corte Nacional Electoral. Available online at http://www.cne.org.bo. Downloaded September 27, 2002.

Dandler, Jorge, and Juan Torrico A. "From the National Indigenous Congress to the Ayopaya Rebellion: Bolivia, 1945–1947." In *Resistance, Rebellion, and Consciousness in the Andean Peasant World, 18th to 20th Centuries.* Ed. Steve J. Stern. Madison: University of Wisconsin Press, 1987.

Del Pilar Gumucio, Maria. "U.S. and Bolivia at a Crossroads: Between Cooperation and Collision." Master's thesis, Florida International University, 1995.

"Desarrollo humano de Bolivia mejor que dos últimos años." *El Diario,* July 10, 2001, n.p.

Dunkerley, James. *Rebellion in the Veins: Political Struggle in Bolivia, 1952–1982.* London: Verso, 1984.

Enever, Andrew. "Bolivian Leader Declares War on Poverty." BBC News Online. Available online at http://news.bbc.co.uk/. Downloaded August 8, 2001.

———. "Open Economy Hits Bolivia's Industry." BBC News Online. Available online at http://news.bbc.co.uk/. Downloaded April 2, 2002.

Fagg, John Edwin. *Latin America: A General History.* New York: Macmillan, 1963.

Farcau, Bruce W. *The Chaco War: Bolivia and Paraguay, 1932–1935.* Westport, Conn.: Praeger, 1996.

———. *The Ten Cents War: Chile, Peru, and Bolivia in the War of the Pacific, 1879–1884.* Westport, Conn.: Praeger, 2000.

Farthing, Linda, and George Ann Potter. "Bolivia: Eradicating Democracy." *Foreign Policy in Focus* 5, no. 38 (March 2001): 1–3.

Fellmann Velarde, José. *Historia de Bolivia.* 3 vols. La Paz: Editorial Los Amigos del Libro, 1978–81.

Francovich, Guillermo. *La filosofía en Bolivia.* Buenos Aires: Editorial Losada, 1945.

Gabai, Rafael Varón. *Francisco Pizarro and His Brothers: The Illusion of Power in Sixteenth-Century Peru.* Trans. Javier Flores Espinoza. Norman: University of Oklahoma Press, 1997.

Galeano, Eduardo. *Genesis.* Trans. Cedric Belfrage. New York: Pantheon Books, 1985.

———. *Faces and Masks.* Trans. Cedric Belfrage. New York: Pantheon Books, 1987.

Gamarra, Eduardo A. "Crafting Political Support for Stabilization: Political Pacts and the New Economic Policy in Bolivia." In *Democracy, Markets, and Structural Reform in Latin America: Argentina, Bolivia, Brazil, Chile, and Mexico.* Eds. William C. Smith, Carlos H. Acuña, and Eduardo A. Gamarra. Miami: North-South Center, University of Miami, 1994.

———. "Fighting Drugs in Bolivia: United States and Bolivian Perceptions at Odds." In *Coca, Cocaine, and the Bolivian Reality.* Eds. Madeline Barbara Léons and Harry Sanabria. Albany: State University of New York, 1997.

———. "Paz Estenssoro, Víctor." In *Encyclopedia of Latin American History and Culture.* Vol. 4. Ed. Barbara A. Tenenbaum. New York: Charles Scribner's Sons, 1996.

Garcilaso de la Vega, El Inca. *Royal Commentaries of the Incas and General History of Peru.* Trans. Harold V. Livermore. Austin: University of Texas Press, 1966.

Guevara, Ernesto "Che." *The Bolivian Diary of Ernesto Che Guevara.* New York: Pathfinder, 1994.

———. *Che: Selected Works of Ernesto Guevara.* Cambridge, Mass.: MIT Press, 1969.

———. *Guerrilla Warfare.* New York: Random House, 1969.

Gumucio, Jorge A. *El enclaustramiento marítimo de Bolivia en los foros del mundo.* La Paz: Academia Boliviana de Historia, 1993.

———. "Toward a Sociology of International Relations: The Case of Bolivian Quest for an Outlet to the Sea." Ph.D. diss., University of Pittsburgh, 1987.

Guzmán, Humberto. *Estéban Arze, caudillo de los valles.* Cochabamba, Bolivia: n.p., 1948.

Harris, Richard L. *Death of a Revolutionary: Che Guevara's Last Mission.* Rev. ed. New York: W.W. Norton, 2000.

Hausmann, Ricardo. "Prisoners of Geography." *Foreign Policy* (January/February 2001): 45–53.

Healy, Kevin. "Coca, the State, and the Peasantry in Bolivia, 1982–1988." *Journal of Interamerican Studies and World Affairs* 30 (1988): 105–26.

Healy, Kevin, and Susan Paulson. "Political Economies of Identity in Bolivia, 1952–1998." *Journal of Latin American Anthropology* 5 (2000): 2–29.

Hillman, Grady, with Guillermo Delgado P. *The Return of the Inca: Translations from the Quechua Messianic Tradition*. Austin, Tex.: Place of Herons Press, 1986.

Hudson, Rex A., and Dennis M. Hanratty, eds. *Bolivia: A Country Study*. 3d ed. Washington, D.C.: Government Printing Office, 1991.

Inter-American Development Bank. *Development Beyond Economics: Economic and Social Progress in Latin America, 2000 Report*. Washington, D.C.: Inter-American Development Bank, 2000.

Klein, Herbert S. *Bolivia: The Evolution of a Multi-Ethnic Society*. 2d ed. New York: Oxford University Press, 1992.

————. *Orígenes de la revolución nacional boliviana: La crisis de la generación del Chaco*. La Paz: Librería y Editorial Juventud, 1968.

————. *Parties and Political Change in Bolivia, 1880–1952*. London: Cambridge University Press, 1969.

Kohl, Ben, and Linda Farthing. "The Price of Success: Bolivia's War Against Drugs and the Poor." *NACLA Report on the Americas* 35 (July/August 2001): 35–41.

Kornbluh, Peter. "The Death of Che Guevara: Declassified." National Security Archive, George Washington University. Available online at http://www.gwu.edu/~nsarchiv/NSAEBB/NSAEBB5/.

Krauss, Clifford. "Bolivia Wiping Out Coca at a Price." *New York Times*, October 23, 2000, p. A10.

Krickeberg, Walter. *Mitos y leyendas de los aztecas, incas y mayas*. Mexico City: FCE, 1971.

Lagos, Maria L. "Bolivia la Nueva: Constructing New Citizens." Paper presented at the International Congress of the Latin American Studies Association, Guadalajara, Mexico, 1997.

Langer, Eric D. "Bolivia: Since 1825." In *Encyclopedia of Latin American History and Culture*. Vol. 1. Ed. Barbara A. Tenenbaum. New York: Charles Scribner's Sons, 1996.

Lehman, Kenneth. D. *Bolivia and the United States: A Limited Partnership*. Athens: University of Georgia Press, 1999.

Lockhart, James. *The Men of Cajamarca: A Social and Biographical Study of the First Conquerors of Peru*. Austin: University of Texas Press, 1972.

Lynch, John, ed. *Latin American Revolutions, 1808–1826: Old and New World Origins*. Norman: University of Oklahoma Press, 1994.

Mace, Gordon, and Louis Bélanger. *The Americas in Transition: The Contours of Regionalism*. Boulder, Colo.: Lynne Rienner Publishers, 1999.

Malloy, James M. *Bolivia: The Uncompleted Revolution.* Pittsburgh, Pa.: University of Pittsburgh Press, 1970.

Malloy, James M., and Eduardo Gamarra. *Revolution and Reaction: Bolivia, 1964–1985.* New Brunswick, N.J.: Transaction Publishers, 1988.

Marín Ibáñez, Rolando. "Bolivia y la integración de América del Sur." In *Bolivia: Temas de la agenda internacional.* Ed. Alberto Zelada Castedo. La Paz: Unidad de Análisis de Política Exterior (UDAPEX), Ministerio de Relaciones Exteriores y Culto, 2000.

Menzel, Sewall H. *Fire in the Andes: U.S. Foreign Policy and Cocaine Politics in Bolivia and Peru.* Lanham, Md.: University Press of America, 1996.

Mesa Gisbert, Carlos D. "Historia de Bolivia, época republicana (1900–2000)." *Acerca de Bolivia.* Instituto Nacional de Estadística. Available online at http://www.ine.gov.bo/iwd010305.htm. Downloaded March 14, 2001.

Mitchell, Christopher. *The Legacy of Populism in Bolivia: From the MNR to Military Rule.* New York: Praeger Publishers, 1977.

Morales, Waltraud Queiser. "Barrientos Ortuño, René." In *Biographical Dictionary of Latin American and Caribbean Political Leaders.* Ed. Robert J. Alexander. Westport, Conn.: Greenwood Press, 1988.

———. "Bolivia." In *Latin America and Caribbean Contemporary Record.* Vol. 5, *1985–1986.* Ed. Abraham F. Lowenthal. New York: Holmes & Meier, 1988.

———. *Bolivia: Land of Struggle.* Boulder, Colo.: Westview Press, 1992.

———. "Bolivian Foreign Policy: The Struggle for Sovereignty." In *The Dynamics of Latin American Foreign Policies.* Eds. Jennie K. Lincoln and Elizabeth G. Ferris. Boulder, Colo.: Westview Press, 1984.

———. "A Comparative Study of Societal Discontent and Revolutionary Change in Bolivia and Paraguay: 1930–1941." Ph.D. diss., Graduate School of International Studies, University of Denver, 1977.

———. "La geopolítica de la política exterior de Bolivia." In *Documentos de Trabajo PROSPEL.* Santiago, Chile: Centro de Estudios de la Realidad Contemporánea, 1984.

———. "Militarising the Drug War in Bolivia." *Third World Quarterly* 12 (1992): 353–370.

———. "The War on Drugs: A New U.S. National Security Doctrine?" *Third World Quarterly* 11 (1989): 147–169.

Norton, Robert E. "Jeff Sachs—Doctor Debt." In *Money Doctors, Foreign Debts, and Economic Reforms in Latin America from the 1890s to the Present.* Ed. Paul W. Drake. Wilmington, Del.: Scholarly Resources, 1994.

Oria Arredondo, Ramiro. "Bolivia: La diplomacia del mar en la OEA" and "El derecho internacional y las negociaciones marítimas con Chile." In *Bolivia: Temas de la agenda internacional.* Ed. Alberto Zelada Castedo. La Paz: Unidad de Análisis de Política Exterior (UDAPEX), Ministerio de Relaciones Exteriores y Culto, 2000.

Osborne, Harold. *Bolivia: A Land Divided.* New York: Oxford University Press, 1964.

Painter, James. *Bolivia and Coca: A Study in Dependency.* Boulder, Colo.: Westview Press, 1994.

Paulson, Susan, and Pamela Calla. "Gender and Ethnicity in Bolivian Politics: Transformation or Paternalism?" *Journal of Latin American Anthropology* 5 (2000):112–49.

Platt, Tristan. "The Andean Experience of Bolivian Liberalism, 1825–1900: Roots of Rebellion in the 19th-Century Chayanta (Potosí)." In *Resistance, Rebellion, and Consciousness in the Andean Peasant World, 18th to 20th Centuries.* Ed. Steve J. Stern. Madison: University of Wisconsin Press, 1987.

Querejazu Calvo, Roberto. *Bolivia y los ingleses.* La Paz: Editorial Los Amigos del Libro 1973.

———. *Guano, salitre, sangre: Historia de la guerra del Pacífico.* La Paz: Editorial Los Amigos del Libro, 1979.

Quiroga Ramírez, Jorge. "Mensaje de S.E., Ing. Jorge Quiroga Ramírez, Presidente de la República, en el día de su asunción al mando de la nación." *Discursos,* Señor Presidente de la República. Available online at http://www.rree.gov.bo/DISCURSOS/DISCURSOS2001/discurso%20PDteJQ7-8-2001.htm. Downloaded August 2, 2001.

Robins, Nicholas A. *El mesianismo y la semiótica indígena en el Alto Peru: La gran rebelion de 1780–1781.* La Paz: Hisbol, 1998.

Ryan, Henry Butterfield. *The Fall of Che Guevara: A Story of Soldiers, Spies, and Diplomats.* New York: Oxford University Press, 1998.

Sabine, George H. *A History of Political Theory.* Rev. ed. New York: Holt 1950.

Sanabria, Harry. "The Discourse and Practice of Repression and Resistance in the Chapare." In *Coca, Cocaine, and the Bolivian Reality.* Eds. Madeline Barbara Léons and Harry Sanabria. Albany: State University of New York, 1997.

Shultz, Jim. "War on Drugs Becomes War on Poor." *Sacramento Bee,* August 1, 1999, n.p.

Siles Guevara, Juan. *Bolivia's Right to the Pacific Ocean.* La Paz: Fundación Manuel Vicente Ballivián, 1960.

Spencer, Bill, with Gina Amatangelo. "Drug Certification." *Foreign Policy in Focus* 6, no. 5 (March 2001). Available online at http://www.foreign policy-infocus.org/.

Spitzer, Leo. *Hotel Bolivia: The Culture of Memory in a Refuge from Nazism.* New York: Hill & Wang, 1998.

St John, Ronald Bruce. "Same Space, Different Dreams: Bolivia's Quest for a Pacific Port." *Bolivian Research Review* 1 (2001), electronic journal, http://www.bolivianstudies.org, (accessed 9 July 2001).

———. "Hacia el Mar: Bolivia's Quest for a Pacific Port." *Inter-American Economic Affairs* 31 (1977): 41–73.

Stern, Steve J. "The Age of Andean Insurrection, 1742–1782: A Reappraisal." In *Resistance, Rebellion, and Consciousness in the Andean Peasant World, 18th to 20th Centuries.* Ed. Steve J. Stern. Madison: University of Wisconsin Press, 1987.

Stokes, Charles E., Jr. *The Amazon Bubble: World Rubber Monopoly.* Fort McKavett, Tex.: n.p., 2000.

Thorn, Richard S. "The Economic Transformation." In *Beyond the Revolution: Bolivia since 1952.* Eds. James M. Malloy and Richard S. Thorn. Pittsburgh, Pa.: University of Pittsburgh Press, 1971.

Toranzo Roca, Carlos F. "Informal and Illicit Economies and the Role of Narcotrafficking." In *Coca, Cocaine, and the Bolivian Reality.* Eds. Madeline Barbara Léons and Harry Sanabria. Albany: State University of New York, 1997.

United States Central Intelligence Agency. "Bolivia." *The World Factbook 2000.* Available online at http://www.cia.gov/cia/publications/factbook/geos/b.html. Downloaded September 7, 2001.

Vargas, Tambor Mayor. *Diario de un soldado de la independencia altoperuana en los valles de Sicasica y Hayopaya.* Sucre, Bolivia: n.p., 1952 [1954].

Vázquez Machicado, Humberto, José de Mesa, Teresa Gisbert, and Carlos D. Mesa Gisbert. *Manual de historia de Bolivia.* 3d ed. La Paz: Editorial Gisbert, 1988.

Vittone, Luis. *Las fuerzas armadas paraguayas en sus distintas épocas.* Asunción, Paraguay: Editorial El Gráfico, 1969.

Von Hagen, Victor W. *The Ancient Sun Kingdoms of the Americas: Aztec, Maya, Inca.* New York: World Publishing Company, 1957.

―――. *Highway of the Sun*. Boston: Little, Brown, 1955.

―――. *The Incas: People of the Sun*. New York: World Publishing Company, 1961.

Voss, Stuart F. *Latin America in the Middle Period: 1750–1929*. Wilmington, Del.: Scholarly Resources, 2002.

Wilkie, James W. *The Bolivian Revolution and U.S. Aid since 1952*. Los Angeles: Latin American Center, University of California at Los Angeles, 1969.

―――. "U.S. Foreign Policy and Economic Assistance in Bolivia, 1948–1976." In *Modern-Day Bolivia: Legacy of the Revolution and Prospects for the Future*. Ed. Jerry R. Ladman. Tempe: Center for Latin American Studies, Arizona State University, 1982.

Wolf, Eric. *Sons of the Shaking Earth*. Chicago: University of Chicago Press, 1959.

―――. "Sons of the Shaking Earth." In *Crossing Currents: Continuity and Change in Latin America*. Eds. Michael B. Whiteford and Scott Whiteford. Upper Saddle River, N.J.: Prentice-Hall, 1998.

Zimmerer, Karl. "Commentary: Social Science Intellectuals, Sustainable Development and the Political Economies of Bolivia." *Journal of Latin American Anthropology* 5 (2000): 179–89.

Appendix 4

SUGGESTED READING

This brief history has been written for nonscholars and general readers. Many topics merit more in-depth coverage. These selected suggested readings in English provide additional resources across many disciplines. Information on Bolivia also appears in works that are not exclusively dedicated to the country. And the bilingual reader will discover that excellent works are available in Spanish.

Books and Other Resources Spanning Major Periods

Acerca de Bolivia. Instituto Nacional de Estadística (INE). Available online at http://www.ine.gov.bo/iwd010305.htm.

Alexander, Robert J. *Bolivia: Past, Present, and Future of Its Politics.* New York: Praeger, 1982.

Andean Information Network. Available online at www.scbbs-bo.com/ain.

Barton, Robert. *A Short History of the Republic of Bolivia.* 2d ed. La Paz: Editorial Los Amigos del Libro, 1968.

Benner, Susan E., and Kathy S. Leonard, eds. and trans. *Fire from the Andes: Short Fiction by Women from Bolivia, Ecuador, and Peru.* Albuquerque: University of New Mexico Press, 1998.

Carter, William E. *Bolivia: A Profile.* New York: Praeger, 1971.

Fifer, Valerie J. *Bolivia: Land, Location and Politics since 1825.* Cambridge, England: Cambridge University Press, 1972.

Healy, Kevin. *Llamas, Weavings, and Organic Chocolate: Multicultural Grassroots Development in the Andes and Amazon of Bolivia.* Notre Dame, Ind.: University of Notre Dame Press, 2001.

Hudson, Rex A., and Dennis M. Hanratty, eds. *Bolivia: A Country Study.* 3d ed. Washington, D.C.: Government Printing Office, 1991.

Jackson, Robert H. *Regional Markets and Agrarian Transformation in Bolivia: Cochababma, 1539–1960.* Albuquerque: University of New Mexico Press, 1994.

Klein, Herbert S. *Bolivia: The Evolution of a Multi-Ethnic Society*. 2d ed. New York: Oxford University Press, 1992.

———. "Recent Trends in Bolivian Studies." *Latin American Research Review* 31 (Winter 1996): 162–69.

Latin American Network Information Center (LANIC). "Bolivia, Academic Research Resources." Available online at http://www.lanic. utexas.edu/la/sa/bolivia/.

Leonard, Olen E. *Bolivia: Land, People and Institutions*. Washington, D.C.: Scarecrow Press, 1952.

Lindert, Paul van, and Otto Verkoren. *Bolivia: A Guide to the People, Politics and Culture*. Trans. John Smith. London: Latin American Bureau, 1994.

———. *Bolivia in Focus*. London: Latin America Bureau, 1994.

Lora, Guillermo. *History of the Bolivian Labor Movement, 1848–1971*. Cambridge, England: Cambridge University Press, 1977.

McFarren, Peter. *An Insider's Guide to Bolivia*. La Paz: Fundación Cultural Quipus, 1992.

Morales, Waltraud Queiser. *Bolivia: Land of Struggle*. Boulder, Colo.: Westview Press, 1992.

Osborne, Harold. *Bolivia: A Land Divided*. New York: Oxford University Press, 1964.

Sánchez-H., José. *The Art and Politics of Bolivian Cinema*. Lanham, Md.: Scarecrow Press, 1999.

Sanjinés, Jorge. *Theory and Practice of a Cinema with the People*. Trans. Richard Schaff. Willimantic, Conn.: Curbstone Press, 1989.

Santos, Rosario, ed. *The Fat Man from La Paz: Contemporary Fiction from Bolivia*. New York: Seven Stories Press, 2000.

United States Central Intelligence Agency. *The World Factbook*. Available online at http://www.cia.gov/cia/publications/factbook/index.html.

Peoples of South America's Heartland

Allen, Catherine J. *The Hold Life Has: Coca and Cultural Identity in an Andean Community*. Washington, D.C.: Smithsonian Institution Press, 1988.

Buechler, Hans C., and Judith-Maria Buechler. *The Bolivian Aymara*. New York: Holt, Rinehart, & Winston, 1971.

———. *The World of Sofia Velasquez: The Autobiography of a Bolivian Market Vendor*. New York: Columbia University Press, 1996.

Duguid, Julian. *Green Hell: Adventures in the Mysterious Jungles of Eastern Bolivia.* New York: Century Company, 1931.

Gill, Lesley. *Peasants, Entrepreneurs, and Social Change: Frontier Development in Lowland Bolivia.* Boulder, Colo.: Westview Press, 1987.

———. *Precarious Dependencies: Gender, Class, and Domestic Service in Bolivia.* New York: Columbia University Press, 1994.

Hahn, Dwight R. *The Divided World of the Bolivian Andes: A Structural View of Domination and Resistance.* New York: Crane Russak, 1992.

Luykx, Aurolyn. *The Citizen Factory: Schooling and Cultural Production in Bolivia.* Albany: State University of New York Press, 1999.

Mortimer, W. Golden. *History of Coca, The "Divine Plant" of the Incas.* San Francisco: And/or Press, 1974.

Nash, June. *I Spent My Life in the Mines: The Story of Juan Rojas, Bolivian Tin Miner.* New York: Columbia University Press, 1992.

———. *We Eat the Mines and the Mines Eat Us.* New York: Columbia University Press, 1993.

Ochoa, C. M. *The Potatoes of South America: Bolivia.* Cambridge, England: Cambridge University Press, 1990.

Osborne, Harold. *Indians of the Andes: Aymaras and Quechuas.* New York: Cooper Square, 1973.

Pacini, Deborah, and Christine Franquemont, eds. *Coca and Cocaine: Effects on People and Policy in Latin America.* Cambridge, Mass.: Cultural Survival, 1986.

Painter, James. *Bolivia and Coca: A Study in Dependency.* Boulder, Colo.: Westview Press, 1994.

Rivera Cusicanqui, Silvia. *Oppressed but Not Defeated: Peasant Struggles among the Aymara and Qhechwa in Bolivia, 1900–1980.* Geneva: United Nations Research Institute for Social Development, 1987.

Stearman, Allyn MacLean. *Camba and Kolla: Migration and development in Santa Cruz, Bolivia.* Gainesville: University of Central Florida Press, 1985.

———. *No Longer Nomads: The Sirionó Revisited.* Lanham, Md.: Hamilton Press, 1987.

———. *San Rafael, Camba Town: Life in a Lowland Bolivan Peasant Community.* 2d ed. Prospect Heights, Ill.: Waveland Press, 1995.

———. *Yuquí: Forest Nomads in a Changing World.* New York: Holt, Rinehart & Winston, 1989.

Stephenson, Marcia. *Gender and Modernity in Andean Bolivia.* Austin: University of Texas Press, 1999.

Pre-Columbian Peoples

Abercrombie, Thomas A. *Pathways of Memory and Power: Ethnography and History among an Andean People.* Madison: University of Wisconsin Press, 1998.
Cobo, Father Bernabé. *History of the Inca Empire.* Trans. and ed. Roland Hamilton. Austin: University of Texas Press, 1979.
———. *Inca Religion and Customs.* Trans. and ed. Roland Hamilton. Austin: University of Texas Press, 1990.
Kolata, Alan. *The Tiwanaku: Portrait of an Andean Civilization.* Cambridge, Mass.: Blackwell, 1993.
Posnansky, Arthur. *Tihuanacu: The Cradle of American Man.* Vols. 1–2. New York: J.J. Augustin, 1945.
Rostworowski de Diez Canseco, María. *History of the Inca Realm.* Trans. Harry B. Iceland. Cambridge, England: Cambridge University Press, 1999.
Salles-Reese, Verónica. *From Viracocha to the Virgin of Copacabana: Representation of the Sacred at Lake Titicaca.* Austin: University of Texas Press, 1997.
Von Hagen, Victor W. *The Incas: People of the Sun.* New York: World Publishing Company, 1961.

Colonial Bolivia

Arzáns de Orsúa y Vela, Bartolomé. *Tales of Potosí.* Ed. R. C. Padden and trans. Frances M. López-Morillas. Providence, R.I.: Brown University Press, 1975.
Bakewell, Peter J. *Miners of the Red Mountain: Indian Labor in Potosí, 1545–1650.* Albuquerque: University of New Mexico Press, 1984.
Buechler, Rose Marie. *The Mining Society of Potosí, 1776–1810.* Ann Arbor, Mich.: University Microfilm International for Department of Geography, Syracuse University, 1981.
Cole, Jeffrey A. *The Potosí Mita, 1573–1700: Compulsory Indian Labor in the Andes.* Stanford, Calif.: Stanford University Press, 1985.
Cornblit, Oscar. *Power and Violence in the Colonial City: Oruro from the Mining Renaissance to the Rebellion of Tupac Amaru, 1740–1782.* Trans. Elizabeth Ladd Glick. Cambridge, England: Cambridge University Press, 1995.
Ferry, Stephen. *I Am Rich Potosí: The Mountain That Eats Men.* New York: Monacelli Press, 1999.
Godoy, Ricardo. *Mining and Agriculture in Highland Bolivia: Ecology, History, and Commerce among the Jukumanis.* Tucson: University of Arizona Press, 1990.

Hanke, Lewis. *The Imperial City of Potosí.* The Hague: Nijhoff, 1956.

Klein, Herbert S. *Haciendas and "Ayllus": Rural Society in the Bolivian Andes in the Eighteenth and Nineteenth Centuries.* Stanford, Calif.: Stanford University Press, 1993.

Larson, Brooke. *Colonialism and Agrarian Transformation in Bolivia: Cochabamba, 1550–1900.* Princeton, N.J.: Princeton University Press, 1988.

O'Phelan Godoy, Scarlett. *Rebellions and Revolts in Eighteenth Century Peru and Upper Peru.* Cologne, Germany: Böhlau, 1985.

Stern, Steve J., ed. *Resistance, Rebellion, and Consciousness in the Andean Peasant World, 18th to 20th Centuries.* Madison: University of Wisconsin Press, 1987.

Tandeter, Enrique. *Coercion and Market: Silver Mining in Colonial Potosí, 1692–1826.* Albuquerque: University of New Mexico Press, 1993.

Zulawski, Ann. *"They Eat from Their Labor": Work and Social Change in Colonial Bolivia.* Pittsburgh, Pa.: University of Pittsburgh Press, 1995.

Independence Wars and the New Nation

Adams, Jerome R. "Simón Bolívar." In *Liberators and Patriots of Latin America: Biographies of 23 Leaders from Doña Marina (1505–1530) to Bishop Romero (1917–1980).* Ed. Jerome R. Adams. Jefferson, N.C.: McFarland & Co., 1991.

Arnade, Charles W. *The Emergence of the Republic of Bolivia.* New York: Russell & Russell, 1970.

Goodnough, David. *Simón Bolívar: South American Liberator.* Springfield, N.J.: Enslow Publishers, 1998.

Hoover, John P. *Admirable Warrior: Marshall Sucre, Fighter for South American Independence.* Trans. Alicia Coloma de Reed. Detroit: B. Ethridge Books, 1977.

Lynch, John. *Latin America Between Colony and Nation: Selected Essays.* New York: Palgrave, 2001.

Lynch, John, ed. *Latin American Revolutions, 1808–1826: Old and New World Origins.* Norman: University of Oklahoma Press, 1994.

The Age of Caudillo Rule

Hamill, Hugh M., ed. *Caudillos: Dictators in Spanish America.* Norman: University of Oklahoma Press, 1992.

Johnson, Lyman L. "Making Sense of Caudillos and 'Revolutions' in Nineteenth-Century Latin America." In *Problems in Modern Latin*

American History: A Reader. Eds. John Charles Chasteen and Joseph S. Tulchin. Wilmington, Del.: SR Books, 1994.

Lynch, John. *Caudillos in Spanish America, 1800–1850.* Oxford, England: Oxford University Press, 1992.

Republican Rule and the New Oligarchy

Costa du Rels, Adolfo. *Bewitched Lands.* Trans. Stuart Edgar Grummon. New York: A. A. Knopf, 1945.

Farcau, Bruce W. *The Ten Cents War: Chile, Peru, and Bolivia in the War of the Pacific, 1879–1884.* Westport, Conn.: Praeger, 2000.

Fifer, Valerie. "The Empire Builders: A History of the Bolivian Rubber Boom and the Rise of the House of Suárez." *Journal of Latin American Studies* 2 (November 1970):113–46.

Gallo, Carmenza. *Taxes and State Power: Political Instability in Bolivia, 1900–1950.* Philadelphia: Temple University Press, 1991.

Grieshaber, Erwin P. "Survival of Indian Communities in Nineteenth-Century Bolivia: A Regional Comparison." *Journal of Latin American Studies* 12 (November 1980): 223–69.

Klein, Herbert S. "Bolivia from the War of the Pacific to the Chaco War." In *Cambridge History of Latin America.* Vol. 5. Ed. Leslie Bethell. Cambridge, England: Cambridge University Press, 1986.

———. "The Creation of the Patiño Tin Empire." *Inter-American Economic Affairs* 19 (Autumn 1965): 3–23.

———. *Parties and Political Change in Bolivia, 1880–1952.* London: Cambridge University Press, 1969.

Langer, Eric D. *Economic Change and Rural Resistance in Southern Bolivia, 1880–1930.* Stanford, Calif.: Stanford University Press, 1989.

Marsh, Margaret C. A. *The Bankers in Bolivia: A Study in American Foreign Investment.* New York: Vanguard Press, 1928.

The Chaco War and the Road to Revolution

Blasier, Cole. "The United States, Germany, and the Bolivian Revolutionaries, 1941–1946." *Center for Latin American Studies Occasional Papers.* No. 8. Pittsburgh, Pa.: University of Pittsburgh Press, 1974.

Farcau, Bruce W. *The Chaco War: Bolivia and Paraguay, 1932–1935.* Westport, Conn.: Praeger, 1996.

Garner, William R. *The Chaco Dispute: A Study of Prestige Diplomacy.* Washington, D.C.: Public Affairs Press, 1966.

Jones, W. Knapp. "The Literature of the Chaco War." *Hispania* 21 (1958): 33–46.

Klein, Herbert S. "American Oil Companies in Latin America: The Bolivian Experience." *Inter-American Economic Affairs* 18 (Autumn 1964): 47–72.

———. "The Crisis of Legitimacy and the Origins of Social Revolution: The Bolivian Experience." *Journal of Inter-American Studies* 10 (January 1968): 102–10.

———. "David Toro and the Establishment of 'Military Socialism' in Bolivia." *Hispanic American Historical Review* 45 (February 1965): 25–52.

———. "Germán Busch and the Era of 'Military Socialism' in Bolivia." *Hispanic American Historical Review* 47 (May 1967): 166–84.

———. "Social Constitutionalism in Latin America: The Bolivian Experience." *Americas* 22 (January 1966): 258–76.

Zook, David H. *The Conduct of the Chaco War.* New York: Bookman Associates, 1961.

The National Revolution

Alexander, Robert J. *The Bolivian National Revolution.* New Brunswick, N.J.: Rutgers University Press, 1958.

Andrade, Víctor. *My Missions for Revolutionary Bolivia.* Pittsburgh, Pa.: University of Pittsburgh Press, 1976.

Blasier, Cole. *The Hovering Giant: U.S. Responses to Revolutionary Change in Latin America.* Pittsburgh, Pa.: University of Pittsburgh Press, 1976.

Burke, Melvin, and James M. Malloy. "From National Populism to National Corporatism: The Case of Bolivia, 1952–1970." *Studies in Comparative International Development* 9 (Spring 1974): 49–73.

Eckstein, Susan. *The Impact of Revolution: A Comparative Analysis of Mexico and Bolivia.* Beverly Hills, Calif.: Sage Publications, 1976.

Heath, Dwight B., Charles J. Erasmus, and Hans C. Buechler. *Land Reform and Social Revolution in Bolivia.* New York: Praeger Publishers, 1969.

Kelley, Jonathan, and Herbert S. Klein. *Revolution and the Rebirth of Inequality.* Berkeley: University of California Press, 1981.

Knudson, Jerry W. *Bolivia, Press and Revolution, 1932–1964.* Lanham, Md.: University Press of America, 1986.

Malloy, James M. *Bolivia: The Uncompleted Revolution.* Pittsburgh, Pa.: University of Pittsburgh Press, 1970.

Malloy, James M., and Richard S. Thorn, eds. *Beyond the Revolution: Bolivia since 1952.* Pittsburgh, Pa.: University of Pittsburgh Press, 1971.

Ostria Gutiérrez, Alberto. *The Tragedy of Bolivia: A People Crucified.* Trans. Eithne Golden. New York: Devin-Adair Co., 1958.

Siekmaier, James F. *Aid, Nationalism and Inter-American Relations.* Washington, D.C.: Edwin Mellen Press, 1999.

Whitehead, Laurence. *The United States and Bolivia: A Case of Neo-Colonialism.* London: Haslemere Group, 1969.

Wilkie, James W. *The Bolivian Revolution and U.S. Aid since 1952.* Los Angeles: Latin American Center, University of California at Los Angeles, 1969.

Zondag, Cornelius H. *The Bolivian Economy, 1952–1965: The Revolution and Its Aftermath.* New York: Praeger Publishers, 1966.

The Military and Counterrevolution

Barrios de Chungara, Domitila. *Let Me Speak! Testimony of Domitila, a Woman of the Bolivian Mines.* New York: Monthly Review Press, 1978.

Brill, William H. *Military Intervention in Bolivia: The Overthrow of Paz Estenssoro and the MNR.* Washington, D.C.: Institute for the Comparative Study of Political Systems, 1967.

Debray, Régis. *Che's Guerrilla War.* Trans. Rosemary Sheed. London: Penguin Books, 1975.

Dunkerley, James. *Rebellion in the Veins: Political Struggle in Bolivia, 1952–82.* London: Verso Editions, 1984.

González, Luis J., and Gustavo A. Sánchez Salazar. *The Great Rebel: Che Guevara in Bolivia.* New York: Grove Press, 1969.

Guevara, Ernesto "Che." *The Bolivian Diary of Ernesto Che Guevara.* New York: Pathfinder, 1994.

————. *Guerrilla Warfare.* New York: Random House 1969.

Ladman, Jerry R., ed. *Modern-Day Bolivia: Legacy of the Revolution and Prospects for the Future.* Tempe: Arizona State University, 1982.

Malloy, James M., and Eduardo Gamarra. *Revolution and Reaction: Bolivia, 1964–1985.* New Brunswick, N.J.: Transaction Publishers, 1988.

Mitchell, Christopher. *The Legacy of Populism in Bolivia: From the MNR to Military Rule.* New York: Praeger Publishers, 1977.

Prada Oropeza, Renato. *The Breach.* Trans. Walter Redmond. Garden City, N.Y.: Doubleday, 1971.

Prado Salmón, Gary. *Defeat of Che Guevara: Military Response to Guerrilla Challenge in Bolivia.* Trans. John Deredita. New York: Praeger Publishers, 1990.

Von Vacano, Arturo. *The Biting Silence.* New York: Avon, 1987.

Whitehead, Laurence. "Bolivia's Failed Democratization, 1977–1980." In *Transitions from Authoritarian Rule: Latin America.* Eds. Guillermo O'Donnell, Phillipe Schmitter, and Lawrence Whitehead. Baltimore: Johns Hopkins University Press, 1986.

The Challenge of Democracy

Alexander, Robert J. "Bolivia's Democratic Experiment." *Current History* 84 (February 1985): 73–76, 86–87.

Burke, Melvin. "Bolivia: The Politics of Cocaine." *Current History* 90 (February 1991): 65–68, 90.

Conaghan, Catherine M. "Reconsidering Jeffrey Sachs and the Bolivian Economic Experiment." In *Money Doctors, Foreign Debts, and Economic Reforms in Latin America, from the 1890s to the Present.* Ed. Paul W. Drake. Wilmington, Del.: Scholarly Resources, 1994.

Conaghan, Catherine M., and James M. Malloy. *Unsettling Statecraft: Democracy and Neoliberalism in the Central Andes.* Pittsburgh, Pa.: University of Pittsburgh Press, 1994.

Crabtree, John, Gavan Duffy, and Jenny Pearce. *The Great Tin Crash: Bolivia and the World Tin Market.* London: Latin America Bureau, 1987.

Crabtree, John, and Laurence Whitehead, eds. *Towards Democratic Viability: The Bolivian Experience.* New York: Palgrave, 2001.

Dunkerley, James. "The 1997 Bolivian Election in Historical Perspective." In *Warriors and Scribes.* Ed. James Dunkerley. London: Verso, 2000.

Farcau, Bruce W. "Being Dragged: The Bolivian Case." In *The Transition to Democracy in Latin America: The Role of the Military.* Ed. Bruce W. Farcau. Westport, Conn.: Praeger Publishers, 1996.

Gamarra, Eduardo A. "Facing the Twenty-First Century: Bolivia in the 1990s." In *Deepening Democracy in Latin America.* Eds. Kurt von Mettenheim and James M. Malloy. Pittsburgh, Pa.: University of Pittsburgh Press, 1998.

———. "U.S.-Bolivia Counternarcotics Efforts During the Paz Zamora Administration: 1989–1992." In *Drug Trafficking in the Americas.* Eds. Bruce M. Bagley and William O. Walker III. Miami: North-South Center Press, University of Miami, 1996.

Hargreaves, Clare. *Snowfields: The War on Cocaine in the Andes.* New York: Holmes & Meier, 1992.

Healy, Kevin. "Recent Literature on Drugs in Bolivia." In *Drug Trafficking in the Americas.* Eds. Bruce M. Bagley and William O. Walker III. Miami: North-South Center Press, University of Miami, 1996.

Jameson, Kenneth P. "Austerity Programs under Conditions of Political Instability and Economic Depression: The Case of Bolivia." In *Paying the Costs of Austerity in Latin America*. Eds. Howard Handelman and Werner Baer. Boulder, Colo.: Westview Press, 1989.

Lagos, María L. *Autonomy and Power: The Dynamics of Class and Culture in Rural Bolivia*. Philadelphia: University of Pennsylvania Press, 1994.

Léons, Madeline Barbara, and Harry Sanabria, eds. *Coca, Cocaine, and the Bolivian Reality*. Albany: State University of New York, 1997.

Malamud-Gotti, Jaime. *Smoke and Mirrors: The Paradox of the Drug Wars*. Boulder, Colo.: Westview Press, 1992.

Malloy, James M. "The Transition to Democracy in Bolivia." In *Authoritarians and Democrats: Regime Transition in Latin America*. Eds. James M. Malloy and Mitchell A. Seligson. Pittsburgh, Pa.: University of Pittsburgh Press, 1987.

Menzel, Sewall H. *Fire in the Andes: U.S. Foreign Policy and Cocaine Politics in Bolivia and Peru*. Lanham, Md.: University Press of America, 1996.

Sanabria, Harry. *The Coca Boom and Rural Social Change in Bolivia*. Ann Arbor: University of Michigan Press, 1993.

Bolivia and the New Century

Crabtree, John, and Laurence Whitehead. *Toward Democratic Viability: The Bolivian Experience*. Oxford: Palgrave, 2001.

Gill, Lesley. *Teetering on the Rim: Global Restructuring, Daily Life, and the Armed Retreat of the Bolivian State*. New York: Columbia University Press, 2000.

Grindle, Merilee S., and Pilar Domingo. *Proclaiming Revolution: Bolivia in Comparative Perspective*. Cambridge, Mass.: Harvard University Press, 2003.

Lehman, Kenneth. D. *Bolivia and the United States: A Limited Partnership*. Athens: University of Georgia Press, 1999.

INDEX

Page numbers followed by the letter *f* indicate illustrations; the letter *m* indicates a map; the letter *t* denotes a table.